The Rulers of German Africa
1884-1914

HOOVER INSTITUTION PUBLICATIONS

The Rulers of German Africa
1884-1914

L. H. GANN & PETER DUIGNAN

Stanford University Press, Stanford, California

1977

Stanford University Press
Stanford, California
© 1977 by the Board of Trustees of the
Leland Stanford Junior University
Printed in the United States of America
ISBN 0-8047-0938-6
LC 76-54100

Sources of photographs on pp. 131–36: 1, 3, 7, 8: *Das Buch
Deutschen Kolonien* (Leipzig: Wilhelm Goldmann Verlag, 1937).
2: Atlantis Verlag, Zürich. 4, 5: Helmut Bley, *South-West
Africa under German Rule* (Hamburg: Leibniz-Verlag, 1968;
London: Heinemann Educational Books, 1971). 6: Jesko von
Puttkamer, *Gouverneursjahre in Kamerun* (Berlin: Verlag von
George Stilke, 1912). 9, 10: *Die Soldaten Lettow-Vorbecks*
(Harburg: Walther Dobbertin, 1932). 11: Richard Küas,
Togo-Erinnerungen (Berlin: Vorhut-Verlag Otto Schlegel, 1939).

Contents

Six pages of photographs follow p. 130

Appendixes

Tables

Preface

The present work is intended as the first in a multi-volume work designed to elucidate the sociological and functional characteristics, the achievements as well as the shortcomings, of the white empire builders, civilian and military, during the age of the "New Imperialism" in Africa. The present volume on the Germans before 1914 will be followed by parallel studies on the British, the Belgians, the Portuguese, and the French. We shall later deal with the evolution of the colonial establishments, and end with the sociology of decolonization. We have concentrated on the white bureaucrats and military officers, their social backgrounds, general preconceptions, and modus operandi, but we soon found that we could not dissociate the rulers from the ruled, or the bureaucracies from the wider social and economic framework in which they operated. This study then evolved into one that shows how the Germans ran their empire and portrays the colonial elite and their work in Africa. It is meant as a contribution to Euro-African history or to the history of Europe in Africa.

The Kolonialreich extended over four separate and widely dispersed territories. It comprised many peoples—Stone Age hunters in the Kalahari desert, Nama pastoralists, Ngoni warriors with an Iron Age culture, Islamic lords in the Sudan, Swahili-speaking traders, and many others. The colonial dependencies were much smaller than those under British or French sway; nevertheless, they constituted an empire of impressive size. Largely acquired between 1883 and 1884, the African colonies extended over more than 900,000 square miles—considerably more than four times the area of the Reich, with about one-fifth of its population as shown in the following table:

The German Colonial Empire, 1913

Colony	Capital	Area (sq. mi. est.)	White population	Indigenous population (est.)
Togo	Lome	33,700	368	1,031,978
Cameroun	Buea	191,130	1,871	2,648,720
South-West Africa	Windhuk	322,450	14,830	79,556
East Africa	Dar es Salaam	384,180	5,336	7,645,770
Kiau Tschau (China)	Tsingtau	200	—	168,900
Pacific possessions	Rabaul and Apia	96,160	1,984	634,579
TOTAL COLONIES		1,027,820	24,389	12,041,603
German Reich in Europe		208,780	64,925,993	

SOURCE: *Statesman's Yearbook* (London, 1916), pp. 967–68.

This vast colonial empire was of only marginal significance to Germany's metropolitan economy. The various colonialist lobbies gained importance only after acquisition of the empire; Germany's pre-colonial trade with the African continent was small, and although the Kaiser's stake in Africa increased after the turn of the century, the colonies played a negligible part in German trade and foreign investment. German settlers in search of new homes overseas preferred the Americas or the British dominions to the German colonies. By 1913, thirty years or so after the establishment of the Kolonialreich, its European population numbered no more than that of a country town like Konstanz or Reutlingen.

The financial means available for colonial expansion were limited; hence the public treasury was forced to assume a considerable share of the burden. The total amount spent on the colonies by the German taxpayers in the form of imperial subsidies and subventions between 1884 and 1914 was 451.5 million marks. (1 mark = $0.23.) This sum was considerably less than the revenue received from Germany's post and telegraph services in a single year, but it exceeded by a considerable margin the total funds placed in the colonies by private companies (346.6 million marks). Seen in terms of German capitalism as a whole, colonialism was at best a speculative investment and at worst a form of conspicuous consumption to be assisted at the general taxpayers' expense.

The German colonial empire also was marginal to German society.

There was no colonial tradition, no far-flung British-type "old boys' network" of men who wanted their sons to serve their empire overseas; no German ever talked as did his British neighbor of joining a

> . . . Legion that was never 'listed,
> That carries no colours or crest.
> But, split in a thousand detachments,
> Is breaking the road for the rest.

On the contrary, for many years the German colonies were widely regarded as places fit only for idlers and ne'er-do-wells, where young men supposedly met a rapid end from drink, fever, or venery.

German colonialism was not without significance, however, and it profoundly affected the regions brought under its dominion. The changing colonial structure reflected profound changes within German society. German colonialism was begun on a shoestring as a limited-liability venture designed to benefit a few special interest groups. Gradually the Germans established effective rule over the vast territories they claimed for their own. The colonial armies and the colonial administration attracted a substantial number of aristocratic officers and administrators as well as marginal men, but over the years the administrative structure became more bureaucratic in tone and more bourgeois in composition. The rate of capital investment in the colonies increased. Germany made more deliberate attempts to develop her colonies in an economic sense, and Africans increasingly came to be looked upon not as foes to be conquered but as "economic men" to be prized as wage workers, cultivators, and customers.

The German impact was double-edged in its effect. Conquest involved violence and brutality—sometimes on a grim scale. While a people like the Ewe in Togo benefited from increasing Western contacts, the Herero and the Nama of South-West Africa suffered social disaster: their tribal organization was shattered and their lands were lost. But the Germans also made a number of positive contributions. They provided a basic infrastructure of modern transport; they encouraged new forms of economic enterprise; they promoted mining; they stimulated research; they imported new crops; to some extent they promoted peasant agriculture in export crops. They were responsible for the first feeble beginnings of secondary industry in their territories. They made a start, however slight, in providing Western-type education, hospitals, and dispensaries, government research in medicine, agriculture, and veterinary problems. They built a Western-type civil administration; they laid the foundations of new states. Their colonial elite helped to force German Africa into the world economy; they introduced new skills and new occupations, and created new economic needs and new economic opportunities. German colonialism thus was an engine of modernization with far-reaching effects for the future. German rule provided African people with new alternatives and a wider range of choices.

There was a problem of colonial "backwash" to the mother country. Few Germans who served in the colonies settled there. The returning colonialists—angry, discontented—sometimes contributed to right-wing radicalism, and some ex-colonialists later joined the Nazi party; however, we could find no evidence to support Hannah Arendt's thesis linking colonialism to the emergence of fascism. German colonialism was the product of an older tradition; it was created by the Wilhelmian era in Germany, with the strengths and weaknesses of a military empire that has passed into oblivion.

Our account is not an exhaustive one. Had we attempted to write a definitive examination of the German administrative and military impact on all the regions under the imperial flag, we should have had to devote half a lifetime to the perusal of surviving archives in East Germany, West Germany, South-West Africa, Togo, Tanzania, and Cameroun. It would have filled many volumes. Instead, we have tried to produce a briefer, interpretative study, making use of the extensive body of scholarly monographs already in existence. Our work is based on case histories and on selective samples in an attempt to cover Germany's African empire as a whole, but with special attention to East Africa—the largest of the German colonies, reputedly the "German India." Since numerous parallel topics have had to be covered, we have had to accept some repetition.

Our work has been lightened by the generous aid received from many institutions and from many individual scholars. Thanks are due to the respective heads and staff of the Bundesarchiv in Koblenz; to the Militärarchiv of the Bundesarchiv in Freiburg im Breisgau; to the Geheime Staatsarchiv, the Staatsbibliothek Preussischer Kulturbesitz, the library of the Kammergericht, Witzlebenstrasse, the Berliner Senatsbibliothek, and the library of the Museum für Völkerkund—all in Berlin; to the Archiv des Auswärtigen Amtes in Bonn; and to the Bayerisches Hauptstaatsarchiv in Munich.

Professors Franz Ansprenger, Ralph Austen, Gordon Craig, Arthur D. Knoll, Jake Spidle, and Woodruff D. Smith have read parts of our manuscript. Mrs. Agnes Peterson and Mrs. Monika Wölk read our original position paper. This work was made possible through the assistance of a research grant from the National Endowment for the Humanities, but the findings and conclusions here do not necessarily represent the views of the Endowment. We are especially indebted to the Historische Kommission zu Berlin, and particularly to Professors Otto Büsch and Hans Herzfeld, whose advice and whose institutional help—including financial assistance—have been of particular benefit to us.

L.H.G.
P.D.

Stanford, California
May 1977

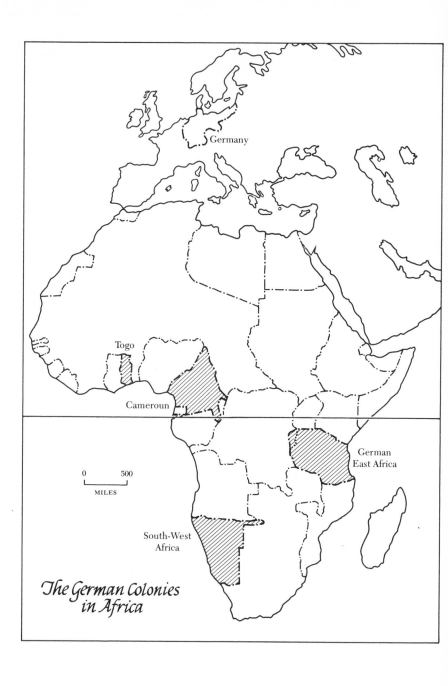

Germany

Togo

Cameroun

German
East Africa

0   500
MILES

South-West
Africa

*The German Colonies
in Africa*

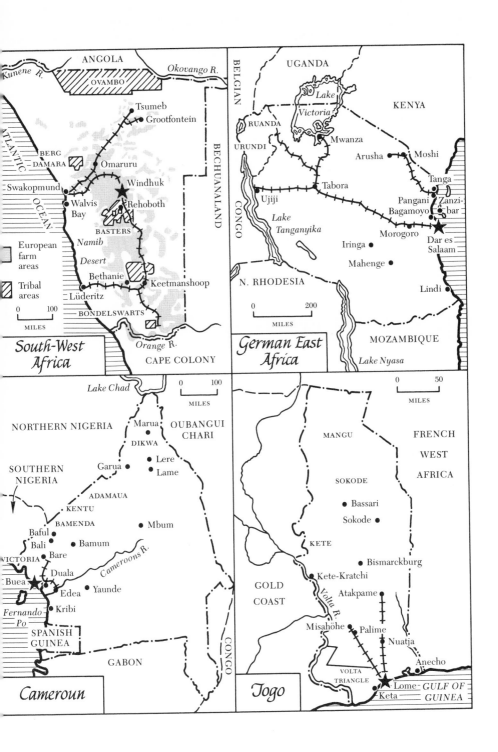

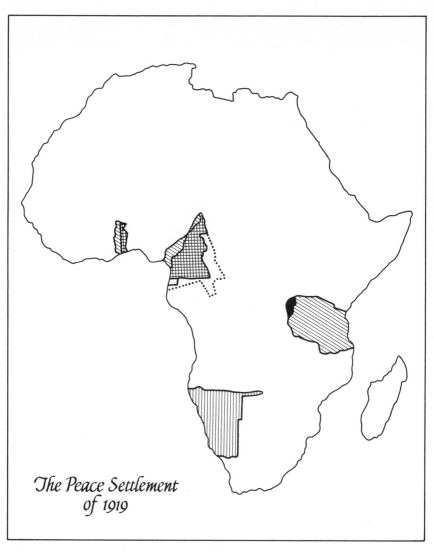

The Peace Settlement
of 1919

 French
Mandate

 British
Mandate

 Belgian
Mandate

 Mandated to Union
of South Africa

The dotted line indicates parts of the former German empire that were reincorporated
into French colonial territory

The Rulers of German Africa
1884-1914

ONE

Introduction

Germany and the German Colonial Service

The Bismarckian empire emerged in 1871 after a victorious war had stripped France of Alsace-Lorraine and deprived her of any claim to European primacy. As a result of unification at home and military victories abroad against Denmark (1864), the Austro-Hungarian Empire (1866), and France (1871), Germany had become the world's most powerful military state, but the Reich was a union of disparate parts characterized by great regional, religious, economic, and constitutional differences.

The Länder (states) retained their separate administrative structures and their own identities. The ethos of a state like Bavaria, which was monarchical and Catholic with a numerous peasantry and a substantial petty bourgeoisie of small traders and craftsmen, differed greatly from that, say, of Baden—a grand duchy in southwestern Germany, which was liberal in its traditions and strongly influenced by the French Revolution—or of a free city such as Hamburg, which was Protestant in religion and dependent on shipping, banking, and overseas commerce. The wide variety of administrative and legal traditions took considerable time to coalesce. The *Bürgerliches Gesetzbuch* (German legal code), for instance, did not come into force in its entirety until 1900—nearly three decades after unification of the Reich.

Rapid economic change added further to the disparities of life in the German empire. Industrial development centered principally in the Ruhr region, Saxony, and Silesia. Urbanization proceeded at a slower pace in the south than in Prussia or in Saxony, and small and medium-sized farms played a much more important part in agriculture there than they did in the east. The Reich, once predominantly an agrarian

TABLE 1

Comparison of the Growth of Key Industries in Germany,
France, and Great Britain, 1870–1914

Industry	Germany	France	Great Britain
Coal production[a]			
1870	34.0	13.3	112.0
1914	277.0	40.0	292.0
Pig-iron production[a]			
1870	1.3	1.2	6.0
1914	14.7	4.6	11.0
Steel production[a]			
1870	0.3	0.3	0.7
1914	14.0	3.5	6.5
Manufacturing (1913 = 100)			
1870	16.0	31.0	44.0
1914	100.0	100.0	100.0

SOURCE: A. J. P. Taylor, *The Struggle for the Mastery of Europe* (Oxford, 1954), pp. xxix–xxxi.
[a] Millions of tons.

state, became the greatest industrial power of Europe (see Table 1). By 1914 the Germans had taken the lead in Europe in many branches of industry—steel-making, chemical engineering, electrical enterprises; German shipyards were capable of building the largest and fastest vessels in the world, such as the giant passenger liners of the *Imperator* class—270 meters long and 30 meters broad, displacing 50,000 tons.

When the Franco-German War broke out in 1870, the total population of the various German states was 41 million, compared with 36 million in France, and in economic terms the struggle between France and Germany was a contest between equals. Forty years later, the economic power of France was considerably overshadowed by that of her neighbor across the Rhine, and Germany's population of 65 million was larger than that of any European country except Russia.

The German empire was dominated by Prussia, the largest and wealthiest state within the Reich. Prussian traditions, with their emphasis on efficiency, economy, and military might, pervaded the administrative practices of the Reich and had considerable influence even within the smaller south German states. As shaped by Bismarck and his successors, Prussian power rested on a tacit alliance between the various segments of the rural aristocracy and the more conservative upper middle classes. The nobility, which continued to play a major (though a gradually declining) role within the Germany of Wilhelm I and II, was a highly diverse body. The great magnates of Silesia with stakes in mining and manufacturing had little in common with the noble-born landowners of Pomerania or Brandenburg, who were traditionally more modest than the magnates in their tastes and their income, but they also were a group of heterogeneous composition. The upper stratum of the middle class was another mixed group. Bankers, shipowners, and merchants—many of them free traders of an anglophile cast—they were very different in their outlook from the magnates in the iron, coal, and steel industries, who were inclined to protectionism and nationalism of the most militant kind. But however disparate in its composition, the so-called reichstreue Elemente—the supporters of Bismarck's Reich—tended to look down on outsiders: Catholics, Social Democrats, ethnic minorities, and Jews.

The fluctuating alliance between landowners and industrialists was cemented by a new system of tariffs in 1879. During the early 1890's the two parties in the alliance fell out for a time, but in 1902 Germany adopted an even more thoroughgoing system of customs duties under the terms of which both agrarians and industrialists obtained protection from overseas competition. The liberal, free-trading traditions inherited from an earlier era had steadily weakened. The bulk of the German bourgeoisie admired the Prussian army, and far from wishing to challenge the power of the state, they looked to the state for social reform, for support against socialist revolution at home, and for backing against commercial competition abroad.

The decline of liberalism was reflected in many ways, particularly within the German administrative system. In 1881 Robert von Puttkamer—father of Jesco von Puttkamer, a German governor of Cameroun [Kamerun]—became Prussian minister of the interior and purged the Prussian civil service of its more liberal members. Senior administrators had to be noblemen from an approved background or middle-class people trained to a rigid code of loyalty and obedience in duelling student fraternities and in the reserve officer corps. This pattern was not universal, of course. The south German Länder had a more egalitarian ethos than the other states in the Reich, and many municipal administrations in south Germany remained sanctuaries of liberalism. But Prussia predominated within the Reich, and the Prussian ethos remained supreme throughout the Wilhelmian era.

According to the Prussian dispensation, the army and the civil service were the main pillars of the state. The prestige of the German army derived mainly from its series of rapid victories in three wars between 1864 and 1870. Its social status was enhanced by its aristocratic connections—a feature that the German army shared with the armed forces of Austria-Hungary and Great Britain, though not with those of smaller western European countries such as Holland and Norway. The proportion of aristocratic officers began to drop during the latter part of the nineteenth century, however, as manufacturing enterprises grew in number and in size, as specialist services increased within the army, and as the armed forces expanded too quickly for the aristocracy to supply sufficient candidates to fill the available posts (see Table 2).

Nevertheless, Germany—the most advanced industrial state in Europe—continued to rely on an army with an officer corps suffused by aristocratic values; these values seeped into civilian society through many different channels. The German bourgeoisie was partially militarized in large part through the reserve officer corps, which represented, so to speak, the more conservative burgher in arms. No applicant was considered eligible for admission to the corps unless he was acceptable to the officers in the regiment to which he applied. Exceptions were made in Bavaria and in some minor states, but in general every candidate—as well as his wife—was expected to be at least a nominal Christian. The aspirant had to have at least a high school education—the so-called Einjährige qualification, which permitted its holder to complete his service in the army in only one year instead of the two years expected from an ordinary conscript. (By 1914, the German reserve officer corps numbered about 120,000, as against 33,000 regulars. Qualitatively, the reserve officer corps was undoubtedly the best of its kind then in existence, as was the German General Staff.)

Germany's emphasis on military virtues had far-reaching consequences. Ambitious civil officials were expected to manifest the qualities required of successful platoon or squadron commanders in the army. Established professional men would do anything for the privilege of adorning their visiting cards with the title "lieutenant of reserve." Above all, a reserve officer—like a regular officer—was expected to have a special degree of loyalty toward the Kaiser (the Su-

TABLE 2

Proportions of Social Classes in the German Army Officer
Corps, Selected Years, 1824–1911

Year and social class	Elite officers (percent)	Total corps (percent)
1824	$N = 111$	$N = 5,230$
Nobility	97%	58%
Middle class	3	42
1870	$N = 178$	$N = 11,034$
Nobility	94%	49%
Middle class	6	51
1898	$N = 254$	$N = 14,778$
Nobility	81%	40%
Middle class	19	60
1911	$N = 263$	$N = 16,979$
Nobility	67%	33%
Middle class	33	67

SOURCE: Guy van Gorp, *Le recrutement et la formation des candidats officiers de carrière à l'armée belge* (Louvain, 1969), p. 47, citing figures supplied by Morris Janowitz.

preme War Lord) and authority in general. In return, he enjoyed a so-cial prestige unequalled in any other European country.

The Wilhelmian system owed perhaps as great a debt to the regular noncommissioned officer as to the commissioned officer. The regular sergeant—the foreman within the military machine—was an important, though inadequately documented, member of the German lower middle class.[1] He was apt to be a junior high school graduate—very different from the semiliterate barracks-room oaf of antimilitary fiction. Having attended a special Unteroffiziersschule for a period of three or four years, the German sergeant was, on the average, better educated than his confrère in other European armies. A regular company sergeant-major could exert enormous influence because he was likely to remain with the same unit while his officers might be posted around. In the colonial service a sergeant was sometimes placed in charge of a remote outstation where he wielded great power. But however able, a regular sergeant could never aspire—in peacetime—to an officer's epaulets. A career such as that of Sir William Robertson—who rose from footman to field marshal in the intensely class-conscious British society of the late nineteenth century—would have been inconceivable in the German military establishment of that era.

At the expiration of their army service, regular noncommissioned officers received preferential treatment in the lower ranks of the civil administration. Hence the ranks of junior officials, customhouse inspectors, postmen, and the like contained a considerable proportion of former noncommissioned army officers who brought something of their military outlook into the routine of government offices. Wherever he went in later life, the regular sergeant was likely to bring the habits and prejudices of the sergeants' mess, with its respect for authority and for *Haltung*—that untranslatable German term signifying a proper physical and moral posture with its peculiar mixture of obedience and stiff-backed stoicism.

But militarism was far from universal. Military ideals had little appeal for members of the "free professions" or for Social Democratic workmen (though even many workers were proud of their army service, and active Social Democrats—the aristocracy of the working class—were usually model soldiers: reliable, punctual, and clean). Wilhelmian Germany derived a good deal of her tone from merchants and professional men who proudly put their reserve officer's sabre with its golden tassel in the umbrella rack at the entrance hall of their homes and hung Menzel's engraving of Frederick the Great on the wall of their stairways. On a lower level, Wilhelmian Germany helped to shape—and in turn was shaped by—a great mass of conscripts who drank their beer from regimental mugs and who commemorated their military service with elaborately framed photos displayed above the sofa in the parlor, showing the man of the house in a corporal's dress uniform, with an illuminated rhyme that—with variations according to regiment—went:

> We all give praise, with one consent
> To the Second Bavarian Regiment.

Given the heterogeneous nature of Wilhelmian Germany, it is easy to exaggerate the impact of militarism. Nevertheless, imperial Germany was surely the only country in Europe where a retired company commander might make a social call on a former sergeant, a Jewish master tanner, so that the two elderly gentlemen could spend a pleasant time discussing religion and doing rifle drill with walking sticks. Nowhere but in Germany would the military authorities in wartime refuse to give up a captured British brigadier general in exchange for a German governor, offering only a British captain instead.[2]

The threefold military status divisions into officers, noncommissioned officers, and privates were reproduced in the civil administrative field. The road to advancement started from the position of Regierungsreferendar—the post of an unpaid but academically qualified trainee with a background in law, political economy, and related subjects. Regierungsreferendare who had completed the required in-service training and passed the state examination advanced to the post of Regierungsassessor, the starting point for the highest positions in the administrative hierarchy. An Assessor, unlike an aspirant to a British colonial career, was trained as a specialist. He usually had a doctor of jurisprudence degree, and was appointed to probationary status in a Land or Reich department where his training emphasized law and administrative procedure. By the time he was through the mill of professional training he was about thirty, and he tended to be set in his professional and social behavior. Throughout their careers, Assessors were taught to believe in the power and dignity of their posts. (According to a Stammtisch joke, the Tsar of all the Russias, having fallen victim to delusions of grandeur, dreamt one night that he had become a Prussian Regierungsassessor.) The successful Assessor rose by steps into the higher ranks of the bureaucracy, whose members exercised considerable authority. A Prussian Landrat enjoyed substantial powers of independent decision-making; he presumably could tackle anything: "Ein Landrat kann alles."

Civil service morale was reinforced by high status. Admission to the upper ranks of the bureaucracy, including the teaching posts in high schools and universities, was a coveted honor. Germany provided the strange spectacle of a thriving industrial country where men who had done well in business or in the professions behaved as if they were still members of an administrative bourgeoisie deriving advancement from princely favor. While an English Croesus might aspire to the social position of a landed squire, his German equivalent (or the German's spouse) was more likely to seek a pseudo-bureaucratic title such as "commercial privy councillor" or, even higher, a "truly privy commercial councillor."

The system was sustained by an elaborate hierarchy of titles, orders, medals, and insignia—about a hundred for Prussia alone and another hundred or so for the different German Länder. This maze of honors, Byzantine in its complexity, involved elaborate distinctions and highly intricate notions of social precedence. There was an acknowledged difference between "The Grand Cross of the Order of the Red Eagle with Oak Leaves and Swords and with Swords on the Ring" and, more modestly, "The Grand Cross of the Order of the Red Eagle with Oak Leaves and Swords." These exalted degrees, in turn, stood a world apart from "The Order of the Red Eagle, Fourth Class"—not to speak of humbler distinctions.[3] The Germans thus had an elaborate system of psychic rewards, as satisfactory to the ambitious as it was beneficial to the treasury.

Given such measures of competitive prestige, the loftier strata of the civil service continued to attract numerous applicants of high caliber, including many men with academic ability. The official status groups were rigidly defined by wealth, however. By and large, only parents who were reasonably well-off could afford to send their children to universities. Scholarships existed, but they were hard to get, and a considerable proportion of them went to theologians (generally one of the most poorly remunerated academic groups in Wilhelmian Germany), just as many an impecunious officer's son was able to get an inexpensive education at a military academy.

Once having joined the civil service, a young Referendar, like a youthful lieutenant in a good regiment, needed an income of his own to live. Hence, economic considerations alone were sufficient to exclude applicants from the working classes. Promotion from the ranks of the Subalternbeamten, the lower civil servants who had completed only a high school education, to the higher civil service was unthinkable—as unthinkable as was the promotion of regular noncommissioned officers into the ranks of the officer corps. In this respect Germany was a far more caste-ridden country than France or Belgium, where regular sergeants could aspire to rise into the officer corps. In Wilhelmian Germany only a technical service such as the Reichsbank had a unified bureaucracy without separate socioeducational status groups to impede internal mobility.

From Influence to Conquest: East Africa

The German Reich had no colonial traditions. German propagandists of empire were wont to complain that Germany was a latecomer on the imperial scene and had thereby missed a "place in the sun" that rightfully should have been hers. This is far from the truth. If from its inception in 1866, the North German Confederacy and, five years later, the unified German empire had embarked on an active colonial career, the Germans would have had many opportunities for overseas conquest. They were not interested in such ventures at the time, however, but preferred a policy of free trade and indirect commercial expansion.

A change in German colonial policy only came during the early 1880's. Debates on the wellsprings of Bismarckian colonialism fill many library shelves, and need not be recapitulated here. Scholars have assessed Bismarckian imperialism in many different ways: it has been interpreted as an instrument of foreign diplomacy, as a response to chauvinism and anglophobia, as a form of conspicuous consumption on a national scale, as a means of freezing the existing social order and of cementing an anti-socialist alliance at home.[4] It has also been described as a device for aiding Germans abroad by active state interference and as a real estate speculation designed to secure a lien on territories whose value, however small, might appreciate in years to come.

Bismarck, by training and tradition, would have much preferred to support German traders abroad by means of an "open door" policy of the kind he advocated in China and the Congo, but by the early 1880's the era of free trade seemed to be drawing to a close. Having suffered serious loss during the economic depression of the later 1870's, Germany seemed to require a form of financial insurance against an uncertain future which might see colonial competitors shut her out of valuable new markets overseas. These fears proved to be unwarranted. Imperial development and consolidation by the European powers benefited international commerce in general; for instance, during the twenty years preceding World War I—1893 to 1913—German exports to British India, unquestionably a British preserve, more than trebled.

But the German anxieties were real, and they stimulated her colonial expansion. Colonialism was in part a surrender to special interests—to missionaries anxious to work under the protection of the German eagle and to merchants, especially traders on the west coast of Africa who looked for imperial protection at a time when falling world prices for African products forced them increasingly to move toward the interior so as to reduce their overhead by cutting out African middlemen. However interpreted, Bismarckian colonialism had but a slender material base—a theme to be discussed later in the text. Throughout this era Germany had little capital to spare for investment in the tropics, and her trade with Africa was negligible (see Appendix Table E. 1). Within the hierarchy of German capitalism as a whole, the magnates of African trade were pygmies.

Colonialism did not play a major part in German domestic politics during the Bismarckian era.* As far as Bismarck was concerned, colonial ventures were of marginal significance. Once having acquired the bulk of Germany's overseas possessions, Bismarck soon lost all interest in their fate; he even spoke of selling the colonies. His indifference to them increased as the domestic situation in Germany worsened during the 1880's and 1890's. There is scant evidence that the governing groups attempted to exploit colonial successes to diminish the appeal of Social Democratic or Catholic politicians opposed to Bismarck's iron rule. Bismarck was so little interested in the colonial experiment that he did not bother to mention it in his reminiscences, *Gedanken und Erinnerungen*, a work much concerned with the machinations of Liberals, Guelphs, Jesuits, Poles, interfering royal women, and other assorted enemies of the Reich.

Bismarck had no intention of using the nation's elaborate administrative machinery for the purpose of ruling distant, little-known, and as yet ill-defined possessions. He disliked the French system of empire-building by military and bureaucratic methods; instead he wished to colonize by means of chartered companies, as the British had done in North Borneo. Chartered rule by independent merchants, Bismarck assumed, would throw the financial and diplomatic risks of colonization onto private capitalists whom he might later disavow. Chartered enterprises would make it unnecessary for the Reich government to seek grants from the Reichstag and thereby add to the power of the legislature.

* According to a thesis brilliantly argued by Hans-Ulrich Wehler, Bismarck used colonialism primarily as a tool of social manipulation. The German "Establishment," composed of the great industrialists and landed aristocracy, was determined to exclude the lower orders from power. This exclusion supposedly became increasingly difficult during the economic depression that struck the Reich during the 1870's. Colonial expansion served as a means not only of tightening social bonds and of furthering trade (as did the protective tariffs introduced in 1879), but also of diverting the people's attention from domestic misery to foreign glory. Wehler's interpretation of history resembles Cecil Rhodes's and Carl Peters's in greatly exaggerating the importance of the colonial factor in metropolitan politics.

But the German colonies were not to become comparable with India or even with South Africa. Much to the chancellor's regret, the German bourgeoisie was incapable of shouldering the task they were meant to assume in his plan. The established German traders at Zanzibar carried on a substantial trade in textiles, guns, and ivory, but they had neither the means nor the will to become rulers; for the most part they preferred to remain on good terms with the local sultan, on whom they relied to protect their commerce. There were no large-scale entrepreneurs like Rhodes—men with a great stake in Africa, capable of financing colonization at least in part from the revenue from diamond and gold mines. And the metropolitan capitalists were at first disinclined to risk their money in colonial ventures.

The initial impetus for colonization in East Africa came from small investors with a patriotic bent. The Gesellschaft für Deutsche Kolonisation, later reformed into the Deutsch-Ostafrikanische Gesellschaft (DOAG), received an imperial charter in 1885. Its initial support—unlike that of the British South Africa Company with its directorate of mining capitalists, bankers, and great landowners—was financially unimpressive. The DOAG at first had to rely on the backing of patriotic professors, army officers, professional men, and a sprinkling of minor entrepreneurs. (There were other important differences between the DOAG and the British South Africa Company, which received a charter in 1889 to administer the area north of the Limpopo River. Bismarck, in contrast to the British Parliament, did not impose any restrictions on the German company: he did not seek to protect African rights and customs, he did not restrict the sale of alcohol, and he did not regulate the company's rule of the territory assigned to it.) Carl Peters (1885–1918), the DOAG's founder, was no businessman. He shared with Rhodes an upbringing in a country parsonage, a visionary-romantic streak, ruthlessness, and a touch of megalomania. But Peters was an intellectual, not a capitalist. Photographs of him show a slightly built, professorial-looking man with a pince-nez and a well-kept moustache—the kind of man who could best the brightest student in an argument on some obscure point of metaphysics. He had, in fact, published a doctoral dissertation under the title "Willenswelt und Weltwille," shaped by the philosophy of Schopenhauer.

Unlike Rhodes, Peters had no money of his own before he went into the business of colonization. Moreover, he was a social climber and a snob, willing to humble himself in the presence of the great in a way that Rhodes would have found incomprehensible. An outspoken racist, he had a streak of brutality, which Rhodes did not have; in 1897 he was dismissed from the imperial service for "exceeding his powers"—a euphemism for his cruelty. His patriotism had a resentful, whining quality quite foreign to British chauvinists of the Victorian era. Peters was consumed by a peculiar love-hate relationship with Great Britain that characterized many German imperialists of his time. He returned from his first stay in London full of envy: "I got tired of being accounted among the pariahs and wished to belong to the master race." In this statement he gave expression to a widespread sense of inferiority felt by Germans of the middle class with regard to the British. A congenital liar, Peters repelled the more sober type of businessman, so that the DOAG had to be started as a shadow enterprise.

Beginning in 1887 substantial private banks like Mendelssohn-Bartholdy and Delbrück, Leo und Co. put money into the DOAG, as did important manufacturers such as Krupp.[5] The company's capital at first amounted to no more than 3.5 (later 8) million marks, a sum which proved to be quite inadequate for the purpose of turning its East African paper claims—acquired by Peters and other explorers—into commercial assets. Worldly wise investors argued that such speculations were attractive primarily because eventually the Reich was bound to take over the concern, enabling the funds to be invested in more profitable enterprises.[6]

The task of conquering East Africa was formidable. The colony often figured in popular travel books as a "German India"—a fertile land of splendid rain forests with luscious fruits and birds of paradise arrayed in gorgeous colors. The realities were very different. Drought remains to this day a major problem in much of the area that was once German East Africa—most of it now making up the post-colonial Republic of Tanzania. There are few permanent rivers, and only about half the area has natural water throughout the year. Much of the soil is poor in quality and easily leached. The vegetation varies from evergreen forests on mountain slopes to grim mangrove swamps south of the Rufiji river delta. Depending on the soil and the amount of rainfall, the bulk of the country is covered by parklike savanna or by bush and scrub; in parts of central Tanzania this tangle may form an impenetrable *maquis* of bushes and small, spiny, twisted trees. In drier areas the bush gives way to thornland and dry steppe. The coastal zone has substantial rainfall, and like the Kilimanjaro and Meru areas has a lush plant cover, as has the island of Zanzibar.

East Africa's most substantial indigenous state was the sultanate of Zanzibar, a Muslim kingdom linked by history to southern Arabia. In pre-colonial times Zanzibar's prosperity, such as it was, depended on plantation agriculture, the export of cloves, and trade in slaves, ivory, and other merchandise brought from the interior. Armed Muslim caravans penetrated far inland to raid, to trade, and sometimes to create their own suzerainties. Muslim lordlings set up trading centers and fortified stockades along the caravan routes; some became petty sovereigns on their own account, resolving ultimately to retire to Zanzibar with the money they made from farming, commerce—peaceful or warlike—and from tributes levied on their subjects. Indirect Muslim influence was spread by Swahili-speaking traders who propagated their language, their letters, and their faith into the interior; their advance was part of a great blood-stained drive that extended the influence of petty rulers and slave-dealers as far as the eastern Congo and into what is now northeastern Zambia.

Internally the Zanzibari state, its allies and dependencies, were sharply stratified. The ruling class consisted of Muslim landowners of Arab or Afro-Arab descent who occupied the top positions in government and ran the country. Zanzibar also contained numerous Indians. As merchants in the capital, they sometimes acted as agents of great Bombay houses. Indian traders generated much of their own capital from doing business with Europeans, Arabs, and Africans. Indians also acted as tax farmers who made money from collecting customs duties. Their roots were in India, but they played a vital part in the Zanzibari economy. They acted as bankers; they financed clove plantations and slave-trading caravans; they did most of the technical, clerical, and auditing work in the sultan's administration. Many more eked out a bare living as commercial employees or as petty traders on their own account.

These various Muslim societies all rested on slavery. African serfs worked on the wharfs and on plantations, in homes, in warehouses, and in shops. There was no rigid color bar, and there were many gradations that allowed an intelligent, lucky bondsman to rise in the social sphere. However brutally or sadistically he might be abused as a captive on the march from his village to the coast, he was rarely treated with severity by the owner who bought him. Nevertheless, Zanzibar and its dependencies remained servile societies dependent on a fairly backward form of plantation agriculture, trade, and handicraft production.

In economic terms, the effects of Swahili penetration into the African interior are hard to assess. Slave raiding and looting occasioned widespread misery and destruction. Yet this commerce promoted the importation of new crops and the diffusion of new products—textiles, guns, knives, trinkets—helping to link inland communities with a wider world economy. But trade in men and ivory ultimately depended on wasting assets. The stories told by Europeans concerning the east coast Arabs' luxury were heavily overdrawn. Against the gross profits of the ivory market, for instance, entrepreneurs had to set the high expense of porterage—an early form of wage employment among inland people like the Nyamwezi—the enormous interest on borrowed capital, the expended time, the risk of total loss, and the fluctuations of prices. For all the hustle in the markets of Ujiji and Zanzibar, the total value of East Africa's trade was much smaller than that of West Africa, and conquerors would be hard put to build an empire on its slender returns.

The inland communities differed widely in their mode of livelihood and political organization. The majority consisted of Bantu-speaking peoples familiar with the art of smelting iron and skilled in various forms of shifting agriculture and cattle herding, supplemented by hunting and fishing. Their tools—the axe, the bow, and the arrow— were simple. They had not learned to harness the force of wind, water, or draft animals. In East Africa as elsewhere, inland peoples were unfamiliar with any form of writing. They professed various animistic religions, believed in the existence of a Supreme Being, and were profoundly concerned with the world of spirits and of departed ancestors, who were assumed to influence the living. In work and travel they relied solely on the power of human muscle—be it for hoeing fields, carrying burdens, or paddling canoes. Their resources were slender. Threatened by sickness, animal diseases, periodic raids by their neighbors, droughts and locusts, their lives were harsh; except for some regions like Rwanda (Ruanda), the populations for the most part remained relatively small with only low rates of growth. They were split into a variety of language groups, and were politically disunited.

Governing structures ranged from centralized monarchies to small, stateless societies.

The most highly organized realms were found among the so-called interlacustrine kingdoms. In states like the Rwanda monarchy, the ruling class consisted of Tutsi conquerors who controlled the country's cattle herds, occupied most of the leading positions in the state, and disdained intermarriage with the lower orders. The Hutu made up the vast majority of the population, and were bound to the Tutsi as vassals and clients; they were obliged to provide their lords with tribute and services and to cultivate the bulk of the food crops. There were other warlike communities, including the Masai—a cattle-keeping people who delighted in plundering their neighbors' herds and who exerted considerable influence on Bantu-speaking people like the Gogo, the Hehe, and others.

In the south was another variety of ethnic groups which included the Ngoni, whose ancestors had made their way to what is now Tanzania from distant South Africa, raiding their neighbors for women and for cattle and spreading terror in their path. There were the Yao, skilled traders who established links with Muslim traders and Muslim culture. There were the Nyakusa, the Bena, and many others. The Nkonde, the Luguru, and others in the east and southeast had different forms of social organization; they reckoned their descent through the mother's line and had been affected to varying degrees by Muslim contacts.

Such was the world that the DOAG meant to conquer. Convinced that Germany should follow an anti-Russian and pro-British policy, a new German government headed by Count von Caprivi signed an agreement regarding Africa with Great Britain in 1890. Germany gave up her claims to Zanzibar (where British commercial influence was already supreme), scaled down her claims in East Africa, and received in exchange the island of Heligoland. The treaty was bitterly attacked in Germany as a surrender to Great Britain, but Anglo-German commercial relations in Africa remained close; German tariffs were moderate, and East Africa, like the other German colonies of Togo and South-West Africa, continued to conduct a major share of its commerce with the British Empire.

The DOAG lacked both the men and the means to generate a substantial income of its own. Unlike the British South Africa Company, it was not in a position to finance railways. Its agricultural work was purely experimental and failed for lack of cash and expertise. As a trading concern the company could not compete with Arab merchants or with Indian financiers who knew the country, relied on extensive networks of kinsmen, and were willing to operate with small profits and take high risks. The DOAG therefore had to maintain itself by levying customs duties and imposing tolls on caravans and by confiscating land from coastal owners by dubious legal devices.

Its administrative network was no more impressive than its economic ventures. The company's administrative staff consisted of only a few dozen whites, some of whom were thugs or social rejects; in 1888 it totaled 46 persons scattered over 14 stations. Their social background was varied: eleven former traders, ten officers, eight artisans, six farmers, four sailors, three lawyers, two students, and two clerks.[7] The higher ranks in the administration were held by noblemen more often than by merchant-adventurers. As an instrument of government the company lacked an army to enforce its will—its coercive power was limited to a few unreliable *askari* (African professional soldiers). The DOAG made no attempt to build a local pro-German party; rather it alienated all groups of the coastal population by its economic exactions, bureaucratic chicanery, and showy displays of flags. By 1889 it seemed at the end of its tether. The Muslim official class, the Muslim traders, the Indian financiers, and the Muslims' customers had been thoroughly alienated, and the bulk of the coastal population was up in arms. The DOAG treasury had incurred heavy losses, and the company threatened to go out of business unless Berlin stepped in.

Bismarck, so contemptuous of the German bourgeoisie when it came to governing Prussia, now found that he had held romantic illusions concerning the ability of German businessmen to rule in Africa. Governance by merchant-adventurers was out of the question. At the same time—though no colonial enthusiast—he was unwilling to withdraw from East Africa altogether, and thereby incur serious loss of prestige abroad and bitter nationalist opposition at home. So he let the DOAG get rid of its administrative obligations in return for a favorable financial settlement, and in 1889 he set up a rudimentary administration under imperial auspices. The German taxpayer footed the bill, and with the new political dispensation the company for the first time became a commercially viable concern. Having failed to yield much in the way of dividends during its initial period, it started to pay moderate but steadily increasing profits to its investors, some of its directors, such as Alexander Lucas and Karl von der Heydt, came to play important parts both in colonial finance and in right-wing politics.[8] The Germans established a formal protectorate in East Africa in 1891 and smashed the Muslim opposition to foreigners. As described in subsequent sections of this study, they slowly penetrated inland to extend their power over their newly won possessions.

From Influence to Conquest: South-West and West Africa

South-West Africa seemed an even less valuable acquisition than East Africa. The greater part of it is harsh and arid, a highland enveloped by dry steppe and desert. On the shore of the Atlantic, the Namib region is a desolate area of shifting sand dunes, salt pans, and stark rock; the Kalahari sandveld stretches over much of the eastern portion. Extensive tracts inland and to the south are covered by grass and dwarf trees, the vegetation changing gradually to bush and acacia shrub. To the north, bushland merges into savanna and finally into a forest region, where the rainfall increases. Rainfall in the areas of vegetation is irregular, varying from an average of 300 to 400 mm. in the central Windhuk (Windhoek) region to only 50 to 100 mm. in the southern Keetmanshoop zone. In some 70 percent of the territory even dryland cropping is out of the question. Except in the north, grazing is the major form of agricultural enterprise, but the pastures have a low carrying capacity. Underground water surfaces in the form of springs in some areas, but usually it can be tapped only by sinking boreholes.

In recent years modern technology has greatly increased the country's wealth. South-West Africa has considerable mineral deposits which are now being tapped. Extensive capital investment in the pastoral industry, up-to-date methods of pasture management and disease control along with techniques of stockbreeding, and the introduction of new animal breeds, new varieties of trees, and new forms of forage have helped to make farming a more profitable and less hazardous occupation than in the past. The development of port facilities and rail and road services has revolutionized the economy of a country where nature failed to provide navigable waterways. Modern fishing vessels now exploit the country's fishing grounds along the Atlantic coast.

These improvements, however, required a great deal of time, capital, and technical knowledge unavailable to the pastoral peoples who inhabited most of the territory during the period of German occupation. Pre-colonial communities were few in number, and they had no defenses against the ravages of locusts, rinderpest, or other cattle diseases. Much depended on the possession of adequate springs, and bitter, bloody feuds were fought over cattle and the control of waterholes.

When the Germans hoisted the imperial eagle on the South-West African coast in 1884 they found a strife-torn area. The indigenous people were divided. The Bantu-speaking communities had developed an Iron Age civilization sustained by hunting, pastoral farming, and—where rainfall permitted—shifting agriculture. The most powerful of these groups were the Ambo of the north and the Herero. The latter were constantly at war with the Nama Hottentots—a pastoral Khoisan people who had come to the country from the north and by importing horses had increased their mobility and substantially expanded the range of their military operations. The use of mounts and the introduction of firearms by white traders had led to more destructive warfare than in the days of the bow, spear, and knobkerrie. Other newcomers settled in the area, including the Basters, a people of mixed European and Khoisan descent who spoke Afrikaans and resembled the pastoral Boers in their mode of life. There were also more backward communities such as the San (Bushmen), who made a scant living by hunting game and gathering food from the veld, and the Bergdamara, who had been reduced to virtual serfdom by the Herero and the Hottentots.

The first Germans to reach South-West Africa were evangelists of the Rhenish Mission Society, who worked in the interior among the Herero. In 1868 internecine conflicts persuaded the missionaries to ask for British protection, which was refused. Fifteen years later Heinrich Vogelsang—an agent of F. A. E. Lüderitz, a Bremen merchant—obtained from a Hottentot chief a cession of land at what later came to be known as Lüderitz, but was then Angra Pequena. The merchant Lüderitz had grandiose notions of forming a great colonial empire, but his own financial resources were slight, and Bismarck at first was reluctant to become involved. The chancellor soon changed his mind, however, and in 1884 extended German protection to all of South-West Africa. Lüderitz failed in his hopes of finding gold and diamonds, and his financial position rapidly deteriorated; he finally sold his land rights and later perished on an exploring trip in his imagined El Dorado.

The Bismarckian concept of colonization by private companies which would supply the capital, run the risks, and administer the country was also applied to South-West Africa until about 1890. The intended instrument was the Deutsche Kolonialgesellschaft für Deutsch-Südwestafrika, founded in 1885 with a capital of 500,000 marks (which was soon doubled)—a petty sum in terms of Wilhelmian big business. Gigantic areas were acquired by the Kolonialgesellschaft as well as by other concerns—including the South-West Africa Company, a British enterprise linked to Rhodes's group. (By 1903 the six major concessionary companies in the country, looking to future profits from mining gold and copper, had laid claim to 29.5 million hectares—more than one-third of the entire territory—but they did little or nothing to develop these enormous holdings.)

In 1890 German troops penetrated into the interior and occupied the area around the present Windhuk, then part of the unoccupied no-man's-land between the warring Herero and Nama communities. The region seemed suitable for white settlement, and German authorities began to provide small subsidies in 1891 to encourage sheep farming; the concessionary companies, without sufficient capital to carry out much development of their own, began to anticipate profits accruing from increased land values caused by the influx of white colonists. But not until 1905, after a twenty-year record of almost continual loss, did the Kolonialgesellschaft begin to make substantial profits as a commercial entity.

The Kolonialgesellschaft was unable to govern the country, however. It raised a small African force which deserted in 1888, and the Reich had to intervene. The first of Germany's official representatives in South-West Africa, Heinrich Goering, accomplished little; few military means were available to him, and German missionaries and traders had to conform to the realities of the Nama-Herero power struggles. In 1892 Hendrik Witbooi, perhaps the greatest of all Nama chiefs, concluded a peace treaty with the Herero in order to protect his flanks. Photographs of Witbooi show a small, sparely built man dressed in the fashion of an Afrikaner farmer, with a distinguished goatee and a determined face. He was well-educated and wrote vigorous though ungrammatical Dutch; he was also a natural leader and a born guerrilla fighter. Under Goering's successor—Curt von François, a military man who embarked on an aggressive policy that aroused bitter opposition— the Germans tried to destroy Witbooi's power by a sudden treacherous attack on Hornkranz, his main stronghold. The attack failed. Witbooi escaped and continued mounted partisan operations against the colonizers. Von François's methods were also opposed by German traders, whose commerce was being ruined, and by critics of the German government within the Reichstag. At the end of 1893 he was recalled and replaced by Major Theodor Leutwein, who believed in a more cautious policy of "divide and rule" (to be discussed later in the text). Indirect influence had been abandoned; direct intervention had come to stay.

In West Africa the Germans found themselves in a different world from South-West Africa; they had to colonize in the tropics. Their West African possessions consisted of two separate colonies: Togo and Cameroun. Togo (now called the Republic of Togo) was the smallest of the German colonies in Africa. It has only a small stretch of coastline on the Atlantic, but it stretches inland a distance of more than three hundred miles. The littoral consists of a low sandbar with marshy creeks and lagoons; it has great stands of reeds, mangrove swamps, and pockets of riverine forest. Cocopalms grow well along the coast, supplying the indigenous people with a valuable export that requires little capital for its exploitation. Behind the lagoons rises the Watyi plateau, where scant rainfall and poor soils permit the growth of only drought-resistant vegetation such as the strange-looking baobabs—tough, gnarled trees that can withstand dust and lack of water. Indigenous cultivators grow Indian corn, cassava, and cotton on the tableland and plateau. The mountains are covered by forest, and cocoa and coffee are grown in profusion on cleared land. Savanna country lies to the north.

Togo's population is varied. In the south are Kwa-speaking people —the Ewe, the Watyi, the Mina, and others. In colonial times they were organized into clans and divided into small chiefdoms; their mode of life was somewhat akin to that of the Ashanti of the Gold Coast. Yams, corn, and other food crops provided subsistence; they were skillful fishermen, and they excelled in weaving, ironwork, and pottery. They produced palm oil for export and developed an intricate network of trade and credit that brought them into early contact with merchants from Germany, Great Britain, Brazil, and other overseas countries. Inland there were pastoralists and farmers. The groups in the northern savanna comprised a number of Muslim communities, but the great majority of the population followed various pagan religions. The Togolese polities differed greatly in size and internal makeup, but none was a military power strong enough to overawe all its neighbors.

Cameroun—in German, Kamerun—has even greater topographic and ethnographic variations than Togo. The vegetation ranges from coastal mangrove swamps to rain forest with trees up to 250 feet in height hung with climbing plants. The variety of plant species diminishes toward the drier margins of the forest as the canopy of trees becomes more open and allows more room for the undergrowth. Forest gives way to parkland at higher altitudes, and the northern region forms part of a large savanna belt. In the extreme north Cameroun abuts on Lake Chad—a wide, watery expanse, its coastline broken by bays, peninsulas, and lagoons. The highest elevation is Mount Cameroun, a great peak by the sea, concealed sometimes by tornado clouds or half-hidden by gold, green, and rose-colored vapors tinted by the setting sun.

Ethnographically and politically, Cameroun was probably one of the most fragmented parts of Africa in the late nineteenth century—a feature that greatly facilitated German conquest of its huge area. Most of the people spoke a group of languages remotely related to Bantu, including Duala, Yaunde, Basa, Fang, and many others, but they lacked any sense of political unity. The northern peoples—the Fulani, Hausa, Kanuri, and Shuwa Arabs—led lives which differed widely from each other. Those on the coast, especially the Duala, utilized their geographical position to set up trade monopolies that dominated inland trade: they accepted imported goods on credit from white merchants and bartered this merchandise to the forest peoples in exchange for slaves, ivory, and rubber. As the Duala prospered, the rulers of Akwa and Bell, the chief trading stations, became influential along the coast.

The extreme north of Cameroun formed part of the civilization of the Sudan, and with other Sudanic areas was linked to the world of Islam. Its peoples built walled cities; they used the horse and camel in trade and war; they practiced a variety of crafts, were skilled herdsmen, and farmed. During the eighteenth and nineteenth centuries the Fulani subjugated considerable portions of northern and central Cameroun, where they set up Muslim states such as Adamawa, a powerful feudal state. Their rule depended on serfdom: Fulani armies periodically raided and murdered or enslaved their pagan neighbors. Fulani influence extended to the pagan kingdom of Bamum situated in the grassland south of Adamawa. The military power of the Fulani nobles depended on cavalry, almost invincible in open savanna country but ill-suited for campaigns in dense woodland. Hausa traders of the Muslim persuasion were able to penetrate into the forest land, however, so that such areas of the country were integrated to some extent into the Sudanic economy. The indigenous peoples inhabiting the rain forests were divided mostly into smaller polities dependent on various forms of shifting agriculture and on hunting. They sometimes practiced ritual human sacrifice.

Until the 1880's the Germans had little knowledge of these regions. Their contacts were confined to a few coastal areas of West Africa and depended on the goodwill of Africans. Missionaries of the Basel Mission Society had settled on the Togolese coast, and the North German Missionary Society labored among the Ewe with far-reaching consequences for the future of German colonization in this region. Educated Africans like James Africanus Horton, an Afro-British army surgeon and scholar of Sierra Leonean origin, thought highly of those Teutonic clergymen who set up schools on the Gold Coast, fought disease, brought new crops, sometimes married black women, and proudly called themselves "Germano-Africans." In a very minor way the traffic of ideas had also gone in the other direction. As early as the eighteenth century, for instance, Anton Wilhelm Amo, a native of Axim, had been taken to Germany as a youngster and later pursued his studies at the universities of Halle and Wittenberg. Amo enriched German philosophy with a work of logical criticism with a mechanistic bias; in another work he argued that on historical grounds slavery was contrary to the laws of Europe.[9]

Merchants on the Atlantic coast were as dependent on the goodwill of their customers as were missionaries on the goodwill of local chiefs and the trust of their flocks. Traders adjusting their activities to the vagaries of the market had little occasion to stand upon their dignity. One of Africa's most popular imports during the 1870's and early 1880's was cheap liquor, and German gin became a favorite article of consumption in many parts of West Africa; in East Africa, where Muslim influence was strong, this was not so much the case. Equally important perhaps was the traffic in firearms. Hanseatic firms had no hesitation in selling guns to Africans. Without foreign-made weapons, including some modern breechloaders imported by German and other white traders, nations like the Herero and Nama of South-West Africa could not have resisted the Kaiser's forces with such tenacity. In addition, the Germans made a good deal of money by transshipping British-made goods. (A form of Black English remained the lingua franca of Cameroun and parts of Togo till the end of German rule.)

Not surprisingly, Germany's pre-colonial trade in guns and spirits became unpopular not only with missionaries and humanitarians but also with hard-line imperialists, who thought that rifles would render Africans insolent and schnapps would make them lazy. The Hamburg pioneers thought otherwise, and as long as they confined their activity to the coast—often doing business from the hulks of old ships anchored off the coast of Cameroun—they, like their fellow British merchants, had little desire for official supervision or for governance by Geheimräte. (A majority of the Hamburg senate opposed empire-building as late as 1890, several years after the formal German empire had become an established fact.[10])

The pattern of trade began to change. The volume of commerce expanded as the Germans purchased increasing quantities of tropical goods—especially palm oil, used as a raw material for the manufacture of soap and candles. In 1882 the firm of Woermann, a Hamburg concern with trading posts at many points along the west coast of Africa, established a regular shipping line to West Africa—a venture that signalled major departures in the history of German maritime enterprise. Woermann, among others, realized that the future lay with the steamboat, not the sailing vessel. The steamboat was an expensive investment of a kind that smaller family firms (like the patrician Buddenbrooks in Thomas Mann's novel) could not afford. The olden-day mercantile house had tried to own at least one (or several) sailing ships for family prestige as well as a means of transport. The future lay with more highly capitalized steamship lines whose financial strength and organizational resources went far beyond anything that the Buddenbrooks could muster. Mann attributed the decline of the Buddenbrooks fortunes to loss of *élan vital*. In reality, the firm would probably have gone under because the Buddenbrooks could not adjust to the age of steam and corporate finance.

The old notions of indirect influence ceased to attract the more aggressive German traders when falling prices impelled merchants to push inland in order to reduce costs and beat the competition by circumventing local African monopolies. The Duala of Cameroun, once German allies, became obstacles to German firms. Once commercial houses like Woermann had set up their own plantations and stores on the mainland, they increasingly looked to direct German protection and began to favor territorial expansion. Within the general context of German capitalism, however, the west coast traders were quite insignificant. They were too weak to shoulder the cost of government: there was no German equivalent of the British Royal Niger Company. From the beginning, therefore, the German government had to step in. In 1884 Bismarck took the decisive step: treaties were concluded with a number of Ewe and Duala chiefs, and the Germans embarked on a career of colonial governance in West Africa.

Bismarck's original theories of colonization by private enterprise had been resounding failures; colonialism had to be nationalized, so to speak. Colonial administrators became dependent on funds voted by the Reichstag, which passed on every item of administrative expenditure. As the chancellor had feared, the German legislature used its financial power to try to supervise its colonial empire down to the most minute details—even to the building of a mole (sea wall) in some remote port in South-West Africa. All important decisions were made in Berlin, so that financial rather than bureaucratic constraints began to impose a system of extreme parsimony and centralization on the governance of Germany's African colonies.[11]

The system linked colonial issues with the domestic concerns of German politics. All parties criticized the German colonial administration at one time or another—in particular, the Center party, and even more, the Social Democrats, who had no part in the various governing coalitions. The Catholic Center and the Freisinnige Liberals sometimes provided necessary swing votes, but until 1906 they were apt to by highly critical of Germany's colonial effort. They could be rallied under the slogan "Let those who profit pay the costs of development and rule," but after the failure of the DOAG this position was no longer tenable. Only the National Liberals and the Conservatives could usually be relied upon to support the government for reasons of patriotism, if not for financial gain.

TWO

The Metropolitan Scene

Colonial Pressure Groups

Despite the activities of businessmen-politicians like von der Heydt and Lucas, colonial enterprise was of only marginal significance to the German public and to German capitalists. During the first two decades of Wilhelmian expansion overseas, the Reich spent little capital in colonial ventures, and the pioneering companies rarely made money. In the early period the colonies were devoid of port and railway facilities, markets were scarce, agricultural experimentation was costly, and risks were high. A colonial financier reported in a private letter in 1892 that absolutely no one would touch colonial stock of any kind.[1] The pace of colonial investment picked up somewhat after the turn of the century; even then, however, German investors did not risk much money outside the fatherland. Between 1900 and 1914 only about one-tenth of current savings in Germany went abroad, and the bulk of this was placed elsewhere in Europe. The Austro-Hungarian empire alone attracted as much German capital as the African and Asian continents combined. Only a tiny proportion of Germany's private funds was invested in her African colonies; by 1907 the reserves and share capital of a single major German bank such as the Dresdner Bank or the Diskontogesellschaft amounted to more than all the private capital invested in the empire's African colonies.[2]

The colonial empire accounted for less than one percent of Germany's overseas trade; between 1891 and 1910 the colonial share of German exports increased from only 0.17 to 0.73 percent of the total. Social Democratic critics of imperial colonization repeatedly pointed out that trade with a small country like Norway was worth far more to Germany's commerce than all her overseas dependencies. By 1912 she exported more than five times as much to Belgium as to all her African colonies and eighteen times as much as to South-West Africa, for which so much German blood and treasure had been sacrificed. (The export figures for 1912 were 493.3 million marks for Belgium, 91.323 million marks for the African colonies, and 26.442 million marks for South-West Africa.)

The financial resources available for German colonial purposes were very limited. Seen in terms of German capitalism as a whole, colonialism was more a form of conspicuous consumption on a national scale than an outlet for the investment of surplus private capital. The total amount spent by the Reich on the African colonies in the form of imperial subsidies and subventions exceeded the investments of all German companies in the African colonies (see Appendix Table E.2). Thus German colonialism was as much the child of state capitalism as of private capitalism.

The weakness of Germany's economic enterprise in the colonies reflected the lack of popular support for her overseas expansion in its initial stages. The German colonies were not founded in response to popular agitation; the first colonial lobbies consisted of highly specialized pressure groups. Among the earliest of these were the geographical societies. From the beginning of the nineteenth century, German scholars like Alexander von Humboldt and Karl Ritter had turned the study of geography into a scientific subject with a theoretical underpinning, and through the creation of geographical societies organizational support was provided for their endeavors. These societies included the Gesellschaft für Erdkunde zu Berlin (1828) and the Centralverein für Handelsgeographie (1863), which emphasized the economic value of the geographical sciences. Early German explorers like Heinrich Barth and Emin Pasha had often worked for foreign governments, but later German scholar-explorers increasingly preferred to work in the service of their own government, providing political as well as academic support for German colonial expansion.

German missionary societies were another colonial lobby; like their British counterparts, they had acquired some political influence. Catholic missionary groups had connections with the Center Party in the Reichstag; Protestant groups had close links with supporters at home and with merchants and administrators in the mission field. Though torn by internal dissension, the missionaries as a whole considered that

Germany should expand not only for religious reasons but also for those of Realpolitik: they felt that the German sword should be thrown into the balance against slave traders and heathen warlords. They also made an important contribution to "scientific colonialism." Clergymen such as Jakob Spieth, with his classic studies of the Ewe, and Heinrich Vedder, with his investigations into the history and ethnology of South-West Africa, played a part in the academic "opening up" of the colonies. The combination of missionaries, geographers, and explorers helped to create an informed reading public with an interest in colonial expansion. Colonial enthusiasm, insofar as it existed, immediately followed German empire-building.

The Deutsche Kolonialverein, formed in 1882, was a minor body without national importance which owed its origin to a meeting of the Frankfurt and Offenbach chambers of commerce, a few businessmen, and intellectuals—especially members of the Verein für Geographie und Statistik—who pledged to support colonial commerce, exploration, and expansion. The Kolonialverein recognized that the Reich could not be expected to give priority to the colonial task or to violate the interests of foreign nations. Its primary objective was to prevent the existing interest in colonization from being stifled at a time when Germany had not yet displayed a determination to colonize.[3] In the first year of its existence the league had fewer than 3,000 subscribers; seven years later, in 1889, membership of the society had grown to 17,500. Even so, its political and financial power remained insignificant: its total annual income was slightly less than 105,000 marks, an amount a lucky man might win as first prize in a local lottery.

In terms of institutional support, the Kolonialverein was at first also in an unenviable position. A number of municipalities and chambers of commerce paid for institutional membership, but support came mainly from small towns and villages—places with names like Schweidnitz, Zeitz, and Ziegenhals. Northern and eastern Germany were particularly ill-represented. At a time when public opinion supposedly was forcing Bismarck to embark upon an active colonial policy for the purpose of promoting German trade, the great seaports like Hamburg and Bremen and major industrial centers like Berlin or Essen were not sufficiently interested to participate in the Kolonialverein (see Table 3).

Such influence as the league could initially command derived from

TABLE 3
*Municipalities and Chambers of Commerce in the
Deutsche Kolonialverein, 1884*

Municipalities (Stradtgemeinden)

Chemnitz	Karlsruhe	Plauen i. Vogtland
Cüstrin	Leer	Scheidnitz
Eibenstock	Leisning	Schneeberg
Emden	Mittweiden	Schwabach
Giessen	Oberhausen	Stuttgart
Haimchen	Osnabrück	Zeitz
Hamm	Pirna	Ziegenhals

Chambers of Commerce

Bielefeld	Lüneburg	Siegen
Braunschweig	Mühlheim	Sorau
Heidelberg	Offenbach	Ulm
Köln	Osnabrück	Wesel
Lübeck	Plauen i. Vogtland	Worms

SOURCE: *Deutsche Kolonialzeitung*, vol. 1, Heft 2 (Berlin, 1884), pp. 27ff.

its connections with the upper layers of German bureaucracy, the world of municipal administration, business, and German universities. The executive committee was replete with names such as Landesdirektor R. von Bennigsen, a distinguished Hanoverian civil servant; Dr. Johannes Miquel, the Oberbürgermeister (lord mayor) of Frankfurt, a prominent National Liberal and a former member of the Diskontogesellschaft; Professor Friedrich Ratzel, a well-known geographer; and Gustaf Freytag, an historian and a novelist widely read in his day. In 1887 the Kolonialverein further strengthened its base by merging with Carl Peters's Gesellschaft für Deutsche Kolonisation, becoming the Deutsche Kolonialgesellschaft (DKG)—the chief extra-parliamentary pressure group in favor of colonial expansion and one of the many Interessenverbände (organized lobbies) that played so important a part in Wilhelmian politics.

Within the DKG, as within the Pan-German League, there were practically no industrial workers, and farmers—the men who were supposed to be looking hardest for living space outside the overcrowded Reich—had no interest in it. The DKG derived its membership overwhelmingly from people who had graduated from high school with an Abitur and had served in the armed forces as one-year volun-

teers or as commissioned officers. They were likely to vote for the
National Liberals or the Conservatives, and to make their mark in the
civil service, the army, the professions, or—above all—in commerce
and industry (see Table 4). The DKG was linked to high finance
through bankers such as von der Heydt and maintained ties with industry through businessmen like Karl Supf, a Berlin factory owner. It had
good relations with the navy through dignitaries such as Rear Admiral
Strauch, a retired officer who served as a deputy vice president. It
could draw on support from civil servants and from retired governors such as General Eduard von Liebert, a militant right-winger and
founder of the Reichsverband gegen die Sozialdemokratie, an anti-
socialist propaganda organization. By 1913 the Executive Committee
of the DKG included a great variety of professional men, bureaucrats,
naval officers, retired generals, civil servants, bankers, merchants,
publishers, physicians, clergymen, and manufacturers. Its social
"spread" was equally wide: there were high-born aristocrats such as
Duke Johann Albrecht zu Mecklenburg and businessmen of plebeian
descent; there were great dignitaries of state and minor civil servants
of whom no one had ever heard.

In size of membership, the DKG was not particularly impressive. In
1914 it had no more than 42,000 members—scarcely more than a sec-
tarian body such as the Centralverein deutscher Staatsbürger jüdis-
chen Glaubens (a Jewish defense league) and incomparably less than
that of a right-wing organization such as the Deutscher Flottenverein
(the German naval league) with its 1,108,106 individual and corporate
supporters. The DKG's annual income in 1912 amounted to only
350,000 marks, of which about 200,000 came from membership contributions.

The political influence of the DKG, however, was greater than
would seem warranted by its membership or income. It united within
its ranks the great majority of all Germans with an interest in the colonies. Its only rival, the Deutschnationaler Kolonialverein—a right-
wing group headed by Curt von François, whose membership consisted mainly of retired civil servants, teachers, attorneys, writers,
surveyors, and other professional men—played no serious part in
German colonial affairs. The DKG was well organized. It shaped opinion through its publications (including the *Koloniale Monatsblätter* and
the *Deutsche Kolonialzeitung*), cinematographic performances, exhi-

TABLE 4
Social Composition of the Deutsche Kolonialgesellschaft, 1893

Class or occupation	Number	Percent
High nobility	149	0.3%
Scholars, writers, artists	203	1.2
Clergymen, teachers	1,063	6.1
Civil officials	2,298	13.1
Military officers	1,462	8.3
Judges, attorneys, notaries public	1,115	6.6
Physicians	826	4.7
Merchants, manufacturers	7,099	40.5
Farmers	421	2.4
Pensioners	370	2.1
Miscellaneous professionals	2,477	14.1

SOURCE: Helmut Müller and Hans-Joachim Fieber, "Deutsche Kolonialgesellschaft DKG 1882 [1887]–1933" in *Die bürgerlichen Parteien in Deutschland* (Leipzig, 1968), I:393.

bitions, library work, lectures (including some to school children), and other activities. It sent scientific expeditions to the colonies, provided assistance to German colonial settlers, and attempted to promote the creation of German schools overseas; it also encouraged colonial congresses held in 1902, 1905, and 1910.

Above all, the DKG closely cooperated with the Kolonialwirtschaftliche Komitee (KWK), an autonomous body nominally linked to the DKG that played a major role in promoting colonial research and development. The KWK, founded in 1896, aimed at building up the colonies as producers of raw materials and as markets for German goods; in addition it desired to develop the colonies in such a fashion as to create new forms of industry in Germany (such as factories producing agricultural machinery suited to the tropics), looked to the expansion of a logistic infrastructure (especially railways and shipping), and hoped to promote German settlement.

The executive committee lists of the KWK read like an extract from a German *Who's Who*. Industry was strongly represented through Supf and men like Kommerzienrat C. Clauss and E. Hertle, both of whom were prominent textile manufacturers; shipping had a spokesman in Albert Ballin, one of the great German-Jewish financial magnates of the period and founder of the huge Hamburg-Amerika Linie; Paul Habicht, director of the Ostafrikanische Eisenbahngesellschaft,

provided expertise in railway matters; banking was represented by
Karl Helfferich, a distinguished economist and a director of the
Deutsche Bank. In addition there were leading intellectuals interested
in colonial questions, including Karl Dove, a geographer, and Professor E. A. Fabarius, head of the Deutsche Kolonialschule, Witzenhausen—a very efficiently run institution designed to train planters
and farmers for work overseas. The KWK was organized into nine
separate departments dealing with specialized questions such as arable
and pastoral farming, machine tools, viticulture, and so forth. It was
therefore able to carry out a great variety of tasks connected with promoting the cultivation of cotton in the colonies, producing improved
strains of maize, increasing the supply of artificial fertilizers, and extending the use of agricultural machinery.

The interests represented in the DKG exercised considerable
influence on the German civil administration. Like the French, the
German colonial ministry looked for support not only in the Reichstag
but also among pressure groups with a colonial interest—businessmen,
financiers, journalists, colonial societies, and soldiers. These lobbies
also dominated the Kolonialrat, an advisory colonial council created in
1891 which embodied a wide variety of interests: great aristocrats with
colonial connections, missionaries, civil servants, academics with a
stake in colonial studies, bankers, merchants, plantation owners, and
concessionaires. According to Heinrich Schnee, who had personal experience of the Kolonialrat, its proceedings tended to be too theoretical in character to be of much value to colonial administrators. In any
case, the Kolonialrat was so heterogeneous in composition as to make it
unsuited for the task of formulating policies, but was of considerable
value to the government in that its "independent experts" would provide support for administrative measures approved by the colonial authorities. In addition, major concerns represented within the council,
such as the Neuguinea-Kompagnie, would spring to the defense of
other bodies of a similar nature when they were attacked in public.[4]
The Kolonialrat supplied a forum where opposing colonial interests
might air their views in public and gain a measure of their opponents'
strength.

During the first decade or so of its existence the council was dominated by planters and concession-seekers—men who tended to believe

that Germany could best carry out her civilizing mission in Africa by forcing tribesmen to become proletarians (a theme covered in subsequent sections of this study). Representative examples of this type were Julius Scharlach, a Hamburg lawyer and land speculator, and Major (later Lieutenant General) Aimé Palézieux-Falconnet.

Palézieux was a member of the old Huguenot-Prussian aristocracy, lord chamberlain to the Duke of Saxe-Weimar, and had a financial interest in the Deutsch-Ostafrikanische Plantagengesellschaft, the first German plantation company in East Africa. He devoted much energy to interesting aristocratic investors in the stock of his company, whose early shareholder lists read like excerpts from the *Almanach de Gotha*. Despite its aristocratic connections the company was not unduly troubled by notions of noblesse oblige. It obtained African laborers through the services of a wealthy Indian merchant at Zanzibar and supervised them through the agency of Arab foremen. When the workmen caused serious trouble, the German manager would tie up the malcontents with rope and suspend them all night from the rafters of his veranda. These practices led to protests from "whining philanthropists" at the German consulate at Zanzibar, but they seem to have persuaded the company's laborers to work for ten hours a day at a daily wage of seventy-five pfennigs, a salary that the company determined to lower once locals had become habituated to wage work.[5]

This approach sharply conflicted with an alternative view of African development especially popular among administrators and merchants in Togo, who assumed that Africa should be civilized by means of a partnership between African peasant producers and European traders. Perhaps the most outstanding representative of this school was Johann Karl Vietor, a Togo merchant—the kind of *christlicher Kaufmann* (Christian businessman) found in nineteenth-century Bremen, an Atlantic port strongly influenced by pietistic revivalism. Johann was the son of a poverty-stricken pastor who had thirteen children. Money was so short in the Vietor home that until his fourteenth year young Johann never had butter on his bread. He was fortunate, however, in having two uncles who were doing well in the Togolese trade; Vietor joined them in West Africa. He later founded a firm of his own known for its probity, its refusal to deal in liquor, and its declared policy of dismissing all employees living with a concubine. In 1901 he entered the

Kolonialrat to become the most influential member of the missionary trading lobby, which from 1902 onward obtained support from a majority within the council.

Within the colonies themselves, by contrast, the mercantile-missionary school of imperialism formed a minority interest. Only in Togo, where German colonizers had encountered an indigenous African trading system of long standing, did the interests of German merchants and native cultivators prevail over those of the planters. In Cameroun the planters were generally stronger than the import-export firms, and the West African plantations organized between themselves the Verband der Kamerun- und Togopflanzungen, which became an influential lobby treated with respect by both administrative officers and politicians.

None of the local pressure groups, however, was strong enough to exclude foreign competitors. British capitalists placed considerable sums into German dependencies, especially those of South-West Africa and Cameroun. British merchants accounted for a substantial part of Germany's colonial trade, above all in Togo and Cameroun, where (as noted earlier) a form of Black English was employed widely both in business and in the colonial administration. British and Indian firms shared in the commerce of East Africa, particularly that handled through the port of Zanzibar, which still conducted about one-third of the territory's foreign trade in 1913. The German tariff policy was liberal. In the Kiau Tschau (Kiao Chow) territory in China, Tsingtau was a free port. Elsewhere colonial tariffs were designed to raise local revenue rather than to extend special protection to German firms. Not surprisingly, the Germans enjoyed the respect of British free traders and humanitarians like E. D. Morel, who thought that their countrymen might learn from Germany's technical efficiency.

German humanitarians interested in the colonies—many of them anglophiles—later banded together in the Deutsche Kongo Liga, an association formed in 1910 on the model of the British Congo Reform Association in order to fight abuses in the Belgian Congo and to secure freedom of trade; both organizations were dissolved in 1913 on the grounds that their objectives had been accomplished. The Deutsche Kongo Liga was succeeded by the Deutsche Gesellschaft für Eingeborenenschutz (DGES), structured on the lines of the British Aborigines Protection Society and substantially supported by capitalists such as Eduard Woermann, head of the Woermann shipping line, and Bernhard Dernburg, a liberal banker and former colonial secretary, leading administrators like Karl Ebermeier, the last German governor of Cameroun, and above all by German Protestant missionary societies.

The DGES resolved to fight what it regarded as the "excesses" inflicted by Western civilization upon backward peoples; it sought to counteract the assumed dangers of depopulation in Africa, to promote the education and well-being of Africans, and to assure a form of peaceful coexistence between black and white. According to the DGES, colonial development was impossible without African cooperation, and Germany had a moral obligation to exercise a form of trusteeship over its colonies. The organization published a monthly entitled *Koloniale Rundschau: Monatsschrift für die Interessen unserer Schutzgebiete und ihrer Bewohner*, edited by Diedrich Westermann and Consul Ernst Vohsen, a liberal-minded publisher, which carried contributions from highly placed men like governors Seitz (Cameroun) and Leutwein (South-West Africa) and was supported primarily by Bremen merchants.[6]

The DGES also had supporters within the Reichstag, where both the Deutsche Kolonialgesellschaft and the Kolonialrat lost power to party members after 1905. The Reichstag became increasingly important as a policymaking body for the colonies. Its main control over colonial affairs was monetary, and the budget commission—much as in the French system—was its vehicle for exercising this control. All income and expenditures in the colonies, all loans raised for their use, had to be reviewed annually by the Reichstag, and the colonial budget received detailed attention in a way unknown to the British Parliament.

Settlers in both South-West and East Africa sought to influence colonial policy by pressuring the colonial secretary through rightist parties and politicians in the Reichstag, and the DGES used similar tactics to exert influence through groups sympathetic to its interests. Three members of the DGES were part of the Reichstag budget commission just before the outbreak of World War I. They were an oddly assorted lot. Reinhard Mumm was a Calvinist theologian and a friend of Vietor's; he stood for the Christlich Soziale Wirtschaftliche Vereinigung, a small right-wing group that uneasily blended vague appeals for social justice with a genteel variety of anti-Semitism. Dr. David

Felix Waldstein was a Jewish attorney and represented the Deutsche Fortschrittliche Volkspartei, a liberal splinter group; he died in exile in Great Britain during the Nazi era. Matthias Erzberger was a left-wing Catholic and an influential member of the Zentrum, the powerful Catholic Center party; he was later murdered by right-wing fanatics. The National Liberals and the conservative parties in the Reichstag could generally be relied upon to support colonial causes. A conservative party like the Reichspartei, for example, argued that colonial expansion was consistent with the requirements of a "healthy national egotism"; the National Liberals echoed that colonies were founded to serve the economic needs of the mother country. The Social Democrats opposed colonial expansion in a fairly consistent fashion, although after the "Hottentot" election of 1907 (held in the wake of a great African uprising in South-West Africa) more of them supported a humane colonization. The Center Party and the Freisinnige Liberals tended to be critical, though they could be won over by concessions and especially—after 1906—by reforms. Even right-wingers were apt to castigate individual abuses; the Pan-Germans, for instance, disliked land concessions given to foreigners. The Reichstag became increasingly reformist in its sentiments after 1900—a theme to be considered in a subsequent section.

Romance and Realism in Colonial Credos

Colonial explorers and empire-builders wrote copiously, and some of them wrote well. Between them they produced a new form of literature that helped create a new interest in exotic lands. Missionaries, for instance, contributed to Germany's growing colonial consciousness by writing in mission magazines of distant pagan lands, of deep darknesses, of rosy dawns, and of the Gospel's morning light whose rays were about to pierce the darkness of heathen Africa. Many of these missionaries also had secular notions of Germany's (and Europe's) civilizing mission. Men like Gustav Warneck, a major figure in the German missionary world, argued that the Germans must protect, educate, and convert the indigenous peoples of Africa; he thereby helped to provide an ethical as well as a religious justification for Germany's African enterprise. Missionaries, like administrators, greatly enriched the knowledge of African ethnography and linguistics; their studies included such classics as Jakob Spieth's *Die Ewestämme: Material zur Kunde des Ewevolkes in Deutsch-Togo* (1906). Works of lesser renown by obscure but able clergymen filled many library shelves; these included dictionaries, grammars, and ethnographies—works which were of considerable value to administrators and to scholars.

The German missionary was only one of many professionals—physicians, agronomists, geologists, engineers, and scores of others—who looked to the colonies not only as a source of employment but also as a field for new and creative work. Here were uncharted frontiers where science and technology might solve age-old problems in countless fields of endeavor. Almost without exception these "functional" colonizers assumed that their work could be accomplished only under the flag of a European power, preferably—as far as the Germans were concerned—under the protection of a *Pax Teutonica*.

Of all the professional groups, perhaps the most important were the explorers and geographers who had followed the initial impetus provided by Alexander von Humboldt and Karl Ritter. Between them and their organizations, these men produced an extensive body of written works, from chatty *feuilletons* in the daily press—replete with descriptions of exotic lands and strange peoples—to massive tomes of an encyclopaedic kind. However these writers might differ among themselves, they all tended to convey to German readers the idea that Africa was a mysterious continent full of unknown peoples with curious customs—a vast terrain of boundless opportunities, one of the world's last open frontiers.

The rewards of geographical achievement were unevenly distributed. The top echelon of German geographers was formed by professional scholars like Heinrich Barth (1821–62), a classical philologist turned explorer. Barth's African studies became classics and earned him an appointment to the chair of geography at Berlin University and election to the presidency of the Geographische Gesellschaft. Other leading academic geographers included Friedrich Ratzel, a pharmacist turned traveller, geographer, and political writer, and Ferdinand Freiherr von Richthofen (1833–1905), who held the University of Berlin's chair of geography in 1886 and helped to found its Institute for Oceanography. Both Ratzel and von Richthofen were influential in the formulation of colonial policy.

On a lower level were travellers like Carl Mauch (1837–75), the first

modern European to visit the Zimbabwe ruins in present-day Rhodesia. Mauch, an elementary schoolmaster turned traveller and a self-
taught geographer and geologist, was a remarkable man. At a time
when geographical exploration was beginning to become a profession
supported by substantial grants from learned societies and requiring a
high degree of organization, he covered great distances at negligible
expense, relying on nothing but the help of friendly black chiefs and
accommodating white hunters. While he lacked paper qualifications
and could not get any kind of academic position in the Reich, he gained
a modest degree of fame—and a job in a cement factory whose owners
were impressed by his feats.

Geography catered to an inexhaustible demand for exact information
and a longing for exotic romance; it was also an applied science of immediate value to merchants and military staff officers. Eduard von
Liebert records in his autobiography that his first impetus to a colonial
career came from a burgeoning interest in cartography. A commoner
by origin, Liebert belonged to a new breed of staff officer—untitled
men like August Keim, his contemporary, who took a keen interest in
military scholarship, promoted Pan-German ideas, and played an active part in defense-minded propaganda organizations such as the
Deutsche Flottenverein and the Wehrverein, thereby doing his bit to
influence the German press and call for a militant Weltpolitik.

In the late 1870's, when Russian armies stood before Constantinople, Liebert became increasingly interested in colonial questions
—not because he had a stake in overseas trade, but because he wished
to enhance Germany's power, commerce, and prestige. He was
thus instrumental in founding a geographical society in Hannover
which he hoped would assist German expansion, at least in the ideological field. Through his geographical work he became acquainted with
Dr. Friedrich Lange, one of the editors of the *Tägliche Rundschau*, a
colonialist journal to which Liebert contributed numerous articles. As
a promising staff officer—a junior member of Germany's military elite
—Liebert got to know the major colonial explorers and colonialist politicians of his day; he also became associated with the Deutsche Kolonialgesellschaft.

On a more philosophical level, Liebert, like many others of his generation, was influenced by the musings of Eduard von Hartmann
(1842–1906), an ex-officer forced to take his discharge because of a

troublesome knee, who was a fashionable philosopher during the Wilhelmian period. His philosophy of the unconscious, *Die Philosophie des Unbewussten*, first published in 1869, was printed in eleven editions by 1904. Hartmann tried to reconcile the work of Schopenhauer and Hegel with the findings of the natural sciences; he somehow argued that the Absolute and the Unconscious were linked and that Will was the essential attribute of the Unconscious. However weak its intellectual foundations, this was a system well suited to activists in search of a purposive philosophy.

Esthetically, Liebert—as well as many of his contemporaries—was strongly influenced by the writings of Felix Dahn (1834–1912), a law professor who entertained successive generations of German schoolboys with trashy best-sellers of Teutonic heroism. In Dahn's novels honest, fair-haired Goths battled through five hundred pages or more against treacherous, black-haired Byzantines who won by cheating and not by valor. He also wrote poetry in a verse with a peculiar rocking-horse rhythm which, translated into English, would probably have managed to rhyme "mango" with "tango" or "hyena" with "subpoena." Dahn's "Song of the Germans Overseas" (1887), solemnly recited at patriotic occasions in the Kolonialverein, likened unexplored lands to longing virgins waiting to be conquered by impetuous German lovers.[7]

The work of Dahn and his ilk had the brash vulgarity that distinguished so much of official Germany—a country whose breathtaking and unparalleled economic progress had created a peculiar nouveau riche spirit entirely alien to the German past. It was for this reason perhaps that Dahn could appeal to a man like Liebert who, contrary to the Anglo-Saxon stereotype of the Prussian professional officer, was both well-educated and well-read—probably more so than his average British or French counterpart. Both Dahn and Hartmann corresponded to a peculiar mood in German society. Both warmly supported the colonial cause; they attended learned and not-so-learned congresses that blended colonialism with chauvinism and enjoyed wide support from German banks and industry and from learned societies such as the Zentralverein für Handelsgeographie.

Colonial propaganda was widespread. Many a school auditorium boasted a huge painting that showed the nations of Europe uniting at Germany's prompting against the smoke-belching yellow peril in the distance. Berlin schoolboys could have an instructive afternoon at the great colonial exhibition held at the Lehrter Bahnhof where soldiers in colonial uniform explained the wonders of Africa to the visitors. These suntanned cavalrymen in their broad-brimmed digger hats had an air of romance, not least because of their ability to ride camels. Grownups at cabaret shows could laugh at King Akwa, a stock figure of fun—an African chief dressed up as a *parvenu* with stiff collar, top hat, and a diamond ring on every finger.[8]

In a more serious mood Germans could attend lectures and meetings arranged by patriotic bodies at which the colonies were praised. Nevertheless, the colonial appeal remained limited. Groups like the Deutsche Kolonialgesellschaft or the Alldeutsche Verband (the Pan-German League, an ultra-chauvinist body founded in 1891) were confined largely to middle-class membership. They had little attraction for workmen or peasants, who for the most part remained aloof.

Even the bulk of the bourgeoisie had no direct concern with tropical colonization. Emigration to temperate countries such as the United States was accepted and respectable; "the rich uncle from America," the emigrant who had made good beyond the Atlantic, played an honorable role in German penny-dreadfuls as the deus ex machina whose financial beneficence united parted lovers or restored fallen maidens to the path of virtue. Until the first decade of the twentieth century, however, the young man who sought to make his fortune under the German flag overseas enjoyed no similar prestige in German fiction.

To the German intelligentsia, the experience of commerce and foreign emigration had always been of marginal interest. German writers had created a splendid prose literature during the eighteenth and nineteenth centuries, but nothing in German letters corresponded to the seafaring and colonizing romances of Defoe or Captain Marryat, although works like *Robinson Crusoe* or *Masterman Ready*—the latter translated into German as *Sigismund Rüstig*—were avidly read by generations of German schoolboys, as were Fenimore Cooper's *Leatherstocking Tales*.

Insofar as the Germans did intellectual pioneering in the colonial sphere, they were active principally in the missionary and pedagogic fields. German scholars built up a new academic study styled Missionswissenschaft designed to elucidate the theory and practice of missionary work; the systematizers in this field paralleled other intellectual innovations such as the Wissenschaft des Judentums undertaken by German-Jewish scholars. They also played an important part in the development of what they called Kolonialpädagogik—systematic education for work in the colonies. Only the Germans drew up a comprehensive plan designed to train settlers. The Deutsche Kolonialschule, a residential institute at Witzenhausen run along uncompromisingly German nationalist and Protestant lines, attempted to give prospective colonists a knowledge of African religions and a basic grounding in agronomy, hygiene, business administration, and useful crafts—along with character training based on the virtues of hard work and prayer. This institution resembled attempts of other German educators to set up residential schools (Landeserziehungsheime) where youngsters would acquire practical skills, especially a knowledge of farming, to balance theoretical training.

But interest in Germany's colonies waxed slowly. In newspaper articles or Reichstag debates, intellectuals were ready enough to praise the achievements, real or reputed, of German colonialism, while others censured its abuses. But there were no significant literary works dealing with the colonies, much less works written in the self-critical tradition of Olive Schreiner, George Orwell, or even Rudyard Kipling, some of whose poems belied his reputation as an imperialist by bitterly flaying the British imperial establishment. German criticism of the colonies tended to be detailed and specific. It was innocent of assimilationist notions; unlike many of the French, German intellectuals never believed that Ewe or Hehe farmers could be turned into black Europeans—a conception that would have run counter to the legacy of German romanticism, with its emphasis on *Volkstum*, as well as to Protestant missionary ideas of establishing indigenous *Volkskirchen*. For a generation or so, colonialism remained of literary interest to only a handful of specialists.

Change came when Germans began to settle in South-West Africa, where thousands of soldiers saw military service for the first time. The colonists were romanticized by now-forgotten writers like Gustav Frenssen (1863–1945), a Lutheran pastor turned agnostic who apostrophized Bismarck in hexameter. Another apostle of German colonialism was Hans Grimm (1875–1959), who made his name by a once enormously popular novel entitled *Volk ohne Raum* (nation without space)—a phrase destined to become a political slogan. His stories and novels about Africa stressed the need for expansion. Germany needed

Africa both as a proving ground for her youth and as a means of national self-assertion; Germany required colonies to affirm her dignity, particularly against the British, whom Grimm regarded with that same curious ambivalence evinced by men as different in their respective stations in life as Carl Peters and Kaiser Wilhelm II.

Doubtless the most important purveyor of overseas romance was Karl May (1842–1912), a popular writer who combined the prolificacy of an Edgar Wallace, the anthropological enthusiasm of a Margaret Mead, and the imagination of an Edgar Rice Burroughs. May's books were read by millions of German schoolboys and became the focus of a literary cult. His life story was almost as fantastic as his fiction. Raised in a poverty-stricken household, he descended to the very bottom of the social ladder—convict and recidivist. While in prison he experienced something like a conversion and became a writer of very popular boys' stories that wove genuine ethnographic knowledge into facile adventure plots. In regions as far afield as the North American prairie, the Balkan mountains, and the Sahara sands, his heroes—splendid though unjustly persecuted—defended right against wrong, crushed evildoers, and formed enduring friendships with noble savages.

May's books made him a fortune; his unsavory past was forgotten, and parents, pastors and professors sang his praise as a writer of "wholesome" literature for adolescents. But his imagination was so prodigious that he confused himself with his literary creations and pretended to have personally accomplished some of his heroes' deeds. He was challenged, and lengthy libel actions revealed his real background to shamefaced pedagogues. Schoolboys young and old continued to devour his books, however, which became an important literary component on the romantic side of Germany's colonial tradition.

This romantic aspect clearly had an impact in attracting candidates to the German colonial service. The lure of the German navy was greatest for inland towns; navalism centered on Berlin rather than on Hamburg. Similarly, a colonial career appealed to candidates from Silesia or Swabia rather than to men from Hamburg or Bremen. Of the ten colonial governors listed in Appendix A below, six came from small country towns, one from Berlin, and one—a member of the aristocracy—had been born in Madrid. The mediators of modernity were small-town men; their visions of themselves at best were heroic. They saw themselves as members of a disciplined elite chosen from the best of Germany's youth, trained to a code of obedience and efficiency, and destined to build a new world by transforming society in the colonies. Many German colonial leaders rejected megalopolis. Bourgeois or aristocrat, the overwhelming majority of German colonial governors and Schutztruppen commanders had one thing in common: a rural bias. Liebert characteristically expressed this prejudice in stating that "the country was made by God, the town by man, and the big city by Satan."

The picturesque element in the German colonial tradition was later reinforced to some extent by the Jugendbewegung. German pathfinders, like the British boy scouts, encouraged hiking and tried to get city children into the countryside. Unlike their more practical British confreres, the Germans developed a sentimental worship of nature. They idolized the peasants whose hard work and unromantic lives city children did not share; they revived folkdancing and folksinging; they played folk instruments like the recorder; they encouraged a cult of Innerlichkeit—a preoccupation with the real or presumed qualities of the soul which could be turned all too easily into a way of shirking unpleasant reality. The more nationalistic organizations, like their opposite numbers in Eastern Europe, taught the young that to die for their country was the highest possible honor and (often) that their own people represented the cause of civilization against barbarism.

The influence of these writers remains hard to assess. Romanticism continued to pervade German life in the early twentieth century to a much greater extent than in any other western European country, and German soldiers—as tough and full of common sense as any—marched into battle with songs redolent of blood, honor, and death in a kind of verse that would have moved British guardsmen or American marines to fits of laughter. It is impossible to imagine in a British context the scene described by a German ex-governor when conversation between hard-bitten characters in a German colonial officers' mess gradually ebbed to give way to softly hummed tunes with mournful lyrics about long-departed youth.[9]

German romanticism alternated and sometimes went hand-in-hand with a curious variety of social Darwinism which found expression in a stark form of realism. Probably only in Germany could a retired governor defend his own record by interpreting colonialism in quasi-Marxist terms. "Stripped of all idealistic and humanitarian impediments," wrote Theodor Leutwein,

the final objective of all colonization is to make money. The colonizing race has no intention of bringing happiness to the aboriginal people, the kind of happiness that the latter perhaps expects. In the first instance, the conquerors seek their own advantage. Such objectives correspond to human egotism, and therefore accord with nature. Colonial policy must therefore be determined by the expected profits.

In writing these lines Leutwein was trying to refute the charge that he had been "soft to the Herero."

Yet Leutwein in many ways corresponded to the best type of British official. He was anxious to preserve the tribal structure of the peoples under his control; he would have liked to protect the Herero against a policy of brutal displacement and destruction; he was willing to recognize the soldierly qualities of hostile African warriors; he was ready to admit that Africans had as good a claim to defend their country against the Germans as the ancient Teutons had to defend theirs against the Romans; he was even prepared to acknowledge publicly the great military value of Germany's Herero auxiliaries who had fought on the German side and without whose help the Germans could hardly have conquered the territory. Leutwein prided himself on being a realist in these and other matters, however, and adopted a tone utterly devoid of the moralistic strain that characterized so much of British colonial apologetics. But the realism on which he prided himself ignored the facts of life in his own colony—a territory that accounted for no more than a negligible part of German trade and consistently helped to relieve the German taxpayer of his money (see Appendix Table E.3).

THREE

The Machinery of Central Administration

The Early Period: 1890–1906

In comparison with France, Great Britain, and even Belgium and Portugal, Germany had not done well in the scramble for Africa. Germany's colonial possessions were less extensive than those of her rivals in relation to the size and population of the metropolitan country. The German colonies were immensely varied, however—so much so that an historian is inclined to speak not of one German colonial empire but of a multiplicity of empires. Conditions in the forested southern part of Cameroun were totally different from those in the savanna-clad hinterland; Cameroun in turn was quite unlike South-West Africa, an arid region suitable at best for stock farmers. The Ewe of Togo, an advanced African people long schooled by German and Swiss missionaries, had nothing in common with the Masai of East Africa or with the cattle-keeping Herero who inhabited a considerable part of South-West Africa. Even within the same colony there were enormous contrasts, such as those among the Herero, the pastoral Hottentots—a nation of horsemen—and the Rehoboth Basters (bastards), a Eurafrican people partly of Boer descent.

The development of this heterogeneous empire proceeded slowly. Until 1906 when Bernhard Jakob Ludwig Dernburg (1865–1937) assumed control of colonial affairs (1906–10), German capitalists invested very little in the colonies.[1] Railway development was negligible, with the result that over most of the empire men and material moved at a snail's pace from the coast to the hinterland. The effective occupation of the colonies extended over a period of more than three decades. In Cameroun the conquest of the coastal zone alone required some nine years, from 1885 to about 1895; during this period the governors were Julius von Soden and Eugen von Zimmerer. Under Jesco von Putt-kamer's harsh rule (1895–1907) the Germans occupied the major part of the hinterland. It was only under Puttkamer's successors—Theodor Seitz, Otto Gleim, and Karl Ebermeier—that economic development in Cameroun began to accelerate. By 1914 there were still vast areas in the German colonies—such as the Muslim emirates of northern Cameroun and the Ovambo region of South-West Africa—that the Germans controlled only in the loosest fashion.[2]

The uneven impact of economic development in the German colonies was reflected in the colonial administrative structure. Colonial affairs initially were run in a somewhat haphazard fashion. Responsibility for the central direction of the administration rested with the Auswär-tige Amt (foreign office), where the Politische Abteilung (known by the number 1A) had disparate functions: it looked after foreign policy, personnel matters, and even relations with the press. Colonial matters were dealt with by a handful of civil servants, including one Vortrag-ender Rat and one Ständiger Hilfsarbeiter. In 1890 a relatively subordinate official known as the Kolonialdirigent was placed in charge of a separate Referat (section) within the Politische Abteilung; later that same year a separate department, the Kolonialabteilung (known as Abteilung IV), was set up within the Auswärtige Amt, where it was to remain for seventeen years, headed by a Vortragender Rat as Kolonial-dirigent. Except in issues affecting foreign policy, this official was directly answerable to the Reichskanzler. In 1894 the head of the colonial section was given the title of Kolonialdirektor.

The German colonial administration was improvised and impoverished. The director slowly gained status, but never attained the position or power of a Joseph Chamberlain in Britain or an Eugène Etienne in France. German chancellors were not very interested in what went on in the colonies, and metropolitan policy usually was shaped by commercial and settler pressure groups and depended upon Reichstag monetary allotments. In the early stages of German colonization the Kaiser—in practice, the civil servants of the Auswärtige Amt—was empowered to draw up colonial budgets on his own responsibility. Beginning in 1892, however, budgets for the various territories had to be submitted to the Reichstag and its budget commission, gaining for the legislature considerable influence in colonial affairs. The legislature could ask questions in passing on the budget, but in general the Kolonialdirektor governed as he wished.

Colonial officials occupied a modest position within the social hierarchy of the Auswärtige Amt, where their standing and background corresponded more or less to that of the consular corps—a position analogous to that of engineers, supply corps, and foot artillery in relation to the army: a corps of technicians, worthy and respectable men who did a useful job but were hardly part of fashionable society. As Heinrich Schnee—who became a colonial official and later a governor—found in London, where he was attached for a time to the German embassy, German consular officials lived worlds apart from their more distinguished and aristocratic colleagues in the diplomatic corps. The consuls went to different parties, made different friends, and even lived in a different part of London, where they mingled primarily with local German residents. The diplomats were part of the "great world," and many of them were descended from Germany's most ancient families; the consular officials and civil servants of the Kolonialabteilung were much more bourgeois in origin and outlook.

Between 1881 and 1914 all nine Staatssekretäre in charge of the Auswärtiges Amt were noblemen, whereas five of nine Kolonialdirigenten, Kolonialdirektoren, and Staatssekretäre in charge of the colonies were commoners—some of them upstarts, according to their aristocratic colleagues. Paul Kayser, the first Kolonialdirektor (1890–96), was a Jew who had managed to break into the German administrative hierarchy because of his distinction as a lawyer and his personal connection with Bismarck, whose son he had tutored for the Referendar examination; on leaving office he was appointed to the Supreme Court of the German Reich. His successor, Freiherr von Richthofen (1896–98), was a nobleman, but used the colonial department merely as a stepping stone to higher office. Gerhard von Buchka, Kolonialdirektor from 1898 to 1900 was—like Kayser—a conservative-minded jurist. His main qualification for the task of administering the overseas empire consisted in having written a learned commentary on the German civil code and in regularly paying his dues to and attending the meetings of the Rostock branch of the Deutsche Kolonialgesellschaft. Buchka's appointment seemed so bizarre to the senior officials in the colonial department that they refused to believe the news when they first heard it.

Men like Buchka and Kayser had little parliamentary influence, and their views carried almost no weight within the German bureaucracy —a serious matter at a time when an important ministry like the Reichsschatzamt (ministry of finance) was wedded to a doctrine of low taxation and extreme economy in public administration. Adolf Wermuth, Reichsschatzsekretär in the early 1900's, was suspicious of Weltpolitik and ran his department on the unromantic principle that every item of expenditure must be balanced by corresponding revenue, much as did his counterpart in the British Treasury who managed British colonial expenses.[3]

From the standpoint of the Auswärtige Amt, however, the social and political deficiencies of the Kolonialabteilung officials were of little concern. Competent lawyers and their like were perfectly suited for the relatively modest office of Kolonialdirektor, who was expected to perform a delicate balancing act between the chancellor and the foreign secretary, be competent at drafting new legislation, be knowledgeable about German treaty rights in obscure parts of the globe, write tactful answers to petitions from African chiefs, and draw up a sound departmental budget. Initially there was no specialization within the Kolonialabteilung: each Vortragender Rat was deemed capable of dealing with whatever business came to the department's attention. Apart from a few peak periods when he might have to work late at night, the pressure on the official was light. Life in the Kolonialabteilung, as in the Auswärtige Amt, moved at a leisurely and gentlemanly pace. Dispatches to foreign parts travelled slowly, and the Berlin headquarters seemed infinitely remote to the men who actually carried the German flag to the tropics. Incoming letters were sometimes hard to trace; hence senior civil servants acquired that greatest of all bureaucratic vices—the habit of creating private "hoards" of important files for their own use—with the result that business was apt to proceed in a halting fashion.

In terms of formal training, the senior officials within the Kolonialabteilung—like higher-level German bureaucrats as a whole—had excellent academic preparation. All but one of the heads of the Kolonialabteilung had a doctorate; senior colonial officials were as well-educated as their colleagues in other departments: the title of Dr. Jur. or Dr. Phil. was the rule. After 1900 most staff members had been formally trained in colonial studies at the Handelshochschulen in

Frankfurt or Berlin, at the Seminar für Orientalische Sprachen at Berlin, or at other institutions. According to the findings of Dr. Jake Spidle, much used here, about two-thirds of them had come to the colonial service by following the customary road into the German—usually the Prussian—bureaucracy.[4] A substantial number had seen service in the colonies as military men, technical specialists, scientists, or physicians. Nevertheless, prejudice against the colonial section remained, and many civil servants continued to think of the office as a refuge for incompetents.

The best of the German colonial officials included men like Erich Schultz-Ewerth (1870–1935), a noted scholar-administrator who joined the Kolonialabteilung in 1897, became a district judge in East Africa, and was later governor of Samoa. He subsequently collaborated with Dr. Leonard Adam in editing a massive two-volume study entitled *Das Eingeborenenrecht: Das Sitten- und Gewohnheitsrecht der Eingeborenen der ehemaligen deutschen Kolonien in Afrika und der Südsee* (1929–30), the standard work on customary law in the German colonies. But despite the presence of able people, there was no comprehensive colonial training system until the Dernburg reforms (see below). In contrast, the French had established the *Ecole coloniale* in 1887.

Within the Kolonialabteilung the newly joined Assessoren learned the business of the office by assisting in the preparation of the colonial budgets, occasionally attending the Reichstag debates of the budget commission or the sessions of the Kolonialrat, an advisory council formed in 1890. Junior civil servants grew inured to the almost ceaseless perusal of files on a wide variety of subjects: justice, the affairs of some South Sea island, financial procedure, and especially personnel. Study of these records did not always induce respect for the qualities of Germany's colonial statesmanship. "The Kolonialabteilung was not on good terms with its governors," wrote Heinrich Schnee in a private letter to his friend Wilhelm Solf; Schnee exaggerated. There was a good deal of incompetence, but governors such as Count von Zech, governor of Togo between 1903 and 1910, and Count von Götzen, who was in charge of East Africa between 1901 and 1906, managed to enjoy good relations with headquarters in Berlin.[5]

One case in the various bureaucratic entanglements remembered by Schnee involved Friedrich Freiherr von Schele, who sued the Reich for his return fare from East Africa, where he had served as governor between 1893 and 1895. Von Schele was a military man and an aristocrat with a prickly nature, and he resigned over a matter of precedence. Instead of being allowed to communicate directly with the Reichskanzler, he was expected to report to Kayser, a civilian, a commoner, a Jew, and—worse still—an official not sufficiently advanced in the German hierarchy to be addressed as "Your Excellency." Other incidents reviewed by Schnee illustrate the mixture of nonchalance and ignorance with which large areas of Africa were disposed of—not with a view toward the indigenous population nor even with an eye on Germany's economic advantage, but for the sake of not incommoding Prince Bismarck with untimely memoranda on obscure subjects apt to arouse His Highness's displeasure.[6]

Colonial policy in a wider sense, entailing an agreed upon set of principles regarding African destinies or African development, hardly existed before the turn of the century. Local governors and their subordinates adapted themselves to different local conditions. They enforced their authority as best they might. The governor was in a position in the colony analogous to that of the Kolonialdirektor in the Auswärtige Amt; he made all important decisions and decided policy undeterred by councils or advice from other officials. He had to defer to Berlin, of course, but locally he was supreme. Governors were even able to avoid supervision by deceiving the Reichstag on budget matters; auditing procedures were so lax that some records had not been checked in seven years, a condition that was impossible in a French or British colony. These autocrats were tempered, however, by a chronic insufficiency of funds and a pervasive lack of personnel, and by criticisms of missionaries or opposition speakers in the Reichstag who were anxious to use scandalous or criminal proceedings in the colonies as a means of embarrassing the government of the day.

The formal structure of the central administration was initially simple—much more simple than in Belgium, say, where an elaborate hierarchy was created in Brussels to run the affairs of the Congo Free State. In 1897 the Kolonialabteilung employed no more than four Vortragende Räte, a handful of Hilfsarbeiter (trained experts on short-term appointments), and a few clerks. The department prepared budgets, dealt with personnel questions such as recruitment, pay, and leave, issued directives, and negotiated with the parliament. In addition, the Kolonialdirektor presided over the Kolonialrat and deputized for the Reichskanzler in supervising the Oberkommando der Kaiserlichen Schutztruppe (the high command of the colonial army), which surprisingly came under the jurisdiction of the civilians in the Auswärtiges Amt rather than of the military. However, the Oberkommando was only a modest bureau with a few military officers, technicians, and physicians on its staff.

During the first decade of the twentieth century, the personnel at headquarters began to expand—partly as a result of the great Herero uprising that set South-West Africa ablaze in 1904. By 1906 the number of Vortragende Räte within the Kolonialabteilung had grown to nine, and the Oberkommando der Schutztruppe now required fifteen military officers, three medical doctors, a legal expert, and nine supply department officials to deal with the administration of a large army in South-West Africa—an assignment the German admiralty and ministry of war were equally unwilling to undertake. (The actual command of the troops was vested in the general staff.) Within a few years the Kolonialabteilung had expanded further still, and by the outbreak of World War I corresponded to a full-fledged ministry.

At the same time the department had to cope with increasing responsibilities connected with the building of railways, the promotion of scientific research, the development of trade, and such. There were also changes in personnel. Dr. Oscar Stübel, a former consular official, assumed the title of Kolonialdirektor in 1900—the first incumbent of the office to have travelled widely overseas. He made a remarkable choice in his chief assistant, Dr. Karl Helfferich, a brilliant intellectual not yet thirty years old. Author of several large volumes on economic theory and one of the leading defenders of the gold standard, Helfferich refused a chair at the University of Bonn in order to join the Kolonialabteilung as a temporary civil servant, albeit with the imposing title of Herr Professor.

Helfferich's formal position was a relatively modern one. He became head of a newly created Referat in charge of statistics, where he represented the new drive toward efficiency and rationalization in colonial affairs and the growing interest of German capitalists in the colonies. He improved the statistical services of the department, hoping to gain more support for colonial ventures from businessmen and parliamentarians. He promoted railway development; he reformed the

TABLE 5

Social Origins of Senior Officials within the Kolonialabteilung
and the Kolonialamt, 1899, 1906, and 1913

Year	Commoners	Noblemen
1899	2	2
1906	9	2
1913	13	1

SOURCE: Kolonial-Wirtschaftliches Komitee, *Kolonial-Handelsadressbuch* (Berlin, 1899, 1906, 1913).
NOTE: Senior officials include Staatssekretäre, Unterstaatssekretäre, Vortragende Räte, and Dirigenten.

currency in East Africa (previously dependent on British India) and in West Africa (hitherto based on the Maria Theresien *thaler*, the American half-dollar, and the shilling, along with cowries), and he assisted in the creation of the Deutsch-Ostafrikanische Bank and the Deutsch West-Afrikanische Bank, enterprises closely linked to major German banking houses such as the Dresdner Bank, the Deutsche Bank, and the Diskontogesellschaft. In 1905, when his patron left the Kolonialabteilung to become German minister to Norway, Helfferich also resigned and moved into the greater world of German politics and high finance as a director of the Anatolian Bank, deputy chairman of the Handelsbank für Ostafrika, and (in 1908) as a director of the Deutsche Bank. Subsequently he obtained high office as a member of the Deutschnationale Volkspartei, and helped to restore the German currency after World War I.[7]

In 1907 the Kolonialabteilung finally developed into a full ministry known as Reichskolonialamt, headed by Bernhard Dernburg. By this time the central administration had become more formalized. The duties of the various Abteilungen were now apportioned by topics—general administration, finance, personnel, defense—rather than by geographical area. The social composition of the Reichskolonialamt was even more bourgeois than that of the old Kolonialabteilung, and vastly more so than that of the Prussian administration at large. Under the chancellorship of Prince von Bülow (1899–1913), the percentage of commoners in the higher reaches of the Prussian administration dropped to 25 percent, while the percentage of senior officials of bourgeois origin within the colonial department eventually exceeded 90 percent (see Table 5).[8]

The Dernburg Reforms: 1906–1914

Bernhard Dernburg assumed office in 1906 as Kolonialdirektor, a year before this office became an independent ministry as the Reichs-kolonialministerium (see chapter 9 below). He was a flourishing banker of Freisinnige Liberal leanings. By the time he assumed office he had made his way to the directorial boards of thirty-nine different companies, including the powerful Allgemeine Elektrizitäts-Gesellschaft (AEG). He had been spectacularly successful at the Darmstädter Bank, one of Germany's greatest banking concerns, and had made a name for himself as a financial expert skilled in putting tottering firms on their feet.

In many ways he was an example of Germany's new managerial class—men who did not own the enterprises they managed. This directorial elite was usually well-educated and came largely from middle-class backgrounds. Its members were not, strictly speaking, technical experts; usually they had their degrees in law or economics rather than in scientific subjects. An unusually high proportion were of Jewish origin, and they made their careers in manufacturing or finance, easily passing from one field to another.

Dernburg made a number of major administrative changes in the Kolonialabteilung. The Kolonialrat, an advisory body that had represented the major colonial interest groups, was dissolved. The Zentralverwaltung (central administration) in Berlin was completely reorganized to allow for greater technical expertise. In the pre-Dernburg era the Abteilung had consisted of an undifferentiated body of administrators; Dernburg created four separate divisions within the Reichskolonialamt, each dealing with separate administrative tasks.[9] For his economic advisor he selected the AEG's Walther Rathenau, a brilliant and contradictory man—literary intellectual and captain of industry, socialist ideologue and entrepreneur, German nationalist and self-conscious Jew, yet representative of the "new era."

Dernburg's policy entailed greater decentralization in governance and greater fiscal powers for the colonies. The preparation of budgets for the territories devolved to their respective governors. Colonies were to be financially self-sufficient; instead of the traditional Zuschüsse (Reich subsidies) they would have to raise Schutzgebietsanleihen (loans) from private investors, subject to financial guarantees given by the Reich. Full responsibility for the cost of colonial defense, however, was to be borne by the Reich; hence the considerable expense of maintaining the Schutztruppen was transferred to the nation's military budget, in contrast to the French practice of making the colonies pay for the colonial army.

At the same time, the tone of Germany's colonial administration became more civilian and more bourgeois in character. Dernburg was not the first head of the German colonial administration to visit the overseas empire; Kayser had done so before him. But Dernburg managed to turn his journeys into a political publicity campaign to strengthen the cause of reform. He resolved to make the colonial service more attractive to applicants and more professional in its outlook. The period of conquest was drawing to an end, and after his accession to office no more governorships went to professional soldiers; of nine subsequent gubernatorial appointments, only three went to noblemen.

Until 1910 staff questions concerning salaries, pension rights, and job security remained largely at the discretion of the Kolonialabteilung; the officials within the Abteilung were regular Reichsbeamten whose duties were carefully specified. But officials in the field were not necessarily members of the Reich service; many were known as Kolonialbeamten, assigned by the Kaiser to serve in the colonies only and ineligible for appointment or promotion within the Reich hierarchy. The *Kolonialbeamtengesetz* (8 June 1910), Dernburg's last major achievement, regularized the positions of colonial officials, unified conditions of service, and laid down explicit conditions of tenure, survivors' benefits, and the like. Pay scales improved and became at least comparable to those obtaining at home, if not better.[10]

From 1892 onward Kolonialabteilung personnel had been detailed to attend language classes at the Seminar für Orientalische Sprachen, but the range of courses was widely expanded to include subjects as varied as tropical hygiene and crops, economics, German and foreign commercial policy, African studies, capital investment in the colonies, history of trade in East Africa, colonial law and administration, Islamic studies, and so forth. The typical "new look" graduate of the Seminar, described by Spidle, was sent to Berlin from some branch of the Reich bureaucracy—probably the Reichskolonialamt. On arrival at the Seminar he would already have completed his basic training and would have entered on a term as an Assessor or as a military officer of junior rank in the Berlin offices of the colonial administration. Normally he spent a year at the Seminar studying an African language and other subjects related to his administrative duties. Studies demanded three to six hours every day; the rest of the student's time was spent in the offices of the Kolonialamt. When he had passed his course—or often before—he was sent to the colonies as a middle-range official or a Schutztruppenoffizier.[11]

The prestigious Kolonialinstitut at Hamburg, founded in 1908, was also a product of the Dernburg era. Its purpose was twofold: it trained Reichskolonialbeamten, who attended the school for at least a year, and it comprised a Zentralstelle to coordinate Germany's economic and scientific efforts in the colonies, to diffuse information, and to promote research. The curriculum of the institute combined theoretical with applied work; students had to acquaint themselves not only with the history of the indigenous people in the colonies, anthropology, and law, but also with more practical matters such as shipping and harbor construction, cartography, botany, and tropical animal husbandry.

By the time Dernburg assumed office, the economic depression that had had such a profound impact on the period 1873–96 was over. After the turn of the century the European economies recovered in a startling fashion. Investments, prices, wages, and production figures were on the upswing; new and more "scientific" methods of organization were introduced into business management; science was applied ever more widely in factories; foreign trade and investments expanded. Dernburg's major claims to consideration were his practical experience in banking and his contacts with high finance—contacts which were particularly useful in dealing with Jewish financial magnates, who were moderately liberal in politics and anglophile in outlook, and who played a substantial part in colonial investment.[12] His links with the great German banking firms facilitated the deployment of German capital in the African colonies—a field largely neglected by German capitalists, who had preferred to place their savings in Europe or in North America rather than in the tropics.[13]

FOUR

Administration in the Colonies

The Pioneers

Imperial colonization in its first stages was scarcely more successful than the ill-planned and under-financed ventures of the Deutsch-Ostafrikanische Gesellschaft. The German colonial empire was of negligible economic importance. It ran on a tiny budget, and the total revenue of all the African colonies in 1892–93 was less than that of Berlin University (see Appendix Table E.4). There was no organized colonial service, and its central administration was of the sketchiest character. The system was predicated on the assumption that Germany would not actually administer its overseas dependencies: the Reich would do no more than furnish consular and naval protection in order to safeguard traders, and it would interfere as little as possible with the internal affairs of brown and black potentates, who would continue to rule under the German flag.

The system broke down, however. German capitalists proved unwilling to risk large amounts of money in the colonies. Except for the Jaluit Gesellschaft, which continued to shoulder administrative responsibilities in part of the German South Sea dependencies until 1906, the chartered company system could not be made to work successfully. By 1889 the Reichstag had been forced to vote a substantial sum for the purpose of putting down a widespread Muslim rising in East Africa, and the mechanism of central control had to be strengthened.

The DOAG relinquished its administration in 1891. In Togo and Cameroun, German consuls were initially appointed to act as the constituted authorities on the British pattern, and were to be backed by German warships if necessary. The colonial service attracted a number of men from the foreign office and the army, but to many, Germany's dependencies were no more than a dumping ground for loafers and ne'er-do-wells. Theodor Seitz, a police official from Baden in southwest Germany who was later to become a colonial governor, was warned by no less a person than the head of the personnel section of the foreign office to keep out of the colonies, while Count Leo von Caprivi, then Reich Chancellor, upbraided the young man on the grounds that only idlers sought employment in Africa.[1]

The German colonies' lack of prestige and economic importance was clearly reflected in the colonial administrative structure. The Kolonialabteilung lacked both bureaucratic and political influence. There was no unified colonial doctrine, no proper system of training colonial officials, and no administrative tradition with an accumulation of precedents. Until 1907, when the Reichskolonialamt came into being, there was no colonial ministry. Service in the overseas dependencies did not offer a permanent career, and its appeal was mainly to those who wanted a change from accustomed routine or who looked for an imagined world of exotic attractions. Not surprisingly, the Germans had to rely on a mixed crew: consular officials anxious to speed up their promotion, military officers tired of life in remote garrison towns, civil servants eager to see the world and drawn from a variety of agencies— the navy, the Reich administration, the Länder, the municipalities. Among them were men of many different types, including workhorses, adventurers, ne'er-do-wells, romantics, malcontents, eccentrics, and incompetents.

One important group of pioneers was composed of physicians turned administrators. During the nineteenth century, medicine abandoned its metaphysical cast, preferring empirical observation to a priori reasoning. At that time the natural sciences were much less specialized than they were to become in a later age, and the study of medicine provided a broad training in subjects like physics and chemistry as well as in medicine itself. Medical men were taught the art of accurate observation and diagnosis in a discipline that tended to enhance the value of their nonmedical observations. Physicians were assumed to be able to help themselves in an emergency, and it was useful in a colonial situation that they could prescribe treatment both for their fellow colonists and for the indigenous peoples. The medical profession enjoyed a good deal of social prestige: physicians were members of the middle class and were therefore well suited to act as explorers and to gain the ear of the public. In their capacities as travellers and scientific correspondents, some physicians acquired extensive African experience—knowledge that made them suitable for early administrative appointments.

Among these physician-administrators was Gustav Nachtigal (1834–85), one of Germany's greatest explorers. Like Cecil Rhodes and Carl Peters, Nachtigal was the son of a rural clergyman. Born in the Prussian village of Eichstad in the Altmark, young Gustav was fortunate to receive a state scholarship that enabled him to study medicine and later to join the army as a medical officer. His father and younger brother had died of a lung sickness, and when Gustav contracted the same disease that had struck down his father and brother, he had to resign his commission. Following a widespread custom, he sought relief for his health in the dry, sunny climate of North Africa. Like Rhodes, who also had lung trouble, Nachtigal recovered and embarked on an adventurous career. He began to practice medicine in Algiers, but later went to Tunis, where he served the bey as personal physician and military surgeon and then as interpreter-diplomatist. His background as an Arabist, a trained observer, and an able medical man proved of great value in his subsequent career as an explorer and as one of the founders of Germany's West African empire.

Other physician-administrators included Max Buchner (1846–1921) and Richard Kandt [Kantorowicz] (1867–1918), Germany's first Resident in Ruanda. One of the most colorful was Gerhard Rohlfs (1831–96), a self-made man in every sense of the term—the kind of adventurer who formed a link between Germany's pre-colonial era, the age of exploration, and what might be called "consular colonialism." A doctor's son, he dropped out of high school, joined the Schleswig-Holstein army at the age of seventeen, distinguished himself in fighting against the Danes, and obtained an officer's commission. Later, after studying medicine, he served briefly in the Austrian army, and then deserted to join the French Foreign Legion. In 1861 he took his discharge from the Legion and enlisted as a medical officer in the Moroccan army, where he acquired a knowledge of Arabic as well as an acquaintance with the Moroccan interior. Disguised as a Muslim, he travelled widely through the western Sudan and then down to Lagos on the Gulf of Guinea

(1867), an astonishing achievement at that time. Later he explored Libya, where he would have liked to found a German colony.

With his aptitude for disguises and his fascination with the ways of Islam, Rohlfs resembled Sir Richard Burton, the eccentric yet brilliant Indian Army officer who played such a prominent role in the history of African exploration. In appearance Rohlfs was as unlike the stereotype of the hard-bitten soldier of fortune as one could imagine. Photographs depict a scholarly looking man with a broad forehead, carefully waxed moustache, and nicely brushed goatee. Like so many of his generation—sailors and artillerymen, physicians and pastors—Rohlfs wrote prolifically and well, gaining a wide public for his works concerning exploration, then a popular branch of literature. His personality appealed to Bismarck, who in 1880 entrusted him with an embassy to the emperor of Ethiopia.

Four years later Rohlfs was appointed consul general in Zanzibar, then the main focus of the East African trade, which had considerably expanded since the opening of the Suez Canal in 1869. The Germans had acquired a substantial stake in the island's commerce, and Rohlfs meant to use this influence to induce Germany to play the same role in the sultanate of Zanzibar as France had in Tunis: the part of an imperial protector guiding a dependent oriental monarchy. In 1884 he submitted a memorandum to the German chancellor in which he outlined a policy of indirect imperialism: German merchants should extend their operations from Zanzibar to the East African coast, set up "factories" on the littoral, and acquire land from African princes so as to create a German colony. Bismarck, however, pursued a much more cautious policy; he considered friendly relations with Great Britain infinitely more important than any number of colonial concessions in East Africa. In 1885 Rohlfs returned to Germany, where he continued to write on African questions for a wide circle of readers.[2]

Emin Pasha (1840–92), another physician, had an even stranger career—as melodramatic as any Victorian adventure story. Born Eduard Karl Oskar Theodor Schnitzer in Oppeln, a small Silesian town, he was the son of a respectable Jewish merchant. At the age of six he was baptized in the Lutheran Church, but later he went to a Catholic high school; at the university he studied medicine and the natural sciences. Though he later was to endure incredible hardships, he was adjudged medically unfit for service in the German army, and was also rejected when he tried to enlist as a rifleman in the Mexican army then supporting the claims of Maximilian, the ill-starred Habsburg pretender to the Mexican throne. Thirsting to see the world, the twenty-five-year-old physician finally managed to join the Ottoman service as a medical officer serving in various parts of the Balkans, including northern Albania.

One of many European and Levantine technicians in the Turkish service, Schnitzer learned Turkish as well as many other eastern languages, adopted the fez as his headgear and Islam as his religion, and assumed the name of Emin—"The Faithful"—much to his family's distress. Emin's patron in the Ottoman service was one Ismail Hakki Pasha, whose German-descended wife became friendly with Emin. When Hakki Pasha died, Emin and the pasha's widow, together with her children, travelled to Constantinople, where he helped settle the lady's financial affairs. He subsequently returned to Silesia followed by an imposing train that included the widow—now reputedly Emin's wife—her six children, an Oriental servitor, and two maids, the strangest household ever to have settled in the little country town of Neisse. But his protégée apparently became too exacting in her financial demands; Emin thought the better of his vows and secretly decamped.[3]

Emin made his way to Cairo, and in 1876 was invited by Colonel "Chinese" Gordon to join him at Lado on the upper Nile as a medical officer. Schnitzer, now known as Emin Effendi, carried out numerous missions on Gordon's behalf and in 1878 became governor of Equatoria, a position he retained after Gordon's departure. Continuing to govern the Equatorial province until 1889, he managed to put the sluggish region on its feet economically. In addition to his administrative duties he built up an important ornithological and botanical collection. His journals and official reports reveal the breadth of his mind and the accuracy of his observations; almost every branch of learning—geology, ornithology, ethnography, biology, geography, meteorology—was of interest to him, and many of his observations were published in learned journals overseas.

In 1883 Emin, now a pasha in the Egyptian service, was cut off from the capital by the Mahdist revolt and was forced to retreat to the extreme south, eventually to be isolated at Wadelai, where he reputedly accumulated an ivory hoard of legendary wealth. The German pasha's strange fate became known to the European public through reports brought back by two African explorers, Wilhelm Junker and Gaetano Casati. Being anxious to profit from Emin's predicament, the British-financed Emin Pasha Relief Committee sent out an expedition under Henry Morton Stanley to bring the pasha back to civilization. The committee's most important individual supporter was the Khedive of Egypt, who did not want to lose a servant. Other supporters were British businessmen eager to promote British enterprise and the fortunes of the Imperial British East Africa Company, the Royal Geographical Society, which sought knowledge concerning a remote region in Africa, and philanthropists who were bitterly conscious of Britain's past unwillingness to rescue Gordon from the Mahdi's might and hoped to rescue this white hero. Stanley desired glory and the newspapers wanted headlines.

Stanley's expedition incurred terrible losses. Its arrival at Emin's headquarters helped set off a mutiny among Emin's Muslim troops, who looked to Egypt for salvation. Emin was not eager for rescue, but in the end he had to leave in Stanley's company, and after many vicissitudes they finally succeeded in making their way to the east coast, where Emin found himself courted for his support by both British and German empire-builders. The Kaiser himself sent a laudatory telegram, and for a brief period Emin was one of Germany's most popular men. His renown occasioned some personal complications however: Frau Schnitzer in Germany recognized her husband's picture in a fashion magazine, sued him for alimony, and was awarded ten thousand marks by a German court. Undaunted, in 1890 he enlisted in the German service with a commission to extend Germany's sphere of influence up to Lake Victoria and Lake Albert; soon after the expedition was under way, the Anglo-German agreement of 1890 put Uganda in the British sphere, rendering useless Emin's original design.

Emin continued his travels, however. Disregarding instructions, he hoisted the German flag over Tabora, then a major center of the caravan traffic in the interior of what is now Tanzania. Emin considered that Tabora should become Germany's main inland garrison; Germany's grip would be further strengthened by a network of subordinate stations held by askari recruited among former slaves. The new colony would be sustained through local tribute, the proceeds of the ivory trade, porterage, and other *corvées* levied on surrounding peoples. Emin's project differed little from a design that might have been framed by a Swahili-speaking merchant prince from the coast—a design for an empire based on caravan traffic. In April 1890 he was commissioned to establish German influence in the northwest interior, but three months later the Germans concluded an important convention with Great Britain in which, for diplomatic reasons, they relinquished far-reaching claims inland.

With no role other than to administer what was left of the German sphere on Lake Victoria, Emin decided in 1891 to embark on a fantastically ambitious plan: he would traverse Africa from east to west with the Cameroun coast as his final goal. This scheme, however, was too aspiring even for a man of Emin's resolution, and he could not complete his self-imposed mission. Relations between the Europeans and the Swahili-speaking merchants had gravely deteriorated; Germans and Belgians had begun to take up arms against the Muslims, and the Swahili-speaking slave traders came to regard Emin—a converted Muslim—as a renegade and enemy. Half-blind and desperately sick, Emin got as far as the Congo region, where he was murdered in 1892 at the behest of hostile Muslims. He met his death with composure, saying to his Muslim captors: "Well you may kill me, but don't think that I am the only white man in this country. There are many others who will be willing to avenge my death; and let me tell you that in less than two years from now there won't be an Arab left in the entire country held by your people."[4] It was an apposite epitaph.

Emin's diaries survive,[5] as do many of his published articles, his letters, and photographs showing his dignified features, deep-set eyes, and rabbinical beard. But the real Emin Pasha is hard to reconstruct. Contemporaries described him as a mild-mannered, meticulous, myopic man, strangely compounded of resolution and indecision, frankness and dissimulation, aloof, courteous in the manner of a Turkish notable rather than that of a German empire-builder. Liebert, a Prussian soldier, a fire-eater, and an anti-Semite, described the Jewish-descended pasha with much respect as a gentle, patient, selfless man, personally courageous, but interested only in the natural sciences. If Liebert is to be believed, Emin owed his position among Africans to his skill as a doctor and to his willingness to let events take their course: *in shā'a Allāh*—if God wills.

According to more exacting critics than Liebert, Emin could be utterly ruthless. He had no hesitation about attacking an armed Arab trading caravan or looting a slaving depot when he lacked funds to sustain himself in the interior. In his way he was a marginal man, one of the many outsiders who played an important part in the early era of empire-building. Patriotic Prussian and Ottoman dignitary, Korpsstudent and caravan leader, Jew, Christian, Muslim, and skeptic by turns, Emin apparently never quite got over his apostasy to Islam. Vita Hassan, a chemist in the Sudanese service and a subordinate and admirer of Emin, recorded an incident in which the latter, despite his reserve, revealed something of this aspect of his character. "Listen, my friend," Emin adjured an angry Muslim who railed against converts, "if a man gives up his religion for the sake of a woman, he merits reproof. If he changes his faith for money, he deserves contempt. But if he changes his creed under duress, he is entitled to understanding and compassion, even though his conduct is deplorable and never quite justified."[6]

A second, even more important group of pioneers consisted of professional soldiers turned explorers. The German army, despite its reputation for militarism, was from 1870 to 1914 essentially a peacetime force that did not become involved in a European war. In Germany—as in Belgium and France—service in Africa provided an outlet for ambitious men with a social conscience, anxious to serve the cause of the nation and of humanity against slave traders and cannibals. Service overseas also offered more opportunities for rapid promotion. Above all, overseas service was an opportunity for adventurous men who were tired of life in small garrison towns with the daily round of the Offizierskasino, the petty social tyranny of the colonel's lady, small-minded gossip, and stultifying routine. Many of the east German frontier garrisons were particularly unpopular places of appointment, and a substantial number of volunteers from these more remote posts applied for colonial service.

An appointment to a garrison on the Polish frontier [wrote a Briton who had once seen service in the German army] is about as acceptable to the young Prussian officer as an East End beat is to a young London policeman. The regiments are split up into their component parts and quartered in small villages. The country is flat and unlovely. The towns holding social distractions are few, and miles away from one another. And added to this . . . the constantly recurring batches of stubborn Polish recruits . . . who are working extremely hard in efforts to devise ways and means whereby they can shirk their daily tasks. The effects of this on an officer or a non-com . . . can easily be imagined. It has invariably one result—drink.[7]

Even in more pleasant places a German officer's peacetime life was hard: he had to cope with elaborate drills, intricate ceremonials, and complicated bureaucratic procedures, as well as the threat of disciplinary sanctions, including premature retirement for minor failures on the barracks square:

> More and more demands are made on his efficiency every year, and this leads superior officers to show their zeal by inventing unnecessary work. All work has to be accounted for in writing, and a long list of work done by every squadron must be sent in by each commanding officer. This is what in the British service is described as "eyewash."[8]

In Africa an ambitious soldier might make a career for himself, have independent command, gain a professional reputation and perhaps a measure of national fame. Service in the colonies might also secure a patent of nobility for a successful soldier—a privilege never extended to civilians. The army provided officers with invaluable preparation for overseas duty: the capacity to endure hardships and to lead men, training in mapping and cartography, and instruction in skills like building a fire, a road, or a camp—abilities of which an ordinary graduate in law or the classics remained ignorant. Not surprisingly, then, the armed forces became an important reservoir for colonial leaders.

One such product was Hermann Wissmann (1835–1905). Though of bourgeois origin, Wissmann was the scion of a Prussian military family. He was educated in the harsh school of the Prussian cadet corps, and later received a commission in the infantry and served as an officer in a fusilier regiment. His tenor of life changed in 1879 when he met Dr. Paul Pogge, a noted African explorer. Travel in Africa seemed an attractive alternative to life in his regimental garrison at Rostock, a Baltic seaport with commercial links to Africa. Wissmann left the service, studied the natural sciences and ethnology at the University of Rostock, and then journeyed widely on behalf of the Deutsche Afrika-Gesellschaft. In 1883 he entered the service of Leopold II of Belgium and led two expeditions into the Congo region. He returned to Germany in 1888, a colonial enthusiast and an established writer on African exploration.

His supreme opportunity came in 1889, when the DOAG was no longer able to handle its assignment. Bismarck appointed the young captain—a proud, ruthless man—to be Reichskommissar with extensive powers and simple instructions: "Go out and win." The administrative machinery at his disposal was negligible: the staff consisted of one Assessor in charge of general administration, two financial officials, and four other civil servants. But Wissmann was a man with imagination, and he proceeded to follow Bismarck's instructions. He created an improvised force of mercenaries, the Schutztruppe—a mixed lot among whom were Sudanese soldiers, Somalis, and Zulu migrants from Mozambique.

Wissmann had an exceptional understanding of the men under his command, both white and black. A military commander, he wrote, should make use of the Africans' sense of kinship and ethnic solidarity by respecting their customs, by dividing soldiers into ethnically homogeneous platoons or companies, and by acquiring an understanding of their beliefs in witchcraft and the power of spirit mediums. Like many other soldiers, he had a high opinion of the men with whom he shared so many dangers and hardships. Africans, he explained, were exceptionally good fighting men, distinguished for their physical resilience, for their ability to march for twenty-five or thirty kilometers in difficult country under a blazing sun and loaded down with baggage weighing some thirty kilos. While they were superb in delivering impetuous charges, he felt they were deficient in the self-discipline, the reasoned courage, and the sense of personal initiative that enabled highly trained soldiers to hold their own in rearguard actions or in defeat. To Wissmann, the Muslim creed was a force for good; Islam was a militant religion that worked in support of established authority. Muslims learned to avoid the evils of drink and of most other physical and moral excesses.

Wissmann's military preferences helped to shape his African policies in general. In his opinion whites must never be employed in the tropics as private soldiers; their role was to train Africans and to lead them into action, tasks for which European commissioned and non-commissioned officers should be carefully selected and trained. This was not an easy assignment, for European volunteers were liable to suffer a severe culture shock when they first arrived in Africa with romantic illusions and had to face the realities of loneliness, hardship, and disease. Moreover, a colonial officer, like an eighteenth-century commander, had to cultivate caution and to avoid unnecessary engagements that would deplete his small reservoir of mercenaries, a force hard to train and expensive to replace. A successful officer required a great measure of self-control and patience as well as the ability to inspire the attachment and the confidence of mercenary soldiers, who differed profoundly in temperament and background from their leaders.[9]

The campaigns initiated by Wissmann secured the littoral and then followed the trade routes into the interior. His wars formed part of a wider convergent movement by means of which the Germans, British, and Belgians destroyed the Muslim trade in ivory and slaves and its attendant political power in what is now mainland Tanzania, Malawi, northeastern Zambia, and eastern Zaïre.

Wissmann tried to impose his own "ethic" on the Schutztruppe. He insisted, not always successfully, that the Germans establish good relations with their soldiers and porters; that the officers show a spirit of impartiality, strictness, and fair conduct; that African customs be respected; and that Swahili be used as the standard language. His policy was to utilize existing political institutions for the purpose of government—a policy that involved respect for Islam and the employment of Swahili-speaking Muslims as soldiers, chiefs, and government officials on the coast and over a fairly large portion of the hinterland. In parts of the interior he also appointed chiefs who were not Muslim. The Wissmann line received support from the Seminar für Orientalische Sprache at Berlin University, which expanded the teaching of Kiswahili and sent out researchers to study the customs of the coastal peoples.

Wissmann's subsequent career, however, was unfortunate. In 1891 he was passed over for the governorship of East Africa in favor of Freiherr Julius von Soden, a career diplomatist who had previously headed the administration of Cameroun. Soden, a firm believer in indirect rule through the Swahili-speaking coastal people, was replaced in turn by Colonel Friedrich von Schele, who also ran the Schutztruppe, spending much of his time on military assignments. In 1895 Wissmann at last received the coveted gubernatorial appointment, but by this time his health was giving way; he had become addicted to morphine, an affliction not uncommon among pioneers exposed to the tremendous psychological and physiological pressures of existence in the bush. Moreover, he found that he could not directly control the Schutztruppe, which was under the command of Lothar von Trotha, an officer higher in rank than Wissmann. Wissmann resigned in 1896. His term of office marked the transition from caretaker government to conquest.

The Successors

Local administration within the various colonies was initially run on a shoestring. The incipient settlements were superintended by a Reichskommissar (imperial commissioner), sometimes known also as a Landeshauptmann—equivalent in bureaucratic rank to a Landesdirektor, a fairly modest dignitary elected by the provincial chamber of a Prussian province to deal with a variety of local matters. In practice the powers of a Reichskommissar were very limited. Dr. Ernst Göring, first Reichskommissar in South-West Africa, came to the colony in 1885 with a two-man staff: a Kanzler (chief secretary) and a police sergeant. He took up residence in a mission station and made treaties with various African communities but lacked the means to enforce his authority.

Four years later Captain Curt von François landed with twenty-one soldiers to lend support to the fledgling administration, but Göring's standing among the Herero and Nama rulers of South-West Africa was not enhanced. The Reichskommissar had to deal with indigenous leaders in command of armed hosts well-supplied with firearms, masters of bush-fighting, who could easily have brushed aside his small troop. In 1892 Göring was posted to Haiti as German consul-general and later as minister-resident; this modest appointment to a remote island in the Caribbean amounted to promotion from the South-West African post and earned him a brief mention in the great *Brockhaus* encyclopaedia. (Eventually the name of Göring acquired both fame and infamy through the activities of Ernst's son, Hermann.)

As the machinery of colonial administration grew increasingly complex, the chief executive officer of a colony became known as the Gouverneur, appointed by the Kaiser (though in practice by the Kolonialabteilung). His formal and informal powers were considerable —by no means equivalent to those of British governors but greater than those of the French. As head of the administration the governor represented in his person the might of German sovereignty and was responsible for the execution of Reichsgesetze (laws) passed by the German legislature, the decrees issued by the Kaiser, and the directives of the Kolonialabteilung. He was also commander-in-chief of the local armed forces, the only civilian official entitled to give orders to the military—an arrangement considered by German soldiers to be at best anomalous and at worst offensive.

Within this legal framework the governor could exercise a good deal of initiative. He was able to issue far-reaching Verordnungen (administrative instructions); he was charged with the supervision of all departments except—oddly enough—the postal services, which remained subject to the Reichspost; he exercised full "police powers" concerned with the maintenance of public order; he was able to make a wide range of administrative decisions not yet settled by imperial legislation dealing with matters as varied as land, labor, and settlement. Within limits, then, he could initiate policy, especially concerning any questions on which the central administration had no opinion or of which the Vortragende Räte were ignorant.

Like senior executive officers everywhere in Africa, the governor was expected to read incoming and outgoing correspondence dealing with key issues and to familiarize himself with reports sent him by his subordinates in the field. Visits to outlying stations to meet with the district heads and the more influential "sultans" or chiefs were routine. In addition he had to keep abreast of economic problems, maintain reasonably good relations with the settlers (not always an easy task), and decide on promotions, transfers, and disciplinary proceedings; he also acted as the ceremonial head of government, the supreme arbiter on the finer points of precedence and etiquette—an important function in caste-ridden colonial society—and he played an essential part in dispensing those much-coveted decorations that went to augment a successful administrator's psychic income.

During the thirty years of German rule, East Africa and Togo each had eight chief executives, Cameroun seven, and South-West Africa six. The German governor's average tenure thus was longer than that of his Portuguese or French colleagues (4.4 years compared to three years for the French), resulting in a higher degree of policy continuity.

In administrative terms, the position of a German governor was weaker than that of his British colleagues, who presided over local legislatures capable of passing ordinances. There were no legislative councils in any part of the German colonies, and their governors were unable to play a parliamentary role. In South-West and East Africa they were subjected to local pressures exerted by settlers through conservative deputies in the Reichstag, through sympathetic officials within the Kolonialabteilung, or through pressure groups like the Kolonialgesellschaft. After an independent colonial ministry was established in 1907, governors and local administrations suffered further inroads on their autonomy. Their freedom to grant concessions was circumscribed, although competing groups—both in the metropolis and in the colonies—continued to lobby for contracts, freight concessions, tariffs, labor regulations, and so forth. The colonial ministry now had to be consulted on all such matters. The same situation existed in France but not in Britain.

German governors exercised scant patronage. Governor Puttkamer might write to Kolonialdirektor Kayser from Cameroun asking for a job to be given to a deserving relative, but the bulk of colonial positions were not filled in this fashion. Puttkamer played an active part, as did von Buchka, in giving a major land concession to the Gesellschaft Süd-Kamerun. Direct contacts with the Kolonialabteilung, however, were far more important to a great capitalist than were personal links to a governor, however well-connected.

While a German governor's position as commander of the local armed forces was modeled on the British precedent, his parliamentary position was very different from that of his British colleague. From 1903 the Germans set up Gouvernementsräte for the various colonies, presided over by the governor of each colony and containing a number of senior civil servants and "unofficial members"—settlers or merchants. These bodies were only advisory, however; their effective power was negligible, especially as the larger firms preferred to make their influence felt directly in Berlin through the Kolonialrat or through personal contacts within the government. The Gouvernementsräte, in practice, were little more than debating societies, and they never acquired the legislative and budgetary powers wielded with so much effect by the legislative councils in British colonies.

Initially German governors had to operate with an astonishingly exiguous staff. At the turn of the century the whole of Germany's senior establishment in her four African colonies—South-West Africa,

Cameroun, Togo, and East Africa—amounted to only forty officials, including four governors, nine Oberrichter (senior judges) and Erste Referenten or Kanzler (senior secretaries), and nineteen Bezirksamtmänner (district commissioners). These were assisted by 134 junior and technical officials—a skeleton staff even by the modest British administration standards, and not at all comparable to the large European staff of the French colonial service (see Table 6). The administrative machinery of the various colonies began to expand during the period 1900–1910. While the governor's staff never formed a cabinet comparable to the British executive council—composed of most senior officials and empowered to exercise quasi-ministerial functions—by the outbreak of World War I German East Africa was governed by a fairly complex official hierarchy assisted by a substantial number of trained experts: medical doctors, veterinarians, agronomists, and such.

The Erste Referent was the governor's chief assistant and headed the central administration, carrying out many of the functions of the chief secretary in a British colony or the secrétaire-général in French colonies. In smaller colonies the governor's aide bore the title of Kanzler and combined judicial with administrative functions. The Referenten were responsible for specific tasks such as medical care, forestry, agriculture, customs, veterinary administration, public works, and so forth. Separate bureaus dealt with financial affairs, harbors, and stores.

The more settled districts were organized into Bezirksämter, each in the charge of a Bezirksamtmann. The Bezirksämter were fashioned along the lines of Regierungsbezirke in Germany, and the Bezirksamtmann was entrusted with far-reaching powers. He commanded the district police; he was able to issue Polizeiverfügungen, which were administrative orders concerned with a broad range of issues bearing directly or indirectly on the maintenance of law and order; in the more developed districts he might obtain assistance from specialists such as a government medical officer or a Distriktkommissar—an official appointed in East Africa from 1909 onward to look after labor matters. His subordinate staff included a Sekretär in charge of the office, a Polizeiwachtmeister responsible for the police, and perhaps one or two junior clerks. Each Bezirksamt had one or two subdistrict stations known as Bezirksnebenstellen.

On paper this administrative machine looked impressive, but the

TABLE 6
*The Administration of the German Colonial Empire
in Africa, 1901*

Administrative division	Colonies			
	Togo	Cameroun	South-West Africa	East Africa
Capital	Lome	Buea	Windhuk	Dar es Salaam
Civil districts (Besirksämter)	2	4	5	10
Other civilian stations	8	6	—	—
Military districts (Militärstationen)	—	9	8	14
Number of troops (Schutztruppen)	0 (560 police only)	900	772	1,400
Police districts (Polizeistationen)	—	—	12	13
Population (est.)	2,500,000 (140 Europeans)	3,500,000 (550 Europeans)	200,000 (3,650 whites)	6,000,000 (1,250 Europeans)
Area (sq. km.)	87,200	495,000	835,000	1,000,000

SOURCE: Johannes Tesch, *Die Laufbahn der deutschen Kolonialbeamten* (Berlin, 1902), pp. 1–2.

Germans—like their colonial rivals—were exceedingly thin in the field. Just before World War I the total number of Germans employed in the district administration of all the German colonies in Africa was about 150.[10] At first administrative districts were few and far between; their number was subsequently increased, but the colonies remained very thinly administered. By 1906, for example, South-West Africa comprised only nine districts with an average size of 100,000 square kilometers, while East Africa numbered only eighteen districts at the outbreak of the Maji-Maji rising in 1905 (as shown below). East Africa, the most developed of Germany's tropical colonies—known to enthusiasts as the "German India, the greatest plum available to gubernatorial candidates in the German service"—employed some forty officials in the districts and four hundred in the administration as a whole, including technical departments and central offices. The Germans in East Africa put more whites to work than did the British, who had less trouble recruiting Indians and Africans acquainted with the colonial power's language (see Table 7); compared with the French and

TABLE 7
*Whites and Non-Whites Employed in the Administrations
of German East Africa and British East Africa, 1904*

Department or occupation	German East Africa		British East Africa	
	Whites employed	Non-whites employed	Whites employed	Non-whites employed
Central administration	23	4	6	3
Justice	12	—	11	20
Finance and supplies	39	1	15	22
Customs	17	40	2	52
Medicine and veterinary services	21	1	15	2
Central police administration	23	—	8	7
Ports and public works	52	—	13	23
Forestry	6	—	4	1
Surveys	5	—	2	3
Agriculture, botany, geology	11	3	3	—
District administration	47	—	46	38
Teachers	8	—	—	—
Postal services	16	2	10	46
TOTAL	280	51	135	217

SOURCE: RM. 5, v. 5668 ("Verwaltung") [German naval archives], Bundesarchiv Freiburg (Militärarchiv).

Belgians, however, the Germans employed European staff in the most sparing fashion and only in positions where they exercised a good deal of authority.

Unlike their Belgian colleagues, German governors did not sit on the boards of great corporations, part privately owned and part state-owned—bodies of the kind that wielded enormous influence in the Belgian Congo. Retired German governors might busy themselves with politics or with the activities of colonial pressure groups such as the Deutsche Kolonialgesellschaft, but unlike retired French governors they were not often invited to serve on the boards of commercial companies. There were exceptions. Göring, for example, became a member of the Aufsichtsrat (executive committee) of the Deutsche Kolonialgesellschaft für Südwest-Afrika, where he sat with the great private bankers Paul von Schwabach and Freiherr Alfred von Oppenheim, with noblemen such as Prince von Hohenlohe-Oehringen and the Duke von Ujest, and with representatives of great German financial corporations like the Geheime Oberfinanzrat Müller of the Dresdner Bank. Liebert was a founder of the Deutsch-Englische Ostafrikagesellschaft, a minor concern in East Africa. Retired officers might take jobs in local colonies firms. Eugen Zintgraff, a well-known Cameroun pioneer, and Captain von Besser, a former Schutztruppen officer, both joined the Westafrikanische Pflanzungsgesellschaft Viktoria; Walter le Tannueux von Saint Ilaire, formerly Bezirkshauptmann at Tanga in German East Africa, later became a director of the Ostafrika-Kompagnie in Berlin.

But in a society ridden by differences of degree and status, a retired governor was much more likely to mingle with his own kind than in Great Britain, where the upper classes were socially more unified through the common experience of the public school and the common ideal of the gentleman, a more pervasive concept than that of the Reserveoffizier, with his imitative behavior. From the social standpoint a German governor was not the equal of his British colleague. A British colonial governor could expect a knighthood almost as a matter of course; in the German colonies only an exceptionally successful soldier could aspire to a patent of nobility. German society, at home as well as in the colonies, lacked that homogeneous character that caused members of the British establishment to look upon themselves as gentlemen rather than as members of a functional elite.

Changing Techniques of Governance

Viewed in retrospect, the German administrative structure had an appearance of uniformity that it lacked in reality. Berlin might try to impose fixed financial procedures, a standardized administrative structure, or a uniform law on its possessions, but the legal position of the Africans was settled essentially in accordance with the French model. Africans were not adjudged to be Reichsangehörige (citizens) but Untertanen (subjects). They were not tried under German law but according to special legislation. The Schutzgebietgesetz (colonial statute) of 16 April 1886 and 10 September 1900 permitted the Kaiser to exercise full sovereign powers and to issue Verordnungen (decrees) that laid down the main lines of administrative and judicial policy. The Reichskanzler and the governors were also permitted to issue decrees within certain legal limits.

Germany's colonial subjects were subjected to disciplines not applied within the Reich, such as corporal punishment by means of birching and the rod, detention accompanied by forced labor, and detention in chains; Indians, Arabs, and women were exempt from beatings. The governor alone was permitted to assign the death penalty. Confessions could be obtained only according to the judicial code applicable in Germany herself, and indigenous chiefs and notables had to be present during court proceedings. Theoretically, advanced Africans were allowed to acquire German nationality, but German colonial dominance did not last sufficiently long to permit the emergence of a substantial class of Germanized Africans.

There was not *one* German colonial empire; there were many. In the settled areas of South-West Africa the victorious Germans imposed direct rule of the most autocratic kind on the conquered Nama and Hottentots; the Ovambo in the distant north, however, were largely left to their own devices and were only indirectly affected by the German presence. In kingly states such as Buhaya, Ruanda, and Urundi, remote from the main centers of German power on the East Africa coast, the Germans ruled through Residents, a policy facilitated by German admiration for "aristocratic" peoples like the Tutsi in Ruanda and Urundi and the Fula in Cameroun. In other parts of East Africa the Germans largely copied the Muslim system of governance and enforced their will through Swahili-speaking auxiliaries, *akidas* (political agents) and *jumbas* (headmen), who were integrated after a fashion into the German political system.

The Germans adjusted their rule to differing circumstances in a pragmatic fashion without working out an all-embracing concept of colonial governance. In general their methods were more authoritarian than those of the British. The Assessor, with his legalistic, bureaucratic, and hierarchic training based on a strong sense of precedence and formalism, dominated the secretariats and the leading jobs along the coast. The military element played a strong part in the hinterland, where the Stationsleiter was commonly a former Schutztruppenoffizier; his work, however, was exacting, lonely, and often dangerous. German discipline was harsher than that of the British and relied to a much greater extent on corporal punishment.

German policy was at its most coercive in the settled part of South-West Africa, where the colonists utterly crushed both the Nama and Herero peoples, employing an even greater degree of ruthlessness than the British had in suppression of the Ndebele-Shona rising in

Rhodesia (1896–97). The Germans justified their actions by invoking self-interest, sometimes using a quasi-Marxist apologetic that would seldom have found its way into a French or British gubernatorial statement. Governor Leutwein, himself a moderate, an advocate of indirect rule, and an opponent of unlimited military violence, explained German colonization policy in terms of commercial gain:

As regards the kind of colonization envisaged, there is in the last analysis only one guide, how to make the desired profits in the surest fashion. Some believe that they can gain this objective by depriving the original population of all rights in favor of the intruder. . . . Others wish to allow the original population to occupy "their place in the sun." From the point of view of the expected profits, the decision cannot be made according to a single scheme, but must correspond to circumstances.

According to Leutwein, German military methods failed to serve Germany's long-range aims: "We have expended several hundred million marks and the lives of several thousand German soldiers. As a result we have . . . totally destroyed the pastoral industry of our colony. We have destroyed two-thirds of our native labor. Worse still, we have as yet [by March 1906] been unable to restore peace."[11]

The Germans sought to turn the vanquished into a landless proletariat, stripped of its rights to the soil and of its ancestral institutions. Thus Deputy Governor von Tecklenburg argued in 1904 that tribal cohesion must be broken down and that unsupervised settlements in the bush should not be tolerated lest they provide focal points for tribal revival.[12] German land and labor laws were modeled on those of an occupying army exercising absolute rule over a vanquished population, and the administration was designed to promote the safety and prosperity of the white population. The administrative divisions of Bezirksämter were in the charge of civil officials, and Militärdistrikte in the more remote areas were controlled by the army. The Bezirksamtmänner at first acted as judges as well as administrators, but as the settler population increased in numbers the government had to separate administrative from judicial functions and set up a system of courts run by professional jurists.

Tribal cohesion among the conquered could not be wholly broken down, however, and German power was inadequate to prevent a gradual Herero revival. As more farmers came into South-West Africa and as diamond-mining expanded, the European demand for labor rapidly increased. The defeated Herero gradually left the camps to which they had been confined and drifted back into the regions they continued to claim for their own, even though German immigrants had by now staked out farms on the conquered lands. These white farmers, who needed African manpower, unwittingly assisted the process of ethnic revival by setting up locations (small reservations) for Africans on their estates or by allowing Africans to keep livestock.[13] Finding that they could not effectively run the colony through a single administrative hierarchy, in 1913 the Germans adopted the British system of appointing native commissioners—a step that marked the beginning of the development of separate administrative systems for Africans and for whites.

Ovamboland, in the distant north of the colony, was run from the start on very different principles. The region was remote from the German centers of power, and the Germans interfered little with the resident tribes and their chiefs. The Ambo, for their part, had no wish to meddle with the Germans. Successes attained by the Portuguese in southern Angola during the period between 1900 and 1910 spread consternation among the Ambo, however, and Naude, a prominent Ambo ruler with followers on both sides of the Luso-German border, preferred to move all his people into German territory rather than remain under Portuguese suzerainty. In Naude's eyes his subjects were better off under the Kaiser's sway: the Portuguese had demanded that the chief furnish them with hostages, build a road, and permit the construction of a Portuguese fort.[14]

The Germans were much less exacting than the Portuguese and had accomplished great things—or so Captain Franke explained to the chiefs while touring the Ambo region: they had vanquished all the enemies of Germany, and they had built dams, railways, ports, and whole new cities. The Ambo would profit from the new opportunities created by allowing their young men to work for German employers; the chiefs were required only to sign treaties recognizing the suzerainty of the German Kaiser.[15] An ever-increasing number of Ambo workmen travelled south in search of jobs in the diamond mines and on the railways, and Ovamboland became the colony's most important reservoir of native labor. German settlers were not allowed to own land in the region, however, and Ambo dignitaries largely continued to run local affairs in their accustomed fashion.

In East Africa the Germans at first tried to govern through a system of direct rule that utilized the services of the erstwhile Muslim ruling class. As noted earlier, Hermann von Wissmann, the first imperial commissioner in the colony, admired Islam as a progressive force, and having had experience with the Swahili-speaking coastmen, he relied heavily on the assistance of Muslim akidas and other dignitaries and built the Schutztruppe around a nucleus of Sudanese soldiers. German government schools taught Swahili, and German governors also learned the language, which became the lingua franca of colonial administration, spreading farther afield as German influence advanced.

The first akidas used by the Germans were usually Arabs or Islamized Swahili who were set over a subdistrict or part of the Bezirk. Akidas were also appointed from among local rulers, and increasingly were local people who knew the local customs and languages. The Germans used such people because they were cheap, but since they were not carefully supervised, they padded their incomes by taking bribes and stealing tax revenues. After the Maji-Maji rebellion, the Germans strengthened their administration by training more Africans as junior officials to rule the local peoples, and such abuse and corruption lessened.

Each akida controlled a number of jumbas—government agents in charge of villages. The akida was appointed and paid by the government and—from 1892—was usually trained in a government school. He could demand labor, collect taxes, and try minor offenses. As the functions of government expanded, so did the akida's; eventually he was charged with the distribution of seeds, the supervision of compulsorily planted cash crops, the maintenance of roads, the construction of bridges, and even the planting of trees. His career in some respects resembled that of a German officer: systematic transfers and promotion with a graduated salary scale. The top post for an Arab or African bureaucrat was that of *liwali* (head of a district with several akida posts), but only one African ever reached this position.

Governor Götzen (1901–6) introduced a number of changes into the East African system. He did not like using coastal people to rule as akidas over inland areas, and he wanted to replace them with local people. Governor Albrecht Freiherr von Rechenberg (head of East Africa from 1906 to 1912) made the change by using the newly educated African class emerging from government schools at Tanga, Bagamoyo, and Dar es Salaam. Götzen also became convinced that direct rule would not succeed except on the coast where pre-colonial Arab influence had destroyed the cohesion of the indigenous communities. He therefore attempted to strengthen the indigenous rulers of the interlacustrine region by appointing Residenten to "advise" them. Impressed by the apparent success of British policy in Uganda and Dutch policy in Java, Götzen determined that his Residenten should observe local customs and authority, should raise taxes only through the agency of the local "sultan," and should mediate between the sultan on the one hand and the missions and traders on the other. The Resident should seek to persuade the sultan to introduce a more civilized form of justice, and eventually to turn him into a salaried civil servant.[16]

Götzen's policy imposed stringent restrictions on the activities of German traders and settlers, and involved a number of social contradictions. The Germans supported the Tutsi aristocracy, and the indigenous rulers retained the power of life and death over their subjects, but at the same time white missionaries worked among the Hutu serfs, some of whose sons began to acquire the kind of Western education that their Tutsi masters despised. The governor's policy required an intimate acquaintance with indigenous institutions which the Germans often lacked. For Ruanda, a centralized kingdom, Götzen found an admirable Resident in Richard Kandt, a physician who had once served as the head of a German lunatic asylum. He was equally successful in overseeing a feudal state in Ruanda; his long tenure of office, his sardonic disposition, his ability as an ethnographic observer, and his policy of backing the monarch against all contenders—all contributed to his success, despite the opposition of Catholic missionaries who sympathized with the Hutu serfs against the Tutsi overlords. The Germans were less successful in Urundi, where they apparently misinterpreted the structure of Urundi kingship and supported rebels against the monarch, requiring the use of a good deal of military force.

Among the Haya of Bukoba, in the northwestern part of East Africa, the Germans made use of the traditional *mukama* (king; pl. *bakama*). The mukama's court received official recognition, he retained control over customary law, and he was given jurisdiction over orders issued in compliance with official German directives. He was allowed to whip or to incarcerate offenders, though the right to execute criminals was reserved to the Germans. The mukama was also placed in charge of tax collection; he retained a fixed portion of each payment which he used in part to pay salaries to his subchiefs and clerks. The system proved so successful from the bakama's standpoint that the Germans had no difficulty in raising the hut tax to five rupies without disturbances (one German East Africa rupie equalled 1.33 marks).

For all their theoretical commitment to "direct government," the Germans ended up with an unsystematized form of indirect rule extending over most of East Africa. Before the outbreak of World War I the Residenturen of Urundi, Bukoba, and Ruanda—all of them densely populated regions—comprised something like 55 percent of the entire population in the territory. The less imposing chieftainships of the interior, run by native dignitaries under white supervision, were said to include 33 percent of the country's population. About 10.5 percent of the people were organized in village communities ruled by Swahili-speaking akidas, and only some 1.5 percent—no more than 150,000 persons in all, and most of them urban or "detribalized" people along the coast—were subject to direct administration.[17]

Given the paucity of German resources, there was no alternative to the system of ruling Africans through Africans. A German district was large: in 1914 there were only twenty-one districts in East Africa. The Bezirksamtmann patrolled the area with his armed retinue, but depended largely on traditional African authorities to enforce the peace and to make the people obey government regulations. As head of a district, the Bezirksamtmann had extraordinary powers: he controlled troops and police, and he was judge and executive. Appeals of his decisions were rare and could be made only to the governor. There were few European officials on duty. In East Africa the German budget estimates for 1913 provided for seventy Europeans—from district officers to junior clerks—at a cost of 1.25 million marks (£ 56,000). (In 1928 the Mandatory Power [Great Britain] budgeted £ 300,000 for 150 district officers in an estimated population of five million.)[18] The colonial administration therefore had to continue to use local dignitaries as well as the Schutztruppe, whose military perspective often dominated the local government.

The Germans worked out a system of governance in Togo that greatly resembled the British rule in West Africa. It was Germany's only African colony without a Schutztruppe, and German governors had only a few hundred African military policemen to enforce the imperial will. The German administration was also deficient in staff. August Full, one-time deputy governor of Togo, estimated that in German Togo the ratio of whites to blacks was 1:11,000, while the ratio was between 1:3,300 and 1:4,000 in the French-mandated part of Togo after World War I.

The Germans in Togo were able to build an economy based on a long-established system of trade: the small states of the Slave and Gold Coasts had dealt for centuries in slaves and palm oil. In Togo, German companies had been established even before the partition of Africa, and the foundations for subsequent development already laid. The colony's wealth derived primarily from African peasant cultivators who sold palm oil and coconuts to foreign merchants; the colonial government's main economic function was to construct rail and port facilities. In addition, the German authorities sought to stimulate production by imposing taxes that would force Africans to sell their surpluses or to work for foreign employers, and by developing agricultural instruction and research—especially with respect to cotton—through improved communications and through the influence of the indigenous political authorities. It was thought that Germany, while enhancing her own might, could benefit her African subjects by acquainting them with superior technology, superior economic methods, and superior forms of government. As Full put it:

Colonial governments must, as a matter of course, accept the obligation of raising the native living standards. Only in this fashion can they combat the malevolent forces that, for millennia, have kept down the population to a fraction of the number that the fertile soil and the vast available lands can support. Famine, plague, and insecurity of life in the face of the unknown hostile forces of nature all stand in the way of progress. Hence the first aim of the German administration was to improve the Africans' labor yield, to instruct Africans in utilizing the opportunities provided by climate and soil.[19]

The Germans had to carry out this policy with very sketchy administrative machinery. In 1914 the whole of Togo was divided into five Bezirksämter, each with a few subdistricts, and three Stationsbezirke situated in the remote north. A great deal thus depended on the individual qualities of German administrators, and certain districts became identified with particular officials—for instance, Misahöhe with Dr. Grunner, and Socode-Bassari with Dr. Kersting.

In operating through indigenous institutions the Germans, like their

British counterparts, felt most at home with a hierarchical order of government that corresponded—or seemed to correspond—to their own system of bureaucratic organization. According to the German interpretation, Ewe society, for example, was based on families grouped into clans. The clan-heads and the village headman ruled local settlements, and headmen and chiefs had to be drawn from specific clans. Candidates for the chieftainship were proposed by the heads of a chiefly clan; their election, however, had to be approved by the clan-heads. Villages combined to make up a *du* (circle) headed by a *fia* (chief) or a *fiaga* (senior chief); these circle chiefs were chosen from the ranks of the village headmen, but their appointment had to be approved by the heads of clans. Chiefs might consult popular assemblies on important issues but they were not bound to abide by the assembly decisions. At the top of this hierarchy stood paramount chiefs who exercised sway over as many as eight circles. The Germans perceived that not all circles among the Ewe were subject to paramount chiefs, and that in pre-colonial times many circles had been only loosely united by military alliance, with power resting with village elders rather than with chiefs.

The Germans, however, felt that they could not work through native tradition unalloyed by efficiency, and they determined to accord greater privilege and larger financial rewards to the chiefs. Chiefs received honorary distinctions, they were allowed to recruit workers for their own benefit as a substitute for tribute formerly collected from their subjects, and in exchange for traditional sources of income, such as tolls on caravans, they received fixed annual stipends of varying amounts. A Tsautsho chief of Sokode, for instance, was reimbursed 1,000 marks a year for his lost income and his diminished army. In return for these privileges, chiefs had to supervise tax collection, report diseases, maintain local paths, provide labor to the colonial government, afford hospitality to visiting Europeans, and perform other such duties.

In Togo, indirect rule of the pragmatic type owed a great deal to Count Julius von Zech auf Neuhofen (1868–1914). Zech, a Bavarian, a Catholic, and a *grand seigneur* like Rechenberg, started his career as a soldier. He was first commissioned in the Second Bavarian Infantry Regiment and then promoted to first lieutenant in 1895, when he was detached for service with the Kolonialabteilung. Between 1895 and

1900 he administered the district of Krete-Kratschi, concluded treaties with various indigenous chiefs, and in 1896–97 took part in several expeditions and military actions in Sugu. After travelling in different parts of North Africa, he served as Bezirksamtmann in charge of the Anecho district from 1901 to 1902, when he became Kanzler of Togo. From 1903 to 1905 he was acting governor, and was the colony's governor for the next five years.

Zech was as unlike the Wilhelmian soldier of fiction as could be imagined. A man of great culture, he was an authority on African laws and customs. He was determined to govern through indigenous institutions—as he saw them—and promoted ethnographic studies in order to acquire a better understanding of African jurisprudence. He believed in developing Togo through a combination of Volkskultur (indigenous peasant cultivation) and trade. He opposed the concept of developing the colonies through large-scale plantation agriculture and placed special emphasis on safeguarding African land rights. All unused land in Cameroun was automatically regarded as Crown land, but the Togolese administration was prevented from registering unalienated land unless the local Africans, assisted by a specially selected European official known as the Eingeborenenvogt (superintendent of natives), had first been allowed to plead their case. Government land decisions could be appealed in the courts. Moreover, Africans were not allowed to sell land to foreigners without the governor's consent—a policy that helped prevent the creation of large plantations but possibly retarded economic growth.

According to the German dispensation, the Togolese chiefs were more than merely tolerated: their judicial powers were recognized. Zech pioneered the study of African legal institutions in Togo and instructed his district commissioners to study them in a systematic fashion; he charged Dr. Asmis, one of his most able Assessoren, to make a methodic survey of African law. Native courts consisting of a chief assisted by several co-adjudicators were allowed to settle civil and minor criminal cases and could impose fines up to one hundred marks. Cases were tried according to indigenous law, but the Germans—like the British and French—insisted that cases could be appealed to the Bezirksleiter, that inhuman punishments could not be inflicted, and that evidence obtained through the use of poison, torture, or similar means could not be admitted. The Bezirksleiter tried the more serious criminal cases, but was obliged to call on chiefs and headmen to assist the court in an advisory capacity. Zech made considerable use of his power to banish criminals, "vagrants," and insubordinate chiefs. These men were allotted land in so-called "rehabilitation settlements," where they were able to live as free farmers although not allowed to leave their assigned district.[20]

Zech wished to use indigenous institutions for the purpose of effective governance and as a means of spreading civilization. This policy, however, placed him in a difficult position. German law did not provide for establishing recognized native treasuries of the kind later used by British advocates of indirect rule, and it prohibited institutions such as child marriage or the pursuit of blood feuds. Nevertheless, the governor insisted in a circular:

In many cases the criminal intent required by the German Penal Code is lacking in such cases. In determining the sentence, the courts will not, therefore, be expected to impose the severe penalties laid down by the relevant legislation. It is therefore incumbent on the courts to decide on more appropriate penalties; in doing so, courts are required to take due account of the facts of the case, of the Africans' own notions of justice, and of the need gradually to introduce more civilized ideas of jurisprudence.[21]

Zech's views had much in common with those of Wilhelm Solf, Germany's last colonial secretary, who was a distinguished Sanskrit scholar, an anglophile, an opponent of forced labor, and an advocate of Volkskultur, as Zech had been. While serving as governor of Samoa (1900–1911), Solf had bitterly criticized German plantation cultivation. He insisted that the Samoans were anything but lazy and that they required protection from the exactions of planters. If the Germans were to attempt to adopt a policy of forced labor, the Samoans would resort to passive resistance: they would cease to buy German products, such as clothes and tools, and they would no longer produce copra for German traders; forced labor therefore was both immoral and unprofitable.[22]

As Staatssekretär in charge of the Reichskolonialamt (1911–18) Solf continued to promote Volkskultur, which in his estimation went with indirect rule in the political sphere. He was particularly interested in the British experience. In 1913 he visited northern Nigeria, where he was impressed by Lord Lugard's work, and decided to introduce a similar system in northern Cameroun. In a letter to Lugard he ob-

served that a policy of preserving African law and customs would certainly lead to opposition on the part of missionaries, of petty white
officials, of Europeanized Africans, and of European capitalists; nevertheless, he continued, Lugard's approach was assuredly correct, and
the Fulani and Hausa-speaking peoples of northern Cameroun would
benefit from a system of government modelled on that of northern
Nigeria.[23]

For all the internal contradictions, economic and administrative development in the German colonies entailed an increasing employment
of African auxiliary staff—the noncoms of empire. The Germans, like
their colonial competitors, could not do without the assistance of African police sergeants, court interpreters, clerks, scouts, and other educated Africans. Even in South-West Africa, the settler country par excellence, they could not have suppressed the great African uprisings
without the assistance of African guides and African guerrilla experts.[24]

African education was promoted by the establishment of government schools designed to supply the growing demand for junior officials. By 1911 the number of students in these schools was 4,312 in
East Africa, 833 in Cameroun, and 449 in Togo; about 120,000 Africans
were attending schools of all kinds, mostly missionary institutions.

Little is known concerning this German-speaking native elite in Africa. Had the Germans succeeded in maintaining their empire, they
might have created a germanophone Africa to parallel the francophone
and anglophone Africas on the borders of their colonies. The task
would not have been easy because in East Africa their policy promoted
the use of Swahili, while tongues such as Duala and a form of Afro-
English remained widespread in Cameroun. In any case, they did not
stay long enough to make a permanent imprint on the territories under
their control, except perhaps in the German-settled parts of South-
West Africa or in Cameroun. Robert Cornevin, a French historian by
no means uncritical of the German record, states: "We ourselves, at
the end of the colonial period, often noted Germanophilism in Togo,
expressed not only by certain old men who still spoke a few words of
German and evoked with emotion their youthful memories, but also by
intellectuals in the prime of life whose families had taught them to respect the German colonial achievement."[25] A certain number of young
Camerounians trained in the German schools became "African Prussians," and regarded the brutality of German discipline as a necessary

evil. In the view of Jean Ikellé-Matiba, an African writer, the young Africans—imbued with German culture from their infancy—saw nothing wrong with the Germans' harsh discipline because Africans were treated in the same way as the Germans.

German racial attitudes ranged from undisguised contempt to sincere respect for the Africans. By and large, however, the Germans felt that they were separated from Africans by an insurmountable barrier of color, caste, class, and culture. In Cameroun, Paul Bissome Medza, an aged chief, recalled that the colonizers would not eat in the company of Africans because the Germans were "bad and proud." But there were exceptions. The famous soldier Hans Dominik lived in a simple hut and dined occasionally with Charles Atangana, a paramount chief who had "absorbed European civilization."[26]

Cooperation with the authorities paid off for African chiefs who managed to make use of German power against their local opponents. Service with the Germans also provided a number of career opportunities for adaptable African youth—not merely for the sons of chiefs, but sometimes even for the sons of outcasts and slaves who had managed to do well in German schools. Puttkamer tells the story of Paul Zampa, a Camerounian African who was taken to Germany as a small boy by a Schutztruppenoffizier. Zampa got his military training in the crack Garde Füsilier regiment in Berlin and became an excellent soldier. He had one serious problem: he felt miserable about his black skin. When Puttkamer inspected Yaoundé station, he was both amused and shocked to see the sergeant major—Zampa—on parade painted white: "It was truly a moving and ghostlike spectacle to see the man, face and hands painted snow-white, with his rolling black eyes and thick lips; we lost our composure and burst out in prolonged laughter." Zampa was so bitterly hurt that while he stood rigidly at attention in the best Prussian manner, tears slowly rolled down his cheeks. Later he explained that he had tried to get rid of his hated black color by ordering paint and powder from Berlin, hoping to make himself look more like Hans Dominik, his revered superior. From being a loyal supporter of Germany, Zampa turned into a rebel; he left the Schutztruppe and was eventually executed by the very whites whom he had once worshipped.[27]

Zampa's case was an exceptional one. There were other German-trained African dignitaries who adapted themselves to changing circumstances in a surprisingly flexible fashion. Soumtan Ndengue, a Bere chief appointed by the Germans in Cameroun, received praise from the French successors to the German administration for his chieftainship; Ndengue, an ex-corporal in the Schutztruppe, went on to serve the French to the best of his ability.[28] In East Africa, Ndengue's career in some respects contrasted with that of Francis X. Lwamgira (1875–1950), a Haya chief and a member of the royal Kiziba clan. Lwamgira began his political career in a purely African context as an official at the court of Mutatembwa, a Kiziba chief who attempted to resist the Germans. He first came in closer contact with the Germans when he was sent on an embassy to the German *boma* (government station) at Bukoba, where the Germans were impressed with his intellectual ability. He later served the Germans as a political intermediary, as a court interpreter, and as commander of a *ruga-ruga* unit—armed auxiliaries who were trained, armed, and equipped by the Germans and served with local chiefs for the purpose of collecting taxes, apprehending criminals, and enforcing German regulations with regard to the cultivation of crops and other matters. In 1913 Lwamgira was appointed boma secretary. When the British occupied Bukoba in World War I, Lwamgira was at first reluctant to abandon the German cause, but the British finally succeeded in recruiting him into their service, where he achieved considerable prominence as a local administrator and defender of British imperialism.[29]

FIVE

The Administrators: An Overview

Sociological generalizations concerning the German colonial service cannot be precise. German civil service in the colonies comprised men of widely different backgrounds—physicians turned administrators, lawyers, agronomists, soldiers, and even ex-missionaries. In Togo, for instance, the seven senior district officials in 1905 included two regular officers, a physician, a doctor of philosophy, a former missionary, an architect, and a lawyer who was stationed at Lomé, the capital, where the presence of a qualified legal man was essential.

There was no separate colonial service with an esprit de corps of its own—comparable, say, to the German railway, customs, or postal services. Such a body would have been expensive to set up, and its creation would have run counter to the accepted doctrine of economy as well as to the prevailing conviction that white men should not serve long in the tropics lest their health give way. Until 1910, when the Germans at last passed a uniform colonial civil service code, even the conditions of service varied. The Kolonialabteilung recruited a large portion of its staff from the administrations of the Reich, the Länder, and the municipalities, insisting that applicants should be eligible for reemployment at home upon the expiration of their colonial contracts. A considerable proportion of German colonial administrators were labor migrants who regarded their colonial experience as no more than an interlude in their careers. All this contrasted sharply with the prevailing spirit of British and French colonial administration.

The German colonial service thus tended to attract young men who were worried neither about their health nor about their long-term prospects in the service, and who generally had no intention of making a permanent career in the colonies. They were post-adolescents who liked the open-air life with plenty of opportunity for hunting, riding, and trekking, free from so many of the restraints of bureaucratic or military life at home, and with wide and sometimes unlimited authority over servants and subjects. Naturally there was a high turnover of personnel—much greater, for example, than under the British South Africa Company's regime in Southern Rhodesia, though lower than in the French empire.

This state of affairs was bound to make for administrative instability, exacerbated by frequent and often unnecessary postings. In South-West Africa, for instance, three governors held office during the critical reconstruction era of 1906–14. Between 1896 and 1908 twenty-one district magistrates held office in the little town of Swakopmund; during 1912 no less than seven persons were appointed to the office of district judge in Keetmanshoop.[1] A great deal of unacknowledged authority was invested in junior white officials and, in the "tropical colonies," in African clerks and interpreters, who were likely to stay longer than senior officials at the same job. Finally, the colonial service often suffered from a lack of backbone. For reasons of economy the Germans were reluctant to grant tenure to the majority of their officials, and non-tenured civil servants were liable to be dismissed upon the expiration of their contracts. The service therefore contained a considerable proportion of men who could not afford to criticize their superiors or report abuses, lest they be punished by the loss of their livelihood. From the technical point of view, however, service standards were high.[2]

Worse still, there was little stability of personnel. Those applicants for senior posts who came mainly from the ranks of the Schutztruppenoffiziere and the Assessoren, or who were senior officials in the service of the Reich, the municipalities, or the Länder (Baden and Württemberg provided an unusually high proportion of the civil servants for South-West Africa), as late as 1914 were signing on for periods of three and one-half years in the "tropical colonies." An official might renew his contract for a second or a third tour, but if he did so his career at home was liable to suffer. Should he stay in the colonies, he was not likely to advance beyond the rank of Bezirksamtmann and the relatively modest title of Regierungsrat, and he was apt to have financial difficulties. Sickness was an ever-present problem. The cost of living was so high that the purchasing power of a district commissioner's salary was about half of what it would have been in Germany. Married men with children were financially penalized because there were no secondary schools in the colonies and they had to send their children to expensive boarding schools in the fatherland for a higher education. As for the more senior appointments, the practice of the Germans did not compare unfavorably with that of their colonial rivals. Nevertheless, no German colonial director and no Staatssekretär remained in office for more than six years; three governors managed to run a colony for a total of some ten years, however.[3]

A colonial career did not hold many attractions for the sons of well-to-do merchants and industrialists used to the operas, the theaters, and the concert halls of great cities like Berlin, Leipzig, or Dresden. In 1871, and during the following two decades, the period that witnessed the birth of the age cohort that provided the young Schutztruppenoffiziere and pioneer administrators who conquered the colonies in the 1890's and early 1900's, Germany was mainly a rural country. Of its total population, 63.9 percent dwelled in communities numbering less than two thousand persons; only 4.8 percent lived in cities with more than a hundred thousand people. By 1910 urbanization had made great strides: the rural component had dropped to 40 percent of the population, and the large city element had increased to 21.3 percent. Despite its industrial wealth, however, Germany was still to a considerable extent a land of villages and small towns.

The geographical origins of the German colonial administrators and civil servants reflect the rural orientation of a country long since changed beyond recognition. A high proportion of colonial soldiers and administrators were drawn from relatively poor regions. The borderlands of Silesia, East and West Prussia were the most heavily represented. Eastern Germany's contribution was followed in importance by that of southwestern Germany, another rather unprosperous region that had supplied a high proportion of emigrants in the past. Table 8, drawn from a random sample of the *Kolonial-Lexikon*, indicates the origins in eastern and southwestern Germany of seventy prominent colonial pioneers. The overwhelming majority came from rural communities. Not one came from a great seaport—in contrast to French colonial officers—or from a liberal center of provincial banking like Frankfurt-am-Main. Only a handful were born in major state capitals or

TABLE 8
Geographical Origins of a Random Sample of Colonial Officials
and Soldiers Listed in the Kolonial-Lexikon

Region	No. of officials/ soldiers	Region	No. of officials/ soldiers
Central Germany:		Eastern and East Central Germany:	
Kingdom of Saxony	1	Silesia	13
Braunschweig	1	Provinz Sachsen	8
TOTAL	2	Brandenburg	6
North Germany:		Pomerania	3
Hannover	2	Berlin	1
Schleswig-Holstein	2	TOTAL	37
Oldenburg	1	Southern and Southwestern Germany:	
Mecklenburg	1	Bavaria Palatinate	5
TOTAL	6	Hesse and Hessen-Nassau	4
Northwest Germany:		Baden and Württemberg	4
Rhenish Provinz of Prussia	5	TOTAL	13
Westphalia	2	Countries other than	
TOTAL	7	Germany	5

SOURCE: Heinrich Schnee, ed., *Deutsches Kolonial-Lexikon* (3 vols.; Leipzig, 1920).

industrial cities, including one from Berlin, two from Munich, two from Königsberg, and one each from Breslau, Elberfelde, Düsseldorf, and Posen—this in a nation where something like one-fifth of the population before World War I lived in major urban centers. A substantial number of the sample—twenty-five in all—were noblemen.

The percentage of aristocrats in the higher level of the colonial service gradually diminished, albeit at a slower rate in the colonies than in the central administration. The initially high proportion of the upper class in the colonial establishment hardly seems explicable in terms of parental "pull." Within the German bureaucracy there was no colonial tradition. There was no farflung "old boys" network of men who wanted their sons to serve the empire overseas. During the initial period of colonization, almost any qualified youth could secure employment in the colonies. Applicants were scarce for civilian jobs though not for the military; few civil servants wanted to work in some godforsaken outpost where health conditions were poor and where promotion seemed hard to get.

The reputation of the German colonial service, moreover, was unsavory. High officials were accused of committing atrocities, of rape and murder—scandals which were ventilated in the Reichstag much more than they would have been in the legislatures of other colonial powers such as France, Italy, or Portugal. The facts, bad as they were, were sometimes embroidered by hearsay evidence collected by veteran anticolonialists in the Social Democratic and Center parties. This impassioned publicity worsened the public image of the Kolonialbeamtentum and further discouraged suitable men from applying.

Findings with regard to the German colonial officials and their parental backgrounds confirm those of John Armstrong's monumental work concerning the European administrative elite (see Table 9). Shortly before World War I the typical German colonial governor was a soldier's son like Liebert, or the son of a provincial judge or administrator like Heinrich Schnee. A much higher proportion of British senior colonial officers came from homes where the head of the family was a clergyman or a member of one of the liberal professions; over 30 percent of British colonial governors were sons of parsons.

Along with its complement of misfits, the German service attracted an impressive number of able and resourceful people. German officials working in the colonies—like their French counterparts—were subject to considerable financial constraints imposed upon them by a complex system of accounting concerned with petty items that should have been left to the discretion of the man on the spot, but otherwise they enjoyed a substantial degree of independence, for good or for ill. Service in remote bush stations tended to level social distinctions within the German ruling group—a point noted by many a visitor accustomed to the preoccupation with precedence characteristic of Wilhelmian Germany.

Gradations in rank found expression in many externals, such as the clothing requirements laid down for the different groups. A senior official in Togo, for instance, was expected to arrive with a wardrobe comprising—so the regulations stated—six civilian suits: two of them white, three khaki, and one tuxedo. A subordinate official was supposed to get by with four suits and no dinner jacket. Only a pith helmet was compulsory for all; its possession established a rough kind of sartorial equality.

In terms of salary, the distinctions between the different rank levels were even greater than in clothing (see Table 10). In addition, the

TABLE 9

Fathers' Class/Occupation of Members of the Administrative Elite
in Prussia–West Germany and Great Britain, Pre–World War I

(Percent)

Class/occupation	Prussia–West Germany	Great Britain
Nobility	16	4
High-level official	21	4
Liberal professional	7	12
Businessman or manager	19	25
Teacher	10	12
Clergy	6	19
Low-level official	13	7
Shopkeeper or clerk	4	10
Manual worker	4	7

SOURCE: John A. Armstrong, *The European Administrative Elite* (Princeton, N.J., 1973), p. 91.

TABLE 10

Total Emoluments Received by Members of the German Colonial and
Diplomatic Services in Africa, c. 1913

(Marks)

Rank	Emolument
Colonial service:	
Governor	c. 50,000[a]
Chief secretary/chief judge	12,300–17,100
Engine driver/lady teacher	4,000–6,100
Senior police sergeant	3,800–5,400
Police sergeant	3,600–5,000
Secretary/substation official	2,100–4,500[b]
Diplomatic service:	
Minister-Resident and	
Plenipotentiary	36,000–80,000
Consul General	18,000–55,000
Consul	12,000–27,000
Clerk	2,000–4,500

SOURCE: *Handbuch des deutschen Kolonialwesens* (Berlin, 1914), and H. Schnee, ed., *Deutsches Kolonial-Lexikon* (Leipzig, 1921).

[a] Salary of the governor of a large German colony. By comparison, the governor of an important British colony (e.g., the Gold Coast) received £4,000 in 1910—the equivalent of 80,000 marks; the governor-general of French Equatorial Africa received 100,000 francs—roughly equal to 80,000 marks; a governor of one of the colonies within the Federation of French West Africa received no more than 35,000–40,000 francs.

[b] Average income of skilled worker in Germany in 1913 was c. 1,500 marks.

German service was rigidly divided along functional and educational lines. A secretary, a junior customs official, or an elementary school teacher was worlds apart from a senior civil servant or even a Referendar who had attended a university. A medium-grade official without a university education could no more aspire to attain higher office, such as that of a Bezirksamtmann, than a corporal in the regular army could hope to obtain a commission. In this respect the German system differed sharply from the British, where even a junior district officer was a gentleman by definition; it was also quite different from the French and Belgian systems, in which a clerk or a sergeant could rise into the higher reaches of the official hierarchy by merit.

Within the German district administration, soldiers played a particularly important part, as they did in the French system up to 1914, but as the pioneering period drew to a close, civilian bureaucrats acquired ever-increasing importance in the administrations of all colonial powers. The kind of man who reached high office after 1910 was likely to be a civilian, reformist in temperament, Protestant in religion, and inclined to support the National Liberals in politics (see Appendix B).

A good example is Heinrich Schnee—governor of East Africa from 1912 to 1918—whose roots were in Hannover, a formerly independent kingdom that had fallen under Prussian suzerainty as a result of the Austro-Prussian war of 1866, only five years before Heinrich's birth in Neuhaldesleben, a small town of the kind that produced the great majority of the civil servants who governed the German colonies. His grandfather was a Luthern pastor, his father a Landsgerichtsrat—a respected member of the judicial bureaucracy. Schnee grew up in a family where books were plentiful and education was taken for granted. His father considered himself a liberal and delighted in interpreting the merits of Great Britain's constitutional monarchy and parliamentary system as expounded at the time by Rudolf Gneist, a distinguished legal scholar. "Conservative thought with its stress on authority and on the preservation of tradition," Schnee subsequently wrote in private reminiscences, "stood worlds apart from my own."

Schnee was educated at the local Gymnasium, the kind of German secondary school which placed particular stress on the study of Latin and Greek; the report cards carefully preserved among his papers show he was a hardworking boy whose conduct was "laudable" and whose academic accomplishments varied from "adequate" to "good." As a peacetime soldier in the German army he did as creditably as he had in the Gymnasium, advancing to be an Unteroffizier in Infantry Regiment No. 85 (Herzog von Holstein). He was later commissioned as a reserve officer in the 6th Grenadier Regiment in Posen, attaining that social cachet which so many middle-class Germans of the Wilhelmian period valued more than academic distinction or even commercial success.

Schnee's academic education, like that of all senior German civil servants, was heavily oriented toward legal studies and included work in Rechts- und Staatswissenschaften (jurisprudence and constitutional law) in Heidelberg, Kiel, and Berlin. Germany's leading philosopher of the period was Rudolf von Ihering, whose teachings profoundly affected university policy. Ihering rejected natural law, insisted that the final object of the law was the preservation of the state, and that justice could only be found within the laws of individual states, which provided the moral norms for society—a doctrine well-suited to colonial conquerors determined to make their own legal notions prevail over those of their subjects. Schnee did well in his legal studies and in 1893 passed his examination as a Referendar, placing him on the lowest rung of the administrative hierarchy; a year later he qualified for a doctorate in law, and subsequently mounted to the second level in the official hierarchy by graduating as a Regierungsassessor.

In 1897, at twenty-six, Schnee took the first unconventional step in his life. Entitled to call himself both Herr Doktor and Leutnant der Reserve and meeting all the necessary qualifications for advancement in the legal profession, he decided to embark upon a colonial career. His father was aghast; according to Landsgerichtsrat Schnee, the colonies were places for *verkrachte Existenzen*—people who had failed in their respective professions or who had gotten into trouble at home. His son stood firm, took a course at the Seminar für Orientalische Sprachen at Berlin, and joined the Kolonialabteilung, the first step in what was to be a distinguished career in the colonial service.

He would have liked to secure an appointment in East Africa, but there was no vacancy at the time; he was sent instead to the South Seas. Here he served as district commissioner among the Tolai, a Stone Age people in what is now New Britain—a warlike race organized in small clan groups, engaged in constant internecine struggles, and hard to govern. Schnee hated them with a passionate intensity and soon was posted to Samoa, where he felt much happier; he acquired a respect for Samoan cultivators that he had not felt for Stone Age hunters. He also fell under the influence of Wilhelm Solf, then governor of Samoa and an old friend and colleague. Solf was a proponent of colonial reform; he firmly believed in developing Samoa through indigenous farmers rather than through the enterprise of white planters (see chapter 4).

At the end of his Samoan tour Schnee returned to Berlin, and in 1905 had a brief appointment as a colonial expert to the German Embassy in London. With his good-looking British-born wife and his thorough familiarity with English, he made an excellent impression, and promotion came quickly. In 1906 he advanced to the rank of Vortragender Rat, and in 1911 became Ministerialdirektor in charge of the political and administrative department within the colonial ministry; he was now a member of the German administrative elite. In addition, he had written several books and held a part-time lectureship at the Seminar für Orientalische Sprachen. Entertaining widely, he mingled on easy terms with parliamentarians, scholars, and senior civil servants; many members of his age cohort had now reached important offices—Solf in particular, who had advanced to be Staatssekretär in the Reichskolonialamt. In 1912 Solf offered Schnee the governship of East Africa, and while still a young man of forty-one, Schnee became the head of Germany's most important colony. He now held an appointment that had hitherto gone only to soldiers or to members of the aristocracy; he had "arrived."

Schnee became well-known in colonial circles, but the usual applicants for the lower-grade posts were destined to remain obscure. For example, Georg Lux, Stadtschreiber (a clerk in the municipal administration) in the little town of Kaiserlautern, was the son of a respectable engine driver. He had done well in the local Lateinschule, completed the first class in a Gymnasium, and served to the satisfaction of his superiors in a variety of clerical posts. According to his personnel file, his attachments to the Bavarian constitution, the royal house, the monarchy, and the rights of the Crown were beyond reproach,[4] as were his deportment and his air of self-possession among his equals and superiors. (Examining boards looked askance at candidates whose manners were gauche and who lacked the quality of Haltung, or physical and moral conduct the absence of which supposedly made a man unfit for any position of authority, great or small; shy men accordingly did not go far in the German colonial service.) Despite his impeccable record, Lux was not able to advance beyond the clerical ranks.

An interesting example of a medium-level administrator is Theodor Gunzert. His memoirs provide some valuable insight into the work of a German district official.[5] Born in Baden in 1874, Gunzert qualified as a jurist in 1899; after a trip to England he joined the civil service of his province, then the colonial service of the Reich as an assistant judge. He served in Dar es Salaam in 1902 as district judge, was transferred to Tanga in 1904, from 1905 to 1906 was an administrator for the Pangani district, and then for a ten-year period served as district commissioner in Mwanza.

Mwanza district had about 600,000 people living in an area the size of Bavaria; the main government post was located on a bay on the gulf of Mwanza in Lake Victoria, linked with the outside world by a deep-water pier at which the "Uganda Railway" steamer regularly berthed. The town had about 6,000 inhabitants, many of whom were Indians, and 150 Europeans; its businesses included several large German firms and a few foreign hide exporters.

Gunzert took over the administration from a military commander who had left local affairs in a muddle, having imprisoned a dozen chiefs for a nonexistent revolt. Gunzert set the chiefs free. He reorganized and expanded the administrative staff to include nineteen Europeans, ten white troopers, and two sergeants-major—a modest complement for such a vast area, and proof of the frugality of the imperial government and of the industry of the officials.[6] Gunzert organized his work as unbureaucratically as possible and without the usual amount of paper work, keeping few records, writing few reports, and relying on his memory. He placed great value on keeping in touch with the people he ruled and on trying to gain their confidence by constant tours of his district; a side benefit of these trips was the production of a detailed district map. Although his discipline was strict, during the ten years of his administration he was not involved in any clashes with Africans.

His duties were varied. As judge in his district he made few decisions that were overturned; as registrar he had to conduct marriages and make wedding and funeral speeches. In this latter capacity he became bureaucratic. During World War I, for example, he refused—for lack of personal guarantees—to marry a German girl to her Swiss lover whose child she was expecting; the father went back home, and the deserted mother pressed the small half-Swiss baby on Gunzert's wife when they were in a prisoner-of-war camp, saying "Take it, Madame; your husband is responsible!"

As Bezirksamtmann he managed a large estate which included vehicles, draught and riding animals, workmen and craftsmen; stores of all kinds had to be kept and buildings and roads constructed. During his ten-year tour of duty Gunzert built a new office with storerooms and a prison, hospitals for both races, official quarters, a school, markets, bridges, gravel roads, water supply facilities, police and *katikiro* (tribal representatives) quarters, stabling, and a European cemetery. The money for many of his schemes came from the "self-help fund" into which was paid a quota of the tax receipts of the district. Later, all expenses had to be officially approved, but Gunzert found ways to use his special funds to get things done.

By 1912 he had built himself a house with four rooms, a kitchen, and a large verandah. He was expected to entertain local Europeans and prominent travelers. He imported Rhine wines and "Mumm's Extra Dry" for such occasions; at a party for Colonial Secretary Solf, Gunzert personally uncorked twenty-four bottles of champagne. The "head boy" managed the details of food and decorations. The menu for special guests tended to be the same: tinned hors d'oeuvres, fish, roast sirloin with home-grown vegetables, pudding, and fruit. The occasional mishaps—kerosene taste in the food, scrambled eggs in the chocolate pudding, expensive fresh grapes served in boiling water—he accepted with such equanimity as he could muster. At the end of the work day, local whites often dropped by his house for a drink of bottled beer or whiskey and soda.

Gunzert earned a salary of 9–13,000 marks (one mark equalled $0.24) as a district commissioner. This, he wrote, was more than enough to keep up appearances, save some money, and to live well while on home leave. He noted that Berlin ladies of easy virtue evaluated colonials on furlough differently according to their colony of origin: Camerounian people had money but were weakened by fever; those from South-West Africa were strong but had few savings; East Africans had both strength and money.

Upcountry there were fewer class distinctions than in the European communities on the coast. The white community was close-knit, and

Gunzert's social companions had a variety of skills and interests. His secretary was in charge of the district's financial affairs, and in his spare time assembled the skeletons of African animals. An Alsatian lay brother of the Catholic mission knew all the local dialects and customs; he also directed building and public works. The customs officer played the piano at weekly musical recitals held at Gunzert's home. On the other hand, the postmaster, while a devoted and cooperative assistant, was a periodic drunk. There were prospectors from South Africa and Austrialia who hoped to find gold-bearing quartz seams like those on the Rand. The missionaries were the largest and most mixed group of Europeans: the Catholic White Fathers were usually French, but some Germans also came to East Africa; the Protestants were represented by English, Americans, and Germans. The Europeans preferred the Muslims to the Christian missionaries, who criticized the Europeans' lifestyles.

Gunzert's "native policy" was authoritarian. He preferred to work through traditional authorities in a form of indirect rule, but insisted on direct involvement when tribal rulers failed. He tried to become the driving force of local development, and attempted to win the cooperation of the local people and their clan chiefs. He named the clan heads to be exclusive agents between the administration and the people; he supported the chiefs and gave them as much official prestige as he could. Gunzert felt that traditional authorities were much to be preferred over alien akidas from the coast; these views were generally shared by his colleagues in the interior.

Gunzert increased the productivity of peasant agriculture in his district. After the Maji-Maji rebellion, European officials were forbidden to force cultivation of crops—they were to recommend, persuade, or encourage voluntary efforts. Gunzert, who believed Africans expected orders from Europeans, ignored the circular. Working through chiefs or their assistants, he arranged for each peasant to be allotted an annually increased area to cultivate export crops, and he allowed a choice between groundnuts or rice. Later he added cotton, which was in great demand in Germany. The officially recommended variety of cotton did not do well in his district; on his own initiative he introduced the American Upland variety. After a test year with communal lands, individual cotton plots were planted, and soon Mwanza became the greatest exporter of the protectorate.[7] Other valuable African export goods were cattle, hides, fat, and skins, whose quality Gunzert sought to improve by better skinning and drying techniques.

Not all his efforts succeeded; the colonial government refused funds for an African experimental farm and for water storage, population re-settlement, and tree-planting schemes. Like so many German officials, Gunzert failed to understand the economic function of the Indian bush trader. He ignored the dealer's problems and imagined, quite mistak-enly, that Indians always cheated the African villagers; he insisted that Indians sell only at controlled and regulated market places which he could supervise.

Gunzert worked hard to improve his district's transportation facil-ities: he built simple landing facilities with sheds around the lake to make more use of lake steamers; he used great numbers of "voluntary" workers to build gravelled roads (complete with drains), cement con-duits, and some concrete bridges; he was among the first to complete roads suitable for motor transport. All of this was done to free labor from porterage so that more manpower would become available for ag-ricultural work. He also instituted a variety of health measures to con-tend with malaria, dysentery, plague, sleeping sickness, syphilis, yaws, recurring fever, worms, leg ulcers, coast fever in cattle, and tsetse fly infection. For his work against disease Berlin awarded him the Order of the Red Eagle, IV Class.

The overall German colonial policy was to cause the least possible disturbance to African societies and to attempt to work through existing institutions. Gunzert encouraged traditional rulers to use more efficient methods and to perform new jobs. He tried to build up a local administrative structure chosen from and by local dignitaries them-selves. Katikiros, market police, and agricultural and road construction assistants were appointed as well as clerks for the chiefs to handle the increasing correspondence with the boma, and salaries were paid from the chiefs' fund administered by the government. A $0.12 surtax on the poll tax was assessed for the chiefs' fund that gave local bodies their own financial resources from which to pay tribal officials and to build roads.

Other changes in tribal institutions were the chiefs' school, the dis-trict police, and tribal courts. Gunzert founded a tribal school with a German headmaster for about one hundred boys to be nominated only by the chiefs, partly from among their own children; the boys were

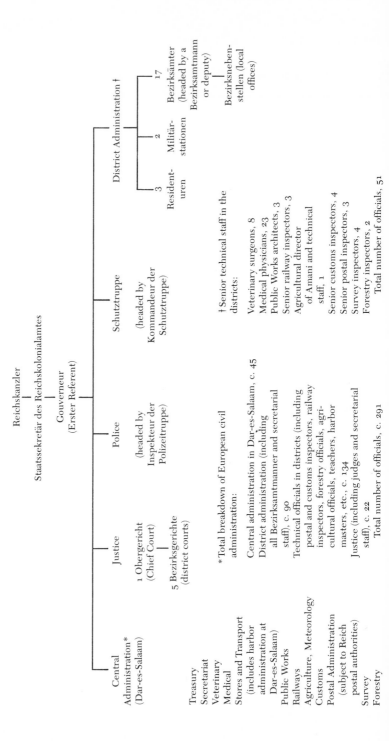

THE CHAIN OF COMMAND IN GERMAN EAST AFRICA, 1913

given free lodging in the houses of the katikiros. After a two- to three-year course, students took positions in the clan administration to assist in carrying on the new functions of local government. Gunzert scrapped the old system of using alien askari to police local people; the old police (mostly ex-colonial troopers) were withdrawn, and a new force was created locally. District police were appointed by the chiefs but were paid by the district administration and trained by German sergeants.

Gunzert did not agree with the German policy of taking away the judicial powers of the chiefs; he rightly saw that this had been one of their main functions and the basis of their prestige. Europeans did not know local languages, customs, or laws; they could not spend long hours as the chiefs had done discussing cases; the European judge ultimately depended on the judgment of the displaced chief or that of the interpreter. Gunzert, therefore, tried to renew the chiefs' former judicial powers. He gave them power to levy fines and to hear all property cases as well as criminal cases that did not involve murder, witchcraft, or breaches of the peace. Appeal to the district commissioner was allowed, and court clerks had to keep a record of the proceedings, the judgments, and the fees. Corporal punishment was reduced, and the prisoners were cared for by their wives.

From the Tanzanian material he has surveyed, Austen concludes that local potentates such as Gunzert were administrators of high quality "capable of managing local political, economic and social development on an independent and responsible basis." Their skills "resulted from a process of selection, training and experience that preceded the Dernburg era, but their continuity at their posts up until the end of German rule" reflected "the concern of the new regime with stability."[8]

There was another side to the German system—an aspect illuminated in a report compiled by Charles Dundas, a British administrator and later governor of Uganda, who investigated German practices in East Africa after the British occupied the territory in World War I.[9] Dundas disliked the Germans and tried to show that they were unfit to rule Africans. He was willing to admit that senior German officials seemed to have been drawn from "a superior type of German" with an excellent education, but he insisted that the Germans were obsessed with enforcing obedience.

German district commissioners were few and far between. They had too much to do, and their responsibilities were too great. The Mwanza district had 600,000 inhabitants, the average district about 148,000. Within his district a Bezirksamtmann was much like a deputy governor, charged with every conceivable kind of task except trying the most serious criminal cases; an excessive amount of work therefore devolved on junior officials, including police sergeants in charge of substations. A Polizeiwachtmeister could, on his own authority, sentence a criminal to two months in jail or to twenty-five lashes, thus wielding the power of a subordinate British court. Even ordinary employers outside the official hierarchy were permitted to beat their workmen in a "moderate" fashion or to confine them for fourteen days—this under the Gewohnheitsrecht (customary law) expounded by the *Bürgerliche Gesetzbuch* (German civil code).[10]

The district officers' judicial powers were so vast and so ill-defined that their exercise was bound to occasion abuses—all the more so because the Germans, like the French, had neither a uniform code of African penal law nor a uniform set of rules for trying criminal cases. Their penal system accordingly suffered from excessive severity, inconsistency, and arbitrariness. At Moshi police station Dundas found that the local police sergeant had tried 348 Africans within a period of nine months; of these, 283 were flogged, receiving a punishment which in British territory would have required confirmation from the High Court.

The German system also was deliberately fashioned as an instrument of class justice. According to a confidential circular issued by von Schele in 1893, "the increasing insolence shown both by male and female proletarians" in the larger centers and the increasing number of disorders and robberies required stronger measures; German officials were henceforth permitted to inflict a maximum of fifty lashes. Reformers later reduced the number of blows that might be administered to an Africa, and Indians and Arabs were exempt from such punishment. Even so, a summons to appear before a German court must have filled many an African laborer with dread. According to the Wilhelmsthal criminal register cited by Dundas, a workman might receive as many as twenty-five lashes for offenses such as neglect of duty, breach of contract, drunkenness, even disobedience to an order to stay up all night with a sick horse.

German justice must often have been excessively summary. In 1909 the Eingeborenenrichter (judge in charge of native cases) at Dar es Salaam tried, on an average, about seventeen persons a day. According to Dundas's calculations, about twelve minutes were given to each prisoner—this in a country where a traditional court might spend several days in trying a serious case. German practice varied widely from region to region and even from station to station. By and large, however, the German regime was authoritarian and even brutal at its worst, especially when account is taken of the unauthorized abuses committed by junior officials—both white and black—and by unsupervised white employers.

SIX

The Armed Forces

When Germany first intervened in Africa, she relied on her navy. The employment of cruisers and gunboats in support of consular representatives on the shores of the Atlantic and the Indian Oceans reflected the needs of German merchants anxious for German support rather than German rule. German trade on the littoral was very limited. The role of the Imperial Kriegsmarine in German colonial expansion was minor in comparison to that of the French navy in the imperialism of France, and the German naval administration, unlike the French, never exercised governmental responsibility in Africa. As long as German trade in West Africa was confined to the Atlantic coast, Hanseatic firms like Woermann were satisfied with indirect forms of protection to safeguard their interests. They looked for support to German consuls and the captains of German warships. Bismarck's navy, though relatively small in numbers of ships and men, was well equipped to supply such backing. Unlike his successors in the twentieth century, the chancellor had no desire to build a battlefleet capable of challenging the Royal Navy in the North Sea. He was anxious above all to protect Germany's foreign trade, and he relied upon cruisers and gunboats to show the flag abroad and strengthen the hand of German consuls and traders in the more exotic regions of the globe. Bismarck thus established both the East Asian and West African squadrons primarily to sustain German commerce.[1]

The German navy was the arm of the bourgeoisie par excellence. Its part in the country's early colonial expansion was represented by men like Admiral Eduard von Knorr (1849–1920), who entered the Prussian navy at the age of sixteen, attained a commission, and during the

Franco-German War made a name for himself as the commander of the gunboat *Meteor* which vanquished a French patrol vessel in a fight off Havana. This engagement, unimportant though it was, fired the imagination of a nation whose naval triumphs had been few, and Knorr advanced rapidly to the rank of rear admiral. In 1884 he was appointed to command Germany's West African squadron, and helped to annex part of the coasts of Cameroun and Togo.

Knorr's intervention, directed against African chiefs who had not signed protectorate treaties with the Germans, led to further promotion. His fortunes advanced briskly at a time when the German navy was rapidly expanding, when navalism was becoming almost a religion for militant German chauvinists, and when naval officers were still drawn largely from the ranks of the bourgeoisie. In 1895 he was appointed chief of the naval staff, and a year later raised to the nobility, thereby attaining a distinction shared by most of the prominent leaders of the Kriegsmarine at a time when the navy showed the way toward "feudalizing" the upper bourgeoisie. After his retirement Knorr was active in various right-wing causes popular among senior officers at the time. Between 1906 and 1920, for instance, he served as president of the Antiultramontaner Reichsverband, which battled against the Center Party on the grounds that the Catholics were conducting an "anti-national" policy against Germany's best interests both at home and abroad.

The navy whose interests Knorr defended in his old age was very different from the fleet which he had joined in his youth. In strategic terms, it had come to rely on battleships designed to engage the British Grand Fleet in the North Sea rather than on light vessels constructed in order to show the flag in distant waters, and politically it had subordinated the Bismarckian policy of protecting German traders to the wider and more aggressive aims of an anti-British and anti-American Weltpolitik that far transcended the more modest aims of the colonial authorities proper. The navy became responsible for running Kiau Tschau, a harbor acquired from China in 1898 as a naval base, a free-trading port, and a stepping-stone to global expansion. The naval administration prided itself on its efficiency, smartness, and social prestige, but "navalism" of the German variety, with its almost paranoid strain, never acquired much importance in the governance of Africa.

TABLE 11

German Military Forces (Schutztruppen) in the African Colonies, 1914

| Colony | Number of units | | | Number of troops | | |
	Field companies	Batteries	Signal companies	Whites	Africans	Total
East Africa	14	—	1	260	2,500	2,760
South-West Africa	9[a]	3	1	1,954	—	1,954
Cameroun	12	—	—	197	1,550	1,747
Togo[b]	—	—	—	—	—	—
TOTAL	35	3	2	2,411	4,050	6,461

SOURCE: Miscellaneous publications and correspondence.
[a] Mounted.
[b] Togo had no Schutztruppen, only armed police.

The navy was well equipped to control the shores of Germany's new possessions. German warships intervened against Swahili-speaking rebels on the East African littoral, and German marines took a minor part in South-West African and East African campaigns without, under unfamiliar conditions, gaining particular distinction. The task of conquering and holding the colonies was essentially left to the army. Colonial enterprise was of marginal importance within the German military establishment as it was marginal in German society. The German public would never have stood for the employment of German conscripts overseas, and the proverbial Pomeranian grenadier had no desire to leave his bones in Little Popoland. The white military establishment in the colonies consisted of volunteers: the bulk of the fighting was done by professional Schutztruppen. Despite their reputation for militarism, the Germans maintained only a small number of troops in Africa. These forces were designed in the main for use against Africans—not against other European colonial powers. German strategists considered that in the event of war the fate of the overseas empire would be decided on the battlefields of Europe—not in Africa. The German colonial forces, which totalled not quite 6,500 before the outbreak of World War I (see Table 11), were considerably smaller than those of France (about 31,000 officers and men in sub-Saharan Africa in 1912), or Belgium (18,000 officers and men in the Belgian Congo), or even Portugal (13,000 men, including 400 officers, 3,500 whites in other ranks, and 9,000 Africans).

Social Background

Within the metropolitan military hierarchy, the status of the Schutz-truppen high command was extremely modest—much more so than that of the Armée Coloniale within the French military establishment. The latter was numerically stronger than the Schutztruppen, and played an active part in both the conquest of empire and the defense of metropolitan France. It also had an ideological character of its own. While the metropolitan forces contained a high proportion of officers with clerical and conservative leanings, the Armée Coloniale—and especially the Infanterie de Marine—attracted officers who came from modest social backgrounds, men who depended on their pay for their living, anti-clericals and convinced republicans who looked askance at "feudalists," whether French or Fula. It also attracted Protestants and officers like Galliéni, foreign in origin—the kind of man superpatriots might deride.

The Schutztruppen, on the other hand, had no ideological orientation to differentiate it from other sections of the German army. It lacked the social prestige of the navy. The high command of the African forces was too insignificant militarily to act as an independent military lobby. Until 1896 the Schutztruppen were subject to dual control by the Reichsmarineamt and the Kolonialabteilung; after that, colonial troops were organized into an independent part of the German armed forces directly subject to the Reichskanzler. They were administered through the Kolonialabteilung and, from 1907, through the Reichskolonialamt, where a special Kommando der Schutztruppen equal in military standing to a Generalkommando looked after their affairs. By 1913 the entire headquarter establishment amounted to no more than the Kommandeur der Schutztruppen, who ranked as major general, eight military officers, three army doctors, and a senior technician. Within each colony the governor—a civilian—acted as supreme commander of the armed forces, an arrangement unheard of in any other part of Germany and one that professional soldiers resented.

Nevertheless, the German colonial officers formed a *corps d'élite*. Service in the colonies was highly sought after at a time when the long peace in Europe seemed endless and when the only shots heard by the average soldier were those discharged on a firing range, but the German officer's predilection for service in the empire was hard to explain. Like everyone else, he had to contend with the high cost of living in the colonies and with the considerable expense of educating growing children in a German boarding school. The colonial establishment was small, and the scale of military operations was petty by European standards. Service was arduous and often dangerous. Between 1894 and 1904—the supposedly peaceful time before the outbreak of the great South-West African uprising (1904–7)—three of eight commanders and adjutants of the South-West African Schutztruppe were killed in action; during the uprising the Germans lost 70 officers and 732 noncommissioned officers and troopers—some 5 percent of the total number of troops engaged.

On the other hand, the pay was good in the colonies—much better than at home. A captain first-class in East Africa received 10,800 marks a year, a lieutenant 6,300, and a sergeant 2,400, in addition to various allowances. By comparison a regimental commander in Germany earned between 6,225 and 9,060 marks a year, and an ordinary lieutenant made 1,284–1,572 marks per year. The director of a big-city Gymnasium (a classics-oriented secondary school) earned between 7,300 and 9,100 marks per year—less than a Schutztruppen captain. For long service a Schutztruppen officer received an additional 3,600 marks in salary and 1,800 marks in housing allowance. The corresponding annual salary for an elementary teacher in a big city was 1,900 to 4,100 marks, plus extras amounting to 900 marks per year.[2]

Life in the colonial forces had other attractions, both imagined and real. A considerable number of enlisted men and sergeants joined the Schutztruppen in total ignorance of African conditions: they envisaged Africa as a dreamland where there would be no more drilling, where an enterprising man might spend his time hunting big game—a land of oranges, dates, and other exotic fruits, of luscious women and golden ten-mark pieces that jingled in a soldier's pocket. The reality was disappointing: most of them never saw a lion or an elephant, the high cost of living soon took care of their salaries (high as their pay might seem on paper), and their time was spent exercising newly enlisted askaris in the blistering sun and fighting various diseases.

Africa still had its compensations, however, even for a junior noncommissioned officer. It was an excellent school for real war, especially guerrilla operations; there were plenty of opportunities for initiative in a country where a station head was required to become a carpenter, builder, engineer, perhaps even a sailor, in addition to serving as a soldier and administrator.[3] And what could be more challenging for a young sergeant than to take command of a column of carriers on a great trek into the interior without even knowing the language or customs, or to assume command of an important post all on his own?

These considerations applied with even greater force to commissioned officers. A large percentage of these officers still came from aristocratic families, but the bourgeoisie's growing wealth and social influence placed the poorer noblemen under increasing pressure. Ambitious young nobles tried to compete with rich commoners in forms of conspicuous consumption, and they often spent more money on clothes, entertainment, and gambling than they could afford. As their parents' income from landed estates declined, aristocratic officers became more dependent on the army for their livelihood and perhaps less willing to criticize their superiors. The pressures of military and social duties increased at the same time, as did the weight of military formalism—a formalism so extreme that a man might have to resign his commission because his unit had made a poor showing at a review. As a fictional character in a controversial novel by Count von Schlicht (Count von Baudissin) entitled *Life in a German Crack Regiment* put it: "I am a dissatisfied aristocrat, and so are we all, from the colonel down to the youngest lieutenant."

Slow promotion and the petty concerns of garrison life were irksome even to men of impeccable political orthodoxy. Ludwig von Estorff, for instance, had all the advantages which birth and ability could afford him. His family belonged to the Lower Saxon *Uradel*—the most ancient nobility—and his father, Eggert von Estorff, was a major general and editor of the influential *Militärwochenblatt*. Ludwig spent a happy youth in his father's garrison towns and at his grandfather's estate at Tyendorf. Despite a somewhat insubordinate disposition, he did well in the Kadettenkorps. Commissioned in an infantry regiment, the young lieutenant soon tired of garrison life: he became convinced that the drill practiced at Altona no longer corresponded to real war, that the famous *Exerzierreglement* was no better than a museum catalog. After taking a course at the Kriegsakademie he served for two years in the general staff, the highest professional distinction that the German army could bestow on a young officer.

Estorff's interest in the colonies was aroused by listening to debates in the Reichstag, and in 1894 he joined the South-West Africa Schutztruppe, where he hoped to emulate the careers of great Prussian soldiers like Moltke and Grolman who had seen a great deal of the world abroad before reaching the top of their profession at home.[4] He distinguished himself in action in South-West Africa, where he was seriously wounded. Later he served in East Africa, but was transferred back to South-West Africa, where in 1902 he became acting commandant of the Schutztruppe. He played an important part in putting down the great uprising of the Herero and the Nama, and made a name for himself by his expertise in mounted counterinsurgency warfare, by the relative humanity of his methods, and by the uncompromising discipline he imposed on his men. In army messes the men smiled at—or derided—his old-fashioned Lutheran piety, but they referred to him admiringly as *der letzte Römer* (the last of the Romans). In 1911 he returned to Germany, where he subsequently reached general officer's rank.

Colonial appointments usually entailed a variety of disadvantages. Within Wilhelmian Germany's military pecking order the status of the Schutztruppen was relatively modest, not comparable to that of a sharp British Guards regiment. In addition there were departmental squabbles. Kaiser Wilhelm, for all his colonial ambitions, preferred his smart Marineinfantrie to the hard-working Schutztruppe.[5] Service in the colonies did not count for much in the race for top jobs; the plums of the German military profession normally went to officers who had seen service on the German general staff. Theodor Leutwein, a major general, was not entrusted with the task of putting down the South-West African rebellion, a task for which he would have been well-suited; instead, command was given to General von Trotha, a protégé of Alfred von Schlieffen's and a narrow-minded military specialist quite incapable of foreseeing the social or economic consequences of his strategy of annihilation.

Nevertheless (as noted earlier) there was no shortage of applicants for colonial service. When Tom Prince, a young infantry lieutenant, decided to volunteer for the newly raised Wissmann force, he travelled to East Africa at his own expense because there were some fifteen hundred other applicants he wanted to beat.[6] In the colonies a young captain might still make his mark, and it was a time when many governorships and numerous jobs as Bezirksamtmänner still went to military officers.[7] The Schutztruppe in the early days attracted some men who later distinguished themselves as technical administrators, such as Franz Stuhlmann, subsequently director of the Kaiserlich-Biologisch-Landwirtschaftliches Institut Amani in German East Africa.[8] A surprisingly large number of officers made contributions to the study of colonial geography, cartography, or ethnography.

The colonial officer corps drew a good proportion of noblemen, usually younger sons of aristocratic families without estates of their own—men who, according to the standards of their class, could find "honorable" employment only in farming, in academic pursuits, or in service to the Crown. In the army, as in the colonial administration at large, the aristocratic component gradually declined (see Table 12). Even so, a Schutztruppen commander was more likely to be a nobleman than was a general or colonel in the metropolitan army during the Wilhelmian period. Of a total of twenty-one Schutztruppen commanders in Cameroun, East Africa, and South-West Africa, fifteen were noblemen. In East Africa—the prize of the German colonial empire—all eight Schutztruppen commanders were noblemen; in South-West Africa, where a great deal of fighting took place, five of seven commanders were high-born; and in Cameroun, the least desirable colony of the four, two of six commanders were aristocrats. By comparison, in the Prussian army there was a considerably higher percentage of commoners among the generals and colonels (see Table 13).

Noblemen also crowded into the lower ranks of the Schutztruppen. In 1912 something like 33 percent of the Schutztruppen lieutenants were noblemen, compared to a proportion of nobleborn infantry lieutenants in the Prussian army of 22 percent in 1908. When the German army was required to make a sudden effort during the great South-West African uprising (1904–7), volunteers flocked to the colors, and the proportion of noblemen in the Schutztruppen rose rapidly. In 1904 the South-West African Schutztruppe was expanded to comprise two mounted infantry regiments with supporting units, mainly recruited from regulars in the home army willing to serve overseas; according to the published *Rangliste der Schutztruppe für Südwest Afrika* (1904), of the combatant officers sixty-two were noblemen (including nineteen Grafen, Barone, and Freiherren) and seventy-nine were commoners.

TABLE 12

Social Class of Schutztruppen Officers in African
Colonies, 1899, 1906, and 1913

Year	Commoners		Noblemen	
	Number	Percent	Number	Percent
1899	58	66%	30	34%
1906	85	69	39	31
1913	174	69	79	31

SOURCE: *Kolonial-Handelsadressbuch* (Berlin, 1899, 1906, and 1913).

TABLE 13

Social Class of Prussian Army Officers, 1860, 1900, and 1913
(Percent)

Year	Commoners	Noblemen
1860	14%	86%
1900	39	61
1913	48	52

SOURCE: Karl Demeter, *The German Officer-Corps in Society and State: 1650–1945*,
trans. Angus Malcolm (New York, 1965), pp. 28–29.

A high proportion of these officers, both noble and commoner, came
from eastern Germany. Of forty-three prominent colonial soldiers
selected from the *Kolonial-Lexikon*, twenty-three were born in Silesia,
West and East Prussia, Pomerania, or the Provinz Sachsen of the Prussian kingdom. The average Schutztruppen officer was likely to be a
countryman or the product of a small city. Like his opposite number in
British colonial units, his ethos tended to be rural, and he often had
little knowledge of—and less sympathy with—the problems of industrial development.

Whatever his class or geographical origin, the social prestige of the
Schutztruppen officer was such that the Germans could afford to be
highly selective in their choices. The Oberkommando der Schutztruppe insisted on picking only candidates distinguished for good conduct, for the ability to make independent decisions, for versatility,
financial probity, and for sound military qualifications. In terms of
career prospects, service in the Schutztruppe was not a bad bet for a

German officer; chances for advancement were somewhat better for a Schutztruppen officer than for his colleague back home. A relatively large number of ex-colonial officers became divisional and corps commanders during World War I, when military preferment for regular officers speeded up and even elderly men found senior employment. Most of these ex-colonial generals had been born during the 1850's; only Paul von Lettow-Vorbeck, the most successful of them all, was in his early forties when the war started.[9] But the German colonies produced no figure comparable in national importance to Trenchard, Kitchener, or Wolseley in the British army, to Galliéni, Lyautey, or Mangin in the French forces, or to Balbo or Graziani in the Italian Fascist establishment.

During the colonial period, service in the colonial forces provided an avenue by which ambitious commoners could acquire a much-envied patent of nobility.[10] The elevated commoners, however, came from families whose outlook differed little if at all from that of the hereditary service nobility. Eduard von Liebert (1850–1934)—a promising staff officer, governor of East Africa from 1896 to 1901, advocate of white settlement in the colony, and later a general—was a characteristic example.

Liebert's father was a regular officer who died in Eduard's childhood, leaving his wife in dire straits. Young Eduard, however, received a scholarship for a cadet academy that educated youngsters for the military profession, and he grew up to be a staunch patriot, deeply grateful to his sovereign for the favors he had received in this youth, with the feeling that the army was his new family. Liebert identified himself completely with the Junker ideal. An extreme nationalist in politics and one of the founders of the Pan-German League, he tried to promote European settlement in East Africa; he became engaged in a long and bitter feud with the missionaries and their parent societies, maintaining that they and their domestic supporters in the Center Party were interfering with the proper development of the colonies. He insisted on implementing a policy of state education and of using Swahili-speaking Africans in government.

Another distinguished colonial soldier later ennobled by the Kaiser was Tom von Prince (1866–1916). Prince was born in Mauritius, the son of a British police officer and a German missionary's daughter; he was orphaned at an early age and was brought up in the Friederizian-ische Ritterakademie in Liegnitz, a military academy and a stepping-stone to a military career.

Men like Liebert and Prince grew up in harsh environments and en-tered an army noted for strictness of discipline, including numerous cases of brutal treatment of private soldiers. Often they were the chil-dren of families where memories were long and cash was short, where conduct was guided by endless lists of do's and don't's, and where all was forbidden unless specifically allowed. Liebert, for instance, went through a harsh school where cadets were unmercifully beaten by stronger boys. Such men usually saw nothing wrong in ruling with an iron fist.

By and large, the German colonial officer made an effective leader. He shared the men's hardships, helped them with their personal trou-bles, trained them, and led them in action—an intimacy made possible by the relatively high proportion of junior officers to private soldiers. Whatever his failings, the average Schutztruppenoffizier lived in close touch with his men. The Germans had considerable respect for the fighting abilities of their African recruits, and apart from a serious mutiny of Dahomean soldiers in Cameroun in 1893 provoked by the cruelty and incompetence of German leadership, they generally man-aged to keep their askaris' allegiance.

These soldier-administrators acted as the trailblazers of German rule, and it was their task to break down the Africans' initial resistance to German governance. There is a world of difference between the en-thusiastic description in the official Schutztruppen field service manual concerning the Africans—their courage, resilience, marching capacity, and knowledge of veld craft—and the accounts of the Africans' reputed wickedness and sloth provided in so many contemporary settler news-papers and missionary journals. The Germans trained their African soldiers, but also learned from them—how to lay an ambush in the forest, how to scout, how to build camouflaged pitfalls lined with bam-boo stakes, how to construct tangled thorn *zaribas* that stopped an as-sault more effectively than barbed wire. By studying the methods of the African tacticians, the Germans became masters at choosing defen-sive positions in difficult country so that their movements could not be seen and their strength could not be assessed, at keeping open many safe lines of retreat, and at suddenly fading away into the bush, only to reassemble at a new point and strike the enemy again with sudden fury.

The most effective German officers managed to forget much of what they had been taught in staff colleges at home. Time-honored formulas such as the Moltkean phrase "March divided, strike in unison" were forgotten in a country like East Africa, where the Germans became skilled at tactical dispersal and in accommodating themselves to the needs of battlefields where there was neither front, flanks, nor rear. Above all, German colonial forces became expert in the use of machine guns, two of which were assigned to each East African company during the Maji-Maji uprising. The machine gun, a weapon as yet neglected by most military theoreticians in Europe, came to dominate the colonial battlefield and—during the Maji-Maji uprising—accounted to a considerable extent for German tactical superiority.[11]

Organization, Functions, and Campaigns

The Schutztruppe, Lilliputian by the standards of contemporary armies, were subdivided into separate regional forces that had little in common. The military element was weakest in Togo, a trader's colony where German economic power depended essentially on an alliance between German merchants, African middlemen, and African peasants. This economic alliance was strengthened by long-standing cultural and religious ties between German missionaries and the Ewe, a people particularly open both to the attractions of the world market and to foreign learning. In Togo, physical force played a very limited part in extending German power. Of all the colonies, Togo alone had no Schutztruppe, but only a military police answerable directly to the governor. The Polizeitruppe was small in numbers—by 1913 it consisted of two German officers, six German Polizeimeister, and 560 African noncommissioned officers and men—but it was highly trained in building roads and railways and in the duties of infantrymen.

As in all other German tropical possessions, the military in Togo was one of the first major employers of long-term labor. The African personnel of the military police in Togo consisted at first of labor migrants from abroad—Hausa, then Grussi, Mossi, Dahomeans, and Wey. Later the force increasingly relied on locally recruited Togolese, including Dakomba, Losso, Kabure, and others—with Ewe as a kind of military lingua franca. Under a system developed by a reserve lieutenant by the name of Klose who reorganized the force in 1894, each Korporalschaft (section) within a platoon was composed of members of the same ethnic group commanded by a corporal able to speak the constables' home tongue. Togo's history was by no means peaceful; the Germans conducted a number of campaigns against various communities, including the Dagomba, who were not finally subdued until 1900. But the paucity of German military resources forced the Germans to be extremely circumspect, and on the whole Togo deserved the appellation of "model colony" bestowed upon it by German colonial reformers.

In Cameroun, where the Germans for a time instituted concessionary regimes of the Belgian Congo variety, the colonizers required a good deal more in the way of military coercion than in Togo. By 1910 the Cameroun Schutztruppe consisted of ten companies—later raised to twelve—each containing about 150 Africans. German methods of recruitment initially seem to have been little different from those adopted by African potentates in building slave armies. When they raised the first Schutztruppe for Cameroun, Captain Freiherr von Gravenreuth purchased 370 slaves from King Behanzin of Dahomey; these slaves, born in many different parts of West Africa, formed the core of the Cameroun military force. They did excellent work despite harsh and brutal treatment that in 1893 led to an anti-German military revolt; floggings were administered even to women.[12]

Conditions of military labor subsequently improved. The Germans secured volunteers willing to serve seven years or longer, including Hausa—who supplied many of the best noncommissioned officers— Yoruba, Wey from Liberia, and Sierra Leonians, who were said to be the most disciplined soldiers in the force. By 1905 half of the troops consisted of local Cameroun men, including Jaunde and Yoki, a development regarded with some apprehension by the Germans, who preferred to seek recruits abroad or among proven Schutztruppen veterans lest the local population acquire too great a proficiency in arms.[13] Service conditions gradually became more standardized. In the various Schutztruppen, African recruits usually signed on for an intial period of five years; thereafter enlistments could be extended on a yearly basis, and many stayed on permanently. White soldiers were accepted only after having served three years in the regular German forces; they had to enlist for periods varying from two years for West Africa to three and one-half years for South-West Africa.

In purely military terms the Cameroun Schutztruppe was not a very formidable force. Only two or three "expeditionary" companies were available for mobile operations—this in a country not much smaller in area than the former Reich, and much of it mountainland or jungle. The rest were scattered throughout the colony in garrisons, where they were supplemented by a police force numbering about 1,300 men. Nevertheless the Germans gradually succeeded in wiping out all indigenous resistance to their rule and put an end to armed inter-ethnic conflicts, slave-raiding, and ritual cannibalism. At the same time they succeeded in building a cohesive military society.

The African military remained loyal to their overlords, even during World War I when Germany's star was on the wane and when many communities, especially the Duala, were looking to the Allies to liberate Cameroun from German rule. After resistance had become hopeless, the bulk of the Schutztruppe, consisting of about twenty-seven whites and several thousand Africans with an equal number of women and children, crossed into Spanish territory where they were interned on the island of Fernando Póo. Even in defeat the Schutztruppe had no disciplinary problems. German officers continued to drill their defeated army, and the Germans supervised fishing, farming, and canoe building, and judged disputes between their black adherents. When the Germans finally departed at the end of the war, many hard-bitten soldiers were in tears as they took leave of their former officers.[14]

In East Africa, as noted earlier, German rule was originally established with the aid of mercenaries from the Sudan and other parts of East Africa. Without the aid of these Muslim soldiers the Germans could not have conquered the colony. The East African Schutztruppe originally bore something of a semi-private character—officers and men signed a personal contract with Wissmann. It was not until 1892 that this mercenary force became officially an imperial force known as the Kaiserliche Schutztruppe. The Sudanese were unemployed ex-soldiers of the Egyptian army, men only too pleased to find new military employment; they formed the core of the original German army, and many of them later settled in the country as traders. They later were reinforced by Zulu-speaking recruits who initially astounded

TABLE 14
*Proportion of Soldiers to Civilians in Selected Colonies of
Belgium, Great Britain, and Germany, c. 1905*

Colony	Colonial power	Proportion of civilians to soldiers[a]
Congo Free State	Belgium	1,110:1
East Africa	Great Britain	1,300:1
Uganda	Great Britain	1,800:1
India	Great Britain	2,775:1
East Africa	Germany	2,650:1

SOURCE: Graf G. A. von Götzen, *Deutsch-Ostafrika im Aufstand: 1905/6* (Berlin, 1909), pp. 39–41.
  [a] Estimated.

their German sergeants by performing war dances when called on parade, and who had to be persuaded with some difficulty that in order to use German weapons they must learn German drill. Manyema from the Congo were also accepted—strangers feared by the local people as man-eaters. Finally the Germans signed on local men, especially Nyamwezi—many of them former carriers used to wage labor—who became the core of the East African Schutztruppe.

The German military in East Africa was run in a highly economical fashion. By 1912 the force consisted of fourteen field companies comprising 226 whites—including 108 officers and physicians—and 2,664 Africans. This hardly seems adequate to the dual task of holding down a country extending over more than 360,000 square miles—an area seven times the size of England—and of protecting the region against attack from abroad. According to contemporary reports, the German colonial establishment had a smaller proportion of soldiers to civilians than any of the other colonial powers in Africa (see Table 14).

Instruments of Coercion

The German training of the askari was based on a simplified version of the 1906 infantry Exerzierreglement, a military regime that tried to assimilate the experiences of the Boer War and stressed independent fire tactics, but as yet failed to appreciate fully the firepower of the machine gun. The askari units were schooled only to operate up to company level; their courses of instruction stressed discipline and musketry rather than technical training. Even the German language was taught sparingly: commands and instructions were given in indigenous tongues, and German served only as the language of the higher command levels. White soldiers were equipped with the most modern arms, including rifle and carbine Mauser Mark 98, machine guns, and light mountain artillery for the South-West African forces; the askari were left to fend with antiquated arms. At the outbreak of World War I most askari units were still armed with obsolescent Mark 71/84 rifles, single-loaders using black powder and lead bullets.

The army served a great variety of functions, and its impact was double-edged. The military generally acted as administrative pioneers, since the Germans habitually put administrative stations under the command of Schutztruppenoffiziere until such time as a region was firmly under German control.[15] In their capacities as civilian administrators many German officers acquired enviable records. In Togo, for instance, there was a whole generation of soldier-administrators who managed to rule with a minimum of force; in East Africa the Schutztruppenoffiziere who initiated German governance on Lake Victoria took care to work through local chiefs where they could.[16] In South-West Africa experienced soldier-administrators like Leutwein and many of his officers were among the most moderate and humane whites in the territory and joined with the most bitter critics of General von Trotha's ruthless policies. Civilian officials like Karl Theodor Heinrich Leist, a sexual pervert later found guilty on criminal charges, or Carl Peters, an unbalanced right-wing intellectual, were more likely to commit atrocities than were soldiers who had lived for some time among the people they governed.

On the other hand, the use of the military provided an element of coercion that in many cases excited the very disorders it was designed to suppress. The local political situation would be influenced by the amount of military force available to the Germans, by logistic factors, by the ability (or the inability) of Africans to resist pressure by means of deception, threats, or violence. In addition, the personal idiosyncrasies of a Bezirksamtmann or a Schutztruppenoffizier might play a considerable role. But no matter whether the local German dignitary was humane or brutal, he could not govern without at least the threat of force in the background. Government entailed the destruction of independent African armies and militias and the disarmament of the population; furthermore, it required the raising of revenues. However sketchy the German administration might be, district officers and their clerks had to be paid in cash. Since colonies were expected to be at least partially self-supporting, administrators were forced to raise local funds in cash rather than kind; taxation forced tribesmen to work for wages or to sell their produce for money. German rule, in this respect, had the same effect on subsistence farmers as any other form of colonial or post-colonial governance dependent on the cash nexus.

The element of coercion became even greater when the Germans tried to speed up development by political means ahead of the economic development produced by the operation of the market alone. When the Germans began to colonize in Africa, the purchasing power of most Africans was very limited, as was the African demand for European goods. The Germans, for their part, were reluctant at first to develop their colonial "estates" by risking capital. Their unwillingness to subsidize the empire, along with their desire for rapid economic rewards and for the prestige derived from "development" as a civilizing mission, drove them toward a policy of force. As an example, for a long time the Germans would not invest capital in railway building; hence they had to use local porters—often unwilling conscripts—to move merchandise by means of human muscle rather than by steam.

The mode of economic coercion varied a great deal from region to region. In East Africa the Schutztruppe first made its mark by a series of campaigns against the Swahili-speakers of the coast; subsequently they turned their attention to the interior, where they defeated communities as varied as the Yao and the Hehe. Between 1905 and 1906 they suppressed a widespread uprising in Tanzania, known as the Maji-Maji rebellion. This was a trans-tribal insurrection occasioned by a variety of grievances, including the hardships caused by taxation, the imposition of labor services designed to maintain bridges and roads, the real or supposed exactions of coastal traders, the abuses committed by local officials (particularly unpopular akidas), the social and religious tensions produced by missionary propaganda, German interference with the traditional powers of chiefs and spirit mediums, and the enforcement of unpopular game regulations that interfered with the livelihood of elephant hunters, who supplied much of the rebel leadership.

The Germans had also alienated many communities by forcing them to grow cotton at fixed prices that left little or no profit to the ordinary villages. However, pressure for cotton cultivation was not a major cause of the uprising; according to Governor Götzen, cotton production was forced in only four of the eight districts affected by the rebellion. Compulsory labor services probably constituted the greatest hardship—it was far more unpopular than domestic slavery. In their despair the rebels looked not merely to the expulsion of the Germans and their reputed Indian and Arab auxiliaries, but also to the creation of a new order. Magic would turn away German bullets, thereby giving African warriors as good a chance to win in battle as German-led askaris. Success in war, sustained by magic, would endow the victors with untold wealth.[17]

In the beginning of the uprising, the Maji-Maji rebels, armed with muskets, a few rifles, poisoned arrows, and spears, attempted to engage large detachments in the open country by means of shock tactics. Failing in this effort and bitterly disappointed when magic was ineffective against the Germans, the insurgents turned to guerrilla warfare. The Germans, however, got the better of the enemy by a combination of political strategy, effective counterinsurgency tactics, and counterterror.

The insurrection was essentially directed against the modernizing elements in Tanzanian society—against Indians and Arabs as much as against the Germans. Hence the social basis of the revolution remained comparatively narrow, and only a few Muslims and Christians joined the rebels. Many of the more advanced people, including the Yao and the Nyamwezi, stayed aloof; indeed the uprising did not spread to the towns or to the economically more developed parts of the countryside where German colonists had made new homes for themselves. The askaris remained loyal.

The Germans found that success in counter-guerrilla warfare did not require gaining the support of the people; the government forces won by a combination of economic, psychological, and military pressure. They seized the enemy's cattle and crops; they ravaged his fields and villages; they captured his women and children as hostages. The key to German victory lay in unified command, in highly disciplined and mobile black troops, in superior weapons, in an effective supply system based on the efficient deployment of carriers, and in the use of African allies such as the Masai, who were more skilled in scouting and in the traditional arts of raiding and plundering than the European-trained Schutztruppe.[18] African losses from battle, hunger, and disease were enormous; precise statistics are of course not available, but contemporary estimates indicated 75,000 or more dead. In the end the uprising was decisively crushed, and German rule was never again seriously challenged.

In South-West Africa the Germans faced a totally different situation. Unlike Togo, it was a thinly populated country climatically suited to European settlement, and the Germans were determined to turn the colony into a white man's country, fighting a series of long and bloody wars to crush the Hottentots and the Nama. As intruders the Germans initially were weak and had to rely on alliances with indigenous chiefs, so they took care not to alienate all native communities of South-West Africa at the same time. The powerful Ovambo people in the north of the territory remained unaffected by German immigration and never took up arms against the whites. The Basters, an Afrikaans-speaking Eurafrican community, sided with the new arrivals, as did some of the smaller black polities that had been reduced to subjection by their more powerful neighbors.

The peacetime military establishment in South-West Africa was organized into three light batteries and nine field companies, including —as a military curiosity in the history of the German army—a company of camel riders. The Germans were convinced that only white soldiers could effectively defend the white presence, and their main reliance was on white mounted infantry supported by light artillery. This policy sharply differed from that of East Africa.

The Herero and the Nama had been engaged in long and bitter conflict over the use of scarce natural resources such as pastures and waterholes; cattle-raiding was a traditional feature of their existence. In the face of the German threat the two communities finally united, presenting the Germans with a formidable task. The great Herero-Nama uprising (1904–7) became Germany's equivalent of the Boer War. The Germans were obliged to fight an extensive campaign requiring deployment of more than 17,000 white volunteers from Germany herself. To quote the official German war history, more objective and less preoccupied with racial stereotypes than the popular literature of the time: "Our enemies were equal in skill and marksmanship to the

Boers, but exceeded them in military efficiency and resolute action."[19] (The economic causes and consequences of the Herero-Nama uprising are covered in chapter 8.)

Lothar von Trotha, commander of the Germans between 1904 and 1905, insisted on assuming dictatorial power and overriding the civilian authorities, including Leutwein. He was the prototype of the pure military technician, concerned only with destruction and not in the least with the political or economic aspects of war. His methods horrified not only Social Democratic and Center Party critics of German colonialism, but also Leutwein—himself a German major-general and not exactly a guilt-ridden intellectual. But Leutwein's views did not prevail; Trotha was supported by Schlieffen, chief of the German general staff and author of the famous Schlieffen plan designed to envelop the French armies in 1914. The Vernichtungsstrategie used by Trotha, culminating in a decisive victory at the Waterberg, was designed to annihilate the Herero in a classic battle of encirclement of the kind taught in German staff colleges. The Herero were partly destroyed, and their scattered remnants reduced to poverty.

The Nama, mounted herdsmen supremely well-adjusted to warfare on the veld, were tougher opponents than the Herero. Partly Afrikaans in culture and origin, their leaders combined literacy in Dutch with a thorough knowledge of bushcraft. Hendrik Witbooi, their greatest captain, was a former school teacher who regarded himself as the divinely appointed king of his people. The Nama's pastoral manner of life had turned them into expert scouts and trackers; hunting had fashioned them into first-class marksmen with a thorough understanding of warfare in a grim and harsh terrain where control over pastures, cattle herds, and waterholes played a vital part in shaping strategy.

Only the best of the Schutztruppen were able eventually to vie with the Nama in the art of laying ambush, in finding their way in bush country, in mobility and in hardihood—skills acquired after a rigorous system of training during which patrols would spend three months at a time in the bush country, returning toughened, lean, and sunburnt, little different in appearance from Basters, wise in the ways of the veld, with ragged clothes.[20] Most of the soldiers who volunteered in Germany as mounted infantry for service against the rebels were, however, far inferior to the Nama in wilderness skills and even in horsemanship, though recruiters tried to give preference to rural people—

coachmen, farm laborers, and peasant sons. The Germans tried to make up for their qualitative deficiencies by numerical superiority, and possibly prolonged the operations by burdening the army with undertrained men.

In the end the Germans won by superior organization and firepower: they had artillery; the enemy had none. The Germans made skillful use of their logistic resources and of traditional strategy of bush warfare involving the seizure of wells and waterholes and enemy herds. The chiefs of western Namaland would not rise against them. In addition, the Germans relied heavily on the employment of indigenous auxiliaries, especially Baster volunteers; without their aid as scouts and trackers, the German military could hardly have functioned at a time when the scout plane and the armored car had not been invented. By the standards of the time, the South-West African campaign involved considerable effort. The original four companies were reinforced and organized into two field regiments, each with four battalions, four batteries, a machine-gun detachment, and technical troops; these were subsequently broken down into small mobile units and grouped into a northern and a southern Bezirk.[21]

Once the fighting had ended, the Germans rapidly withdrew their metropolitan forces from the country, and the colony was left with a small military establishment divided into a few mobile field companies and local district forces fitted for internal police duties rather than for defense. South-West Africa was "secure" in the sense that the indigenous people never tried to challenge the Germans again, even in World War I when the German position became desperate.

But the war and its aftermath occasioned long and bitter enmity on both sides. The Herero and the Nama were in desperate straits, filled with hatred for their German overlords.[22] Their survivors had lost kinsmen and friends; they had been deprived of their beasts and pastures; the future looked so grim that further resistance appeared inconceivable. The settlers' mood was likewise one of bitterness, fear, and wrath; many colonists had been massacred, sometimes under grim circumstances. Some German newspapers added to the prevailing mood of anger and hostility by publishing mendacious accounts of how the Herero had supposedly tortured their prisoners to death—stories repudiated by Captain Franke, an experienced soldier, who privately denied ever having seen a mutilated German corpse. But the colonists believed themselves to be menaced by a treacherous foe who might strike again at any time.

Only a handful of Germans were willing to see the war from the point of view of the conquered; these included a number of soldiers who had learned to respect their former enemies. The most prominent was Ludwig von Estorff, who believed that the Vernichtungsstrategie was an affront to God as well as to mankind. According to Estorff, the conduct of the German authorities in dishonoring promises and in imprisoning captured Nama and Hottentots in unsanitary camps had been outrageous; Germany's subsequent loss of South-West Africa was just punishment for the sins committed by the bulk of Germans in the territory through their incomprehension and lack of charity.[23] But even Estorff did not condemn colonialism as such, and his sincere piety and warmly held humanitarian sentiments did not prevent him from subsequently supporting the Kapp Putsch against the German Republic.

The Army and Society

The Schutztruppe served a variety of functions whose total impact—like that of colonialism as a whole—was full of contradictions. Using military force the Germans created new territorial aggregations —Togo, Cameroun, East Africa, South-West Africa. These consolidated many units of government much larger in size than any of the pre-colonial polities that had existed in these regions before the arrival of the Germans, but the new frontiers also divided peoples and borders.

The scope of administrative action was vastly expanded. The colonial army acquired a semi-monopoly of modern arms; it stamped out all rival centers of independent military power. To a minor extent the army became involved in World War I, when the Germans attempted to defend their overseas possessions against the Allies. By the standards of European warfare the losses suffered by German colonial forces in Africa were small; E. G. Jacob has calculated a loss of just over 7,000 men for the entire colonial period and World War I (see Table 15). This figure, however, excludes the many porters who perished of sickness and hardship during the German colonial campaigns. No one

TABLE 15

*German Military Personnel Losses in the African Colonies
through 1918*

Colony and personnel category	Number lost	Colony and personnel category	Number lost
Cameroun:		South-West Africa:	
Officers	68	Officers	117
Noncommissioned officers	168	German noncommissioned	
African soldiers	1,703	officers and men	1,732
TOTAL	1,939	TOTAL	1,849
German East Africa:		Togo*a*	—
Officers	77		
Noncommissioned officers	345	GRAND TOTAL	7,210
African soldiers	c. 3,000		
TOTAL	3,422		

SOURCE: E. G. Jacob, *Deutsche Kolonialpolitik in Dokumenten* (Leipzig, 1938), p. 480.
a Togo had no Schutztruppen, only armed police.

will ever know how many Africans perished as the direct or indirect result of all these operations; in all probability, however, the overall losses reached six-digit figures.

The Germans succeeded because they had unity of command, because they could always rely on African allies, and because their enemies rarely managed to band together. In Cameroun, for example, the people of the forest zone were inclined to resist the German advance, which threatened their independence and the existence of local trade monopolies, but the forest itself divided them into numerous communities with different customs and languages who could cooperate neither with one another nor with the people of the grassland zone. The Muslim kingdoms of the extreme north were divided both by tensions between individual emirates and by bitter hostility between Muslims and pagans.

Use of the military, however, necessitated an element of coercion that in many cases excited the very disorders it was designed to suppress. Especially in the early days, inefficient supply arrangements at times encouraged looting, and askaris alienated villagers by molesting women or by stealing food. Even where the Schutztruppen were kept under good control, pacification expeditions could impose a heavy economic burden on the countryside at a period when communications were poor and food supplies hard to get. The military would requisition beasts and grain; they would call on local chiefs for carriers and resort to reprisals when the local dignitaries were unwilling or unable to comply with their demands.

The imposition of Western government necessarily entailed the destruction of independent armies and militias; it required the disarmament of the population, the extirpation of the slave trade, of raiding, and of banditry, as well as the elimination of local transit trade monopolies and of tributary relationships between rulers and the ruled. The Germans imposed all kinds of new economic sanctions, sometimes involving the use of conscripted labor, the forced cultivation of crops at fixed prices, and other coercive devices.

From the social and political standpoint, the impact of the Schutztruppe, as it gradually developed into a long-service force, was far-reaching. The military was one of the first employers to use a stabilized form of wage labor on a large scale; the African mercenary became a member of a recognized salaried profession—tough and adaptable. One of the most remarkable of these was Chari Maigumeri, a Beri-Beri from the Maiduguru district who joined the Schutztruppe in Cameroun in 1913, fought with great distinction under the Germans, and won the Iron Cross. He enlisted with the West African Frontier Force after capture by the British in 1915 and served with equal fidelity against the Germans in East Africa. Promoted to Regimental Sergeant Major in 1928, Maigumeri further distinguished himself in World War II, where he won the Military Medal in fighting the Italians and the British Empire Medal in serving against the Japanese. After thirty-six years of service he retired in 1953 with the rank of Honorary Captain, a soldier to the core, still capable—on suitable occasions—of giving a demonstration of German imperial arms drill with the appropriate words of command.[24]

In a wider sense, the army—more so even than the mission societies—was an instrument for spreading Western notions of punctuality, discipline, and time; German employers had good reason for preferring former askaris to untutored villagers. The Schutztruppe, like the mission stations, often provided employment for the disinherited—former slaves, ne'er-do-wells, and orphans. The military profession also appealed to specific ethnic communities such as the Nyamwezi, many of whom had already become used to selling their labor for cash as porters, trading agents, and caravan guides. Within colonial society as a whole the Schutztruppe was a privileged body endowed with outstanding esprit de corps, and this feature of itself gave a military character to much of German administration. According to the private reminiscences of Pater Vieter, a Catholic missionary in Cameroun, Governor von Puttkamer was looked down upon by many officers because he had not been a soldier.[25] Even African soldiers were apt to absorb a military sense of superiority from their white mentors.

The creation of reliable military forces completely altered the character of colonial relationships. During the earliest years of Afro-German contact, the Germans—be they merchants, missionaries, or government envoys—had to rely on the goodwill of African customers, congregation members, or chiefs; the second phase of Afro-German relations increasingly came to hinge on coercion. The element of force was not, of course, applied in a uniform fashion. There were enormous variations between colonies, between regions, and even between districts. Much depended on the nature of the local African polity and its relations with its neighbors. G. C. K. Gwassa wrote, with regard to his Tanzanian homeland:

One of the three methods of German intervention was to seek alliance with those strong or influential chiefs in a locality who professed "recognition" of German authority. Friendship with one group led to division between chiefs. The Germans by their method of alliances made themselves for some time victims of local politics, and instead of achieving a less troublesome occupation, they increased the prospects of war against themselves. Depending on local political circumstances, the African chiefs often found themselves without an alternative; they had to be either "friends" of the Germans or their enemies. When Germans allied with a rival of one chief, rivalry was extended to the Germans themselves. In such conditions some Africans had the sense to use the Germans in the existing political game. In other words, they sought to enlist the Germans in a way that would ensure both the extermination of rivals and the friendship of the Germans.[26]

The new rulers brought new weapons, new tools, and new techniques of governance. But perhaps the most revolutionary concept introduced by white soldiers and administrators, preachers, and farmers alike concerned space and time. Africans, of course, could reckon time most accurately for their purposes by studying the position of the sun and the stars, or by using the growth cycle of a staple crop. But in a village where there were neither printed calendars nor mechanical clocks, the villagers thought of time in terms of the ancient Hebrews who wrote that "to everything there is a season and a time to every purpose under the heaven: a time to be born and a time to die; a time to plant and a time to pluck out that which is planted" (Eccles. 2:1–2).

To the European, however, time was something to be minutely subdivided like a leaf, a commodity for sale. In terms of mechanical devices the Germans had a weapon more potent in the long run than the machine gun: they had a pocket watch. For the first time African warriors clashed on the battlefield with opponents who were punctual, who operated with carefully thought-out timetables, who could efficiently coordinate large bodies of troops. Africans had to fight against men drilled to punctuality from early childhood, by nursery rhymes in their homes, by injunction at school, and by threats on the barrack square.

> Watch the clock, I do repeat—
> Late for dinner, nought to eat.

said the nurse;

> Trouble never was yet made
> For soldiers early on parade.

echoed the sergeant.[27]

As time went on, the Europeans began to teach their time sense to African subordinates—to askaris on drill parade and to mission pupils in the school room—with far-reaching results for the future of Africa. Terms for hours, minutes, and seconds began to percolate into African languages, often—characteristically—in European dress.

Linked to the novel concepts of time was a new sense of space that slowly filtered into the villages. In most parts of Africa there was as yet no shortage of land; land was a continuum that was usually in unlimited supply and seemed to go on forever. In most traditional societies huts were round; gardens naturally assumed oval shapes that were determined by the rhythm of the hoe, as did the outlines of great ancient building complexes like Zimbabwe. The Europeans, and to some extent the Arabs, had different notions; their houses and barrack squares were rectangular, as were their city blocks. They conceived of land as a commodity which was limited in supply and which could be apportioned on the basis of individual tenure. Space was subdivided by imaginary grids, and the resulting squares became marketable pieces of merchandise, like the hours specified in a labor contract. Africans learned to build square houses, to form squares on the drill ground, and to square-off on parade. The intellectual and spiritual impact of these intangibles is hard to assess—more difficult even than the physical impact of the railways, rifles, boreholes, and similar technological innovations. But their long-term influence was profound, and the army was an important agency in deepening their impact.

Governor Schnee and General von Lettow-Vorbeck

Above left: Colonial Secretary Bernhard Dernburg. Above right: Gustav Nachtigal.
Below left: Governor Theodor Leitwein. Below right: Hendrik Witbooi.

ft: Governor Jesko von Puttkamer. Above right: Dr. Carl Peters.
low right: Major Hermann von Wissmann.

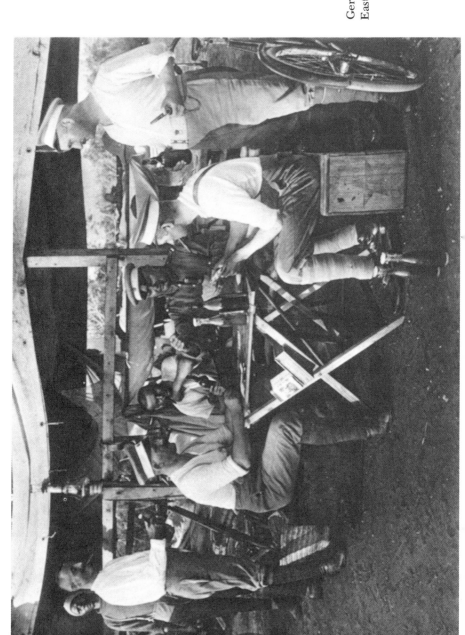

German reservists,
East Africa, 1914

Military band,
East Africa, 1914

Bassari warriors, Togo

SEVEN

The Civilians

The civil administration in the German colonies grew from several distinct strata—explorers, soldiers, career bureaucrats, technicians, and professional men-turned-administrators. Nevertheless, these administrators had a number of features in common. Their ethos tended to be military and bureaucratic; the Germans never thought of employing an outstanding businessman in an administrative capacity in the colonies. The career of Sir Francis Chaplin (1866–1933)—ex-journalist, mine manager, head of the British South Africa Company's administration in Southern Rhodesia from 1914 to 1923, and finally a director of the chartered company itself—would have been quite unthinkable in German colonial history.

An account of the social and regional origins of civilian administrators requires recapitulation of some information provided in the general overview of the German colonial system. A substantial number of German administrators came from eastern Germany, though other parts of the Reich also made important contributions; Württemberg and Baden in particular contributed a high percentage of emigrants for the government and settlement of South-West Africa.[1] However these administrators might differ in their regional affiliation, they usually had one thing in common: the great majority came from rural settlements, from places like Neuhaus on the Elbe (Peters), Strümpfelbronn near Freiburg im Breisgau (Leutwein), or Seckenheim in Baden (Theodor Seitz). The average civil servant in the colonies had childhood memories of the German countryside rather than of the growing cities. A man like Wilhelm Solf (1862–1936)—at one time district judge in East Africa, later governor of Samoa, and finally Staatssekretär at the

Reichskolonialamt (1911–18)—was unusual in having a wealthy Berlin industrialist for his father.

The colonial administrators held political views very similar to those of their colleagues in other parts of the German civil administration. They ranged from the Catholic Center to the extreme right;[2] Social Democrats were excluded, and Freisinnige (liberal free traders) were likely to exclude themselves.

Social differences among the various segments of the service were considerable. Aristocrats continued to play a major part in the colonial administration at a time when the civil service in the Reich itself was becoming increasingly bourgeois in nature. Three-fourths of all colonial governors were noblemen, and aristocrats were particularly important in East Africa (see Table 16). The upper stratum consisted of great noblemen drawn to Africa not so much by the desire to take out a profitable career for themselves as by the urge to gain fame as explorers and publicists.

Highest in rank was Adolf Friedrich (born 1873), Duke of Mecklenburg, son of Grand Duke Friedrich Franz II, ruling prince of the little state of Mecklenburg Schwerin. Adolf Friedrich, a professional soldier, travelled widely in the Middle East and in East and West Africa and wrote several books before being appointed governor of Togo in 1912. Another great nobleman was Gustav Adolf Graf von Götzen (1866–1910) who was born at the castle of Scharfeneck in Silesia, a member of the great Silesian nobility. In 1891 he explored Mount Kilimanjaro and later went to Asia Minor; during 1893–94 he crossed Africa from east to west, an achievement that brought him into the limelight and also provided material for an interesting book. From 1896 to 1898 he served as military attaché in Washington, and three years later was appointed to the governorship of East Africa—a post for which his social connections, his service overseas, and his military experience as well as his literary activities seemed to make him eminently suitable. He resigned in 1906 after the outbreak of the Maji-Maji rebellion, whose origins he may have misunderstood, and became Prussian envoy to the Hanseatic cities.

Perhaps the most outstanding of the East African governors was Albrecht Freiherr von Rechenberg (1859–1930), who was born in Madrid and reared in Russia. Rechenberg was an unusual man. He came from an aristocratic lineage so ancient as to consider the Hohenzollerns

TABLE 16
Social Class of German Colonial Governors, 1884–1914

Colony	Noblemen	Commoners
East Africa	6[a]	1
South-West Africa	3	3
Cameroun	3	4
Togo	4	4
TOTAL	16[b]	12

[a] Includes two commoners raised to the nobility.
[b] Includes one duke, two counts, and four barons.

mere upstarts. The Rechenbergs had been active in the diplomatic corps, and Albrecht was one of the few Catholics to attain gubernatorial office. With a doctorate in law and a reserve commission, he joined the diplomatic corps and was posted to Tanga (1893), Zanzibar (1896), and then to Moscow and Warsaw. Before returning to Africa he became an authority on eastern Europe, an area on which he concentrated after he left Africa in 1911. In 1914 he was elected to the Reichstag, but left government service when he was not appointed Minister for the Occupied Areas ceded to Germany by the Treaty of Brest-Litovsk. He was killed in a traffic accident in Berlin in 1935.[3]

Rechenberg was an aristocrat—paternalistic, arrogant, and sarcastic. He remained an aloof bachelor. A gifted linguist, industrious and expert in whatever he did, he had no taste for popularity, and while in Africa seemed to prefer the company of lordly sheikhs and cultured Asians to that of his fellow Germans. Although he was a colonial governor, he was not a colonialist—he felt Germany's future lay in eastern Europe and not in overseas expansion. Nor was he a liberal humanitarian who tried to uplift Africans: he simply wished to govern East Africa inexpensively. He never sought the help of the Deutsche Kolonialgesellschaft, and clashed frequently with local settlers and planters. In essence, he was "a conservative, professional Prussian bureaucrat administering an occupied area with a minimum of expense and a minimum of force."[4]

Yet his governorship was a great period of reconstruction and development for African peasant farmers. He was determined to prevent another rebellion by pursuing policies that benefitted the indigenous people. He decided—and won Dernburg to his views—against pushing white settlement and plantations and in favor of improving African agriculture, yet the number of settlers more than doubled during his tenure as governor: 315 in 1906, 750 in 1912. East Africa had more whites than did Kenya at that time, and European settlement continued even in the face of official opposition. Afrikaners from South Africa and German Russians came to settle, but neither proved to be good farmers. Rechenberg regarded the colonists as troublesome people who upset African societies. There was not enough labor to satisfy all the demands of government, missions, settlers, and plantations, and during his governorship he resisted efforts to compel Africans to work for the Europeans. In spite of his efforts, various forms of forced labor continued in East Africa; the jumba, akida, and Bezirksamtmann all put pressure on Africans to work for local Europeans. Under this pressure he attempted to organize the supply of migrant workers by government recruiters.

Rechenberg also opposed the forced growing of crops and ordered his officials only to "recommend, persuade, and encourage voluntary efforts."[5] He did not like agricultural experts, believing that they knew far less about peasant farming than the men they were instructing. He opposed the agricultural department's pressure to make Africans use ploughs instead of hoes: he saw rightly that hoe-culture was the only basis for peasant agriculture for some time to come. His solution and the basis for his policies while governor was reform and expand indigenous agriculture.

To increase African productivity he built a railway through the central part of East Africa. He limited and tried to replace settler councils because they kept trying to get tax revenues for their purposes and to extend the northern railway. Rechenberg encouraged Indian traders and retailers because they bought the Africans' produce and sold them goods. He insisted that officials concentrate on tax collecting so that he could have revenue to perform essential government functions and service the railway loan.[6]

In the Rechenberg program the settlers saw dangers for themselves. They organized and sought allies in the colonial societies and in the Reichstag; they demanded more Selbstverwaltung (voice in local affairs) and won seats on the governor's council. They fought Rechenberg on his Indian policies, but he successfully protected Indian rights to enter the colony, to trade, and to buy land. Indians did what he had expected of them: they stimulated trade, and textile imports increased from 6,876,296 marks in 1905 to 16,508,349 marks in 1912. Settlers and government continually fought over the question of African labor and the practice of flogging. In 1910 the settlers forced Rechenberg to accept an extension of the northern railway to Moshi, but he held firm against having the government force Africans to work for Europeans. He tried to protect migrant workers by limiting work periods to 180 days, requiring employers to provide food, housing, medical care, and to pay passage home. Labor regulations were issued in 1909.

Europeans created a territorial league in 1909 to promote their interests and to force the governor to make concessions. It eventually gained a majority of members on the governor's council, but though Dernburg gave in to settler pressures exerted through the Reichstag, Rechenberg steadily held out. Even Friedrich von Lindequist, a friend of the settlers who became the new colonial minister in 1910, could not force Rechenberg to modify his policies, and Berlin could do little about it. As governor he was a successful administrator—he had tripled trade, had reduced the imperial subsidy from 6.964 million marks to 3.618 million, and had kept the peace; he was also a Catholic with Center Party support. When he seemed to bow to heavy pressure from home—he granted settlers an elected majority on the district councils—he nullified their gains on municipal councils by refusing them revenue. Not until he resigned did the Europeans get control of the district and governor's advisory councils.

Rechenberg represented the cause of "Negrophilism" and reform, as did Count Julius von Zech auf Neuenhofen, another Catholic who governed Togo between 1903 and 1910, but generalizations concerning the political leanings of the nobility are as hard to make as those about their economic role and social proclivities. Rechenberg, for instance, was comparable in social standing with Bruno von Schuckmann (1855–1919), governor of South-West Africa from 1907 to 1910. A Prussian Lutheran and owner of the estate of Rohrbeck in the Neumark, Schuckmann had served in high consular appointments before coming to the colonies, but once established in the gubernatorial office he ran South-West Africa like a white farmer and acquired considerable popularity among the European population, who called him Väterchen (little father).

Slowly the nonmilitary and commoner element in the colonial service became more important. During 1896–97 the senior officials—governors, deputy governors, Referenten, judges, Bezirksamtmänner, etc.—numbered forty-two; of these, twenty were noblemen, seventeen were active or reserve officers. By 1912 the administration had expanded and the technical services had grown. Of a total of 117 senior officials, only 16 were noblemen and only 19 had a military background (see Table 17); exactly half of the gubernatorial positions in German African colonies between 1907 and 1914 were held by commoners.

Theodor Seitz (1863–1939) was typical of the sort of man who did well in the later stages of German administration, when bureaucratic skills became increasingly prized. In the course of his career he went through every stage, from the pioneering days to the breakup of the colonial empire. Born in a small town in Baden, he joined the administration of his little Land, advancing to the position of Polizeiamtmann (a medium-grade police official). He then decided to transfer temporarily to the colonial service, despite cautionary remarks on the part of well-meaning superiors who thought that service in Africa was filled with uncertainties and would wreck the young man's career. Seitz's sole training for his new duties consisted of a four-month spell in the Kolonialabteilung in Berlin, where he fell foul of the department because of his south German style and where he had little to do except read through files and attend departmental meetings.

He became particularly interested in the problem of slavery and departed on his first assignment in Cameroun brimming with idealistic notions, determined to wipe out this scourge of humanity. Colonial realities, however, were a revelation. When he arrived in Cameroun in 1895 he was impressed by the high degree of social equality that existed among the indigenous people of the country and by their spirit of sturdy independence. In the mid-1890's, with the German administration in Cameroun still in rudimentary condition, Seitz—in addition to being appointed Bezirksamtmann—was almost immediately given the post of acting Kanzler (deputy of the governor in administrative matters and a judge in the first instance). According to Ralph Austen's findings, he was instrumental in ending the practice adhered to by German administrative courts of enforcing slave contracts. He decided, however, that the abolition of slave status should proceed slowly rather than rapidly on the grounds that the conditions of servile de-

TABLE 17
Noblemen and Commoners among Senior Officials in the German
Colonial Administration, 1896–1897 and 1912

Territory	Noblemen	Commoners	Total	Military or ex-military included in total
1896:				
East Africa	9	7	16	4
Cameroun	5	4	9	5
Togo	4	4	8	7
1897:				
South-West Africa	2	7	9	1
TOTAL	20	22	42	17
1912:				
East Africa	4	35	39	9
Cameroun	2	22	24	—
Togo	6	9	15	5
South-West Africa	4	35	39	5
TOTAL	16	101	117	19

SOURCE: *Handbuch für das Deutsche Reich* (Berlin), issues for 1896, 1897, and 1912. "Senior officials" were governors, deputy governors, department heads, Referenten, judges, district officers, etc.

pendency were not all that onerous, and that the government should avoid social disruption.

An essential aspect of his job was the supervision of African chiefs, and he became an ardent advocate of the system of indirect rule. Theodor Leutwein's son described him as a faithful supporter of the governor and of the Leutwein "system" of using chiefs and of preserving the tribal cohesion of the indigenous people of South-West Africa.[7] He did well in the service, and in 1900 returned to the Kolonialabteilung in Berlin. Between 1907 and 1910 he served once more in Cameroun, this time as governor, before being transferred in a similar capacity to South-West Africa. Here he played a part in improving irrigation facilities and extending railway transport; he was also responsible for the first legislation passed by the Germans concerning the recruitment of Ovambo laborers and the health care of migrant workmen. When World War I broke out he had the job of defending South-West Africa against the South Africans, a hopeless undertaking in view of the Germans' numerical inferiority. In 1915 Seitz surrendered the territory and was interned; he returned to Germany in 1919 an embittered anglophobe, disgusted at conditions in postwar Germany and determined that the Germans must once again battle for their place in the sun.

Another—and certainly one of the most gifted of German "indirect rulers"—was Richard Kandt, who was born in Poznan in 1867. A medical man-turned-explorer, he made his name through his work as an East African geographer, ethnographer, and writer. His study *Caput Nili: Eine empfindsame Reise zu den Quellen des Nils* (1904) remains one of the best travelogues of the time. In 1907 he was appointed Resident in Ruanda, a powerful and highly centralized monarchy so remote from the centers of German power that it had to be controlled more through influence than through physical force. Kandt was profoundly impressed by the Hima ruling group in Ruanda, by the "sublimity of their speech, the tasteful and unobtrusive way of their dress, their noble traits and their quiet, penetrating, often even witty and irritating eyes." He was determined to uphold the power of the monarchy and strongly criticized the local French missionaries on the grounds that missionary interference threatened the very basis of indirect rule. According to Kandt, Germany's "political and colonial interests require that we support the king[s] and uphold the extreme dependence of the great mass of the population. Considering the nature of the country and the character of its people, this arrangement can be reconciled with those humanitarian imperatives which require the elimination of abuses of power and arbitrary rule over subject populations."[8]

Kandt's period of office, however, was cut short by World War I. When the German armies were about to mobilize, he was on leave in Germany; he joined the military as a medical officer and in 1918 died of an infection that he had contracted in treating his patients. His Jewish ancestry and his original family name, Kantorowicz, were soon forgotten, and the supreme irony of his career came long after his death: during World War II the Nazis revived his memory and honored the eightieth anniversary of Kandt, a Jewish psychiatrist turned German proconsul, now transfigured into a Teutonic empire-builder from the eastern marches of the fatherland.[9]

In addition to such reputable men, the German colonial administration contained its underworld—soldiers and officials who abused their enormous personal powers and took advantage of the widespread lack of official supervision. Harsh methods of governance were almost inseparable from colonial conquest; in the treatment of individual offenders the Germans were operating among peoples whose own methods of punishment were commonly brutal. Pioneer governance in the bush at first was conducted within a social framework where there were no prisons, no prison guards, and no reformatories; there was no option but to release a criminal, fine him, beat him, or have him put to death. Like its colonial competitors, Germany had a contingent of perverts and sadists whose doings horrified even the hard-bitten. During the 1890's, for instance, the German public was astounded by a number of colonial scandals involving senior officials like Karl Theodor Heinrich Leist, deputy governor of Cameroun in 1893, and one Assessor Wehlan, a Cameroun judge. Leist helped to provoke an uprising of black askari by torturing prisoners, flogging women, and violating the wives of African soldiers; he was eventually cashiered, emigrated to America, and ended as a well-to-do lawyer in Chicago.

Socialists such as August Bebel, a veteran Reichstag critic of German colonialism who would have been glad to rid the fatherland of its empire, considered that the Leist affair was merely the tip of the iceberg—that the Germans had elevated brutality to a system of governance. Supporters of the colonial system, on the other hand, sought to write off the Leist case and similar affairs as isolated instances of barbarity which might be avoided by more adequate selection and training of officials. Parliamentary inquiries and commission reports naturally emphasized the dealings of officials guilty of offenses rather than of those with blameless records, but whatever the incidence of brutality within the German administration, it is clear that even the best-intentioned selection boards had no means of eliminating potential criminals by checking personnel files and investigating previous records. Paul Kayser, then director of the Kolonialabteilung, argued in the Reichstag in 1896:

When the Kolonialabteilung was founded in 1890, the two officials in question [Leist and Wehlan] had already been in colonial employment. Leist had rendered distinguished service on his previous assignment in the district of Magdeburg [in east Germany], and held excellent references. The same applied to

Wehlan; Wehlan had enjoyed an excellent reputation, and had been praised by his superiors; he had previously worked in another section of the Auswärtige Amt; we had not been able to foresee that these two men might commit the deeds with which they were later charged.[10]

The fault did not lie merely with the excesses committed by individual sadists, but with the widespread nature of coercion occasioned by military and economic necessity. The Germans, like other colonizing powers, were inclined to press-gang carriers to carry supplies for Schutztruppen companies on the march or for officials on tour—an obligation least burdensome in Togo, where the military establishment was negligible. They used forced labor to build roads, bridges, rest houses, and government stations; district commissioners on tour required carriers, food, and accommodations. The total impact of these exactions is hard to measure. They were greatest where military operations were in progress; they were least in the most developed areas, where means of communication were available and where the Germans were able to pay for the supplies and services required.

Compared with a modern state, the machinery of coercion at the disposal of a colonial power was, of course, infinitesimally small. In 1904 the entire administrative establishment in East Africa, Germany's best-administered colony, consisted of no more than 280 whites and 51 non-European civil servants; by comparison, the Americans, British, and French required more than thirty thousand officials to run occupied Western Germany after World War II. The impact of the administrative burdens in the colonies was extremely uneven, but they were probably made worse by the exactions of German agents, including those of chiefs recognized by the Germans. In East Africa, for example, many local dignitaries maintained small forces of their own, known as ruga-ruga, which received uniforms and rifles as well as periodic training in the boma. They assisted chiefs in arresting criminals, collecting taxes, and enforcing German rules. They were looked upon by the Germans as among their most dependable followers, but they might also deal harshly with the chief's enemies, who could not easily revolt against an overlord supported by the colonial power.

Above all, there was economic coercion designed to assure profits to private concerns. According to the Bismarckian concept, the task of colonization was to be accomplished by specially privileged bodies that would supply the capital, run the risks, and administer Germany's newly acquired possessions. Companies such as the Kolonialgesell-schaft für Deutsch-Südwestafrika received huge concessions in order to attract foreign capital, but the bulk of the bourgeoisie was unwilling to risk its savings in colonies where conditions were little known and profits seemed uncertain. The Reichsschatzamt (imperial treasury) was wedded to a doctrine of economy as rigid as the financial creed of the British Treasury, and the Reichstag was unwilling to vote substantial funds for colonies stained by scandals. But capital was needed, and according to men like Gerhard von Buchka, head of the Kolonialabteil-ung from 1898 to 1900, cash could be attracted only by the grant of large-scale concessions. Concessionary monopolies, however, were apt to engender the most brutal forms of coercion.

One of the most extreme advocates of direct coercion was Julius Scharlach (1842–1908), a Hamburg lawyer and colonial land spec-ulator, who felt that the government should not initiate any form of economic enterprise in the colonies.[11] The job should be left to pri-vate investors, who would have to be tempted by the grant of extensive concessions. The African population, he maintained, had no economic value. Colonization was not a matter of civilizing savages, but of push-ing them to the wall and ultimately destroying them. In the view of such men, the colonizers were fully justified in drafting black people for work on European plantations or for the collection of wild crops; where African land was required for settlers, the indigenous people should be dispossessed. Scharlach's philosophy was widely adopted.

Coercion was also linked to primitive methods of administration in posts where subordinate officials were able to rule without much supervision as petty tyrants within their own domain. The literature of early German colonialism is full of material such as the unpublished reminiscences of Father Vieter, a Catholic priest in Cameroun who spent twenty-three years in the country (1890–1913). Vieter records individual misdeeds such as the actions of one Lieutenant Umber, a deputy Bezirksamtmann who took a Catholic girl as his concubine and then sentenced her fiancé to a beating because he dared to complain in the Bezirksamtmann's court. The girl was later released at the behest of Vieter's mission, and Umber was removed from Cameroun. In Yaunde, to give an even worse example, Lieutenant Hans Dominik re-cruited several hundred porters for an expedition inland. The draftees were supplied by local chiefs who were provided with small detach-

ments of soldiers to "recruit" unwilling tribesmen; the prospective recruits fled into the bush, and the soldiers seized their women and cattle
to compel them to report for duty. Military porterage was particularly
unpopular because the porters had to move in disciplined formations,
while porters employed by commercial expeditions were allowed to
march at their own speed even when this procedure entailed some
straggling and slowed down the progress of the entire expedition.[12]

Reform clearly required not only the employment of good personnel
but also a thorough change in the military and economic power structure. It demanded a logistics system dependent on steam-power rather
than on carriers, a military commissariat supplied through central
stores rather than through ad hoc requisitions, and a form of labor
management that utilized skilled and willing workmen rather than unskilled draftees capable of performing only the most simple tasks. Finally, reform could operate only within a colonial framework in which
military power had been effectively monopolized by one ruling power
and all other power centers had been virtually eliminated.

The inspiration for reform came from several different sources.
Many German district officials in the bush disliked the task of "mobilizing" villages for labor dues, a burdensome and unprofitable task for the
administrators, who realized well enough how unpopular these corvées
were among those compelled to work for the Germans. Wissmann, for
instance, was disliked by some of the employers on the ground that his
policy was "weak" on the labor question.[13] There was opposition from
missionaries and from merchants like Johann Karl Vietor, the prominent Togo trader who believed that Africa should be developed by
means of a partnership with the African peasant producers.

Vietor's doctrines appealed to a variety of big businessmen, bankers,
shipowners, and manufacturers who became increasingly convinced
that Africans should be looked upon as customers of German merchandise, not merely as "hands" useful for the production of raw materials.
Similar views were popular among a select group of intellectuals, including men such as Professor Diedrich Westermann, an ethnographer
of missionary background, and Wilhelm Blohm, a Moravian preacher
and author of a fine study of the Nyamwezi people. Men of this kind
helped to popularize a new doctrine of Fürsorge (paternal concern for
the Africans) better adapted to the demands of a developing colonial
system than the Negrophobe notions of the earlier militarized genera-

tion of Africanists such as Hans Zache, to whom the word "Negrophile" was an insulting label.

The Settlers

When Bismarck embarked upon his search for colonies, German—like French—theoreticians developed two distinct models of imperial development. Trading colonies would supply the fatherland with exotic raw materials and would purchase German goods; this model, not unnaturally, appealed to merchants, manufacturers, and also missionaries who believed that commerce and civilization should march hand in hand. In addition, many advocates of overseas expansion called for the creation of Siedlungskolonien—colonies of settlement that would enable Germans to find new homes for themselves under the German flag.

The proponents of Siedlungskolonien argued that Germany was losing millions of her sons and daughters to the United States. German emigration should be directed to her own colonies, where pioneers would build new Germanies beyond the seas. In their struggle against the wilderness the colonists would develop those qualities of independence and self-reliance which townsmen supposedly lacked. Colonists rooted in the soil of newly conquered acres would preserve the preindustrial values of those sturdy peasant farmers and small craftsmen whose economic prosperity was being undermined in Germany itself.

The real settlers bore little resemblance to the images conjured up by academicians. German emigration reached its peak in the 1880's and 1890's, but most emigrants continued to go to the United States. During the 1890's, when the economic depression drew to a close and the Reich became the greatest manufacturing power in Europe, the stream of overseas emigration largely dried up (see Table 18). Far from looking for new lands to cultivate, German peasants moved into the cities. Germany had in fact begun to attract immigrants from other parts of Europe. Only an insignificant number of Germans decided to make their homes in the colonies. By 1914 the white population was 386 in Togo, 1,871 in Cameroun, 5,336 in German East Africa, and 14,830 in South-West Africa—22,405 in all, less than half the population of a small Rhenish town like Koblenz. Even South-West Africa, envisaged by many planners as a new agricultural frontier, had at-

TABLE 18

German Overseas Emigration, 1871–1905

Period	To the United States	Total	Period	To the United States	Total
1871–75	360,536	394,814	1901	19,912	22,073
1876–80	193,303	231,154	1902	29,211	32,098
1881–85	791,019	857,287	1903	33,649	36,310
1886–90	440,120	485,136	1904	26,085	27,984
1891–95	371,506	402,567	1905	26,005	28,075
1896–1900	107,424	127,308			

SOURCE: _Grosser Brockhaus_ (Leipzig, 1929), 2:140.

tracted no more than a handful of colonists, considerably less than the number of Germans who departed to the United States in a single year. The new settlers went out to make money rather than to develop those folksy virtues admired by university professors. Moreover, the majority of those going to South-West Africa were not farmers but workers and professional men, people whose way of life was shaped by the city rather than by the countryside (see Tables 19 and 20).

In both economic and political terms, however, the settlers' impact was far greater than their numbers would suggest. Europeans brought in a great variety of skills—agricultural, industrial, and professional. Whether possessing a formal education or not, they brought to Africa an invisible capital of skills—the ability to handle machinery, or do arithmetic, or draw up a balance sheet. They introduced new notions of what might be technically feasible. Their notions, inherited from a civilization technologically much more advanced than any African culture, included items as varied as the use of humble domestic devices like the outhouse, or horticultural innovations like the ornamental lawn, or technical improvements like dips and dams, or tools like the wheelbarrow, the plow, and the harvesting machine. The best of the colonists accomplished remarkable feats of pioneering—no wonder _Robinson Crusoe_ or _Sigismund Rüstig_ were popular reading matter in many a settler's home. They had to make their living in areas lacking as yet the massive infrastructure of roads, repair shops, stores, schools, pharmacies, and clinics later taken for granted by their descendants.

The settler often began his career in an African-style hut; as conditions improved he might put up for himself a round house built with dried bricks and covered with straw. Finally, he might teach his African laborers to help him in building a homestead with walls of red brick and a corrugated iron roof, with a few imported trees, bougainvilleas, or jacarandas to lend a splash of color to the veld. Such houses often became the model for a new kind of rural architecture, unpretentious and inexpensive, that subsequently was adopted by the more prosperous Africans for their buildings. The settlers planted trees, acclimatized new crops, and laid out fields in the bush; they put up barns; they built fences. They looked after their own and their servants' health; they fashioned their own furniture; they opened farm stores; they attended to the education of their children; they adjudi-

TABLE 19

Occupations of Male Whites in South-West Africa, 1911

Occupation[a]	Number
Artisans, workmen, and miners	2,572
Planters, farmers, and smallholders	1,390
Merchants, shopkeepers, and innkeepers	1,035
Civil servants	881
Missionaries and clergy	70
Other male inhabitants	895
TOTAL	13,962

SOURCE: Andrew R. Carlson, *German Foreign Policy, 1890–1914, and Colonial Policy to 1914: A Handbook and an Annotated Bibliography* (Metuchen, N.J., 1970), p. 57.
[a] Excluding army and police.

TABLE 20

Occupations of Male Whites in East Africa, 1913

Occupation[a]	Number	Occupation[a]	Number
Professional men:		Engineers, technicians, artisans:	
Civil servants	551	Engineers, building	
Missionaries and clergy	498	contractors, technicians	355
Medical men	19	Artisans	523
TOTAL	1,068	TOTAL	878
Planters, farmers,		Total of adult white men	3,536
horticulturists	882	Total of adult white women	1,075
Traders	532	Total of white children	725
Miscellaneous	169		

SOURCE: Heinrich Schnee, ed., *Deutsches Kolonial-Lexikon* (3 vols.; Leipzig, 1920), 1:386–87.
[a] Excluding army and police.

cated in quarrels of their servants. They were at best men of middling degree, for the rich did not emigrate to make a hard and risky living in the bush. But for all their prejudices—social and racial—the best of the settlers, at any rate, acquired a real sense of *bourgeoisie oblige*.

In South-West Africa the whites adapted a variety of fruit, including grapes and dates, as well as grain and vegetables. The newcomers planted many varieties of new trees, including the eucalyptus, whose presence in the countryside helped to change both its appearance and its ecological features. They imported such strains of animals as the karakul sheep from Bokhara and southern Russia, herds which flourished under South-West African conditions and developed into a valuable industry. White farmers constructed fences, dips, and dams; they introduced the art of breeding cattle (see Table 21). In short, the immigrants recreated a pastoral economy that was a great deal more productive than that destroyed by German conquest.

The Germans also introduced modern mining methods to South-West Africa. The mining industry was left to private enterprise because administrators like Seitz soon became convinced that it was too complex and too risky to be run by the state. The discovery of diamonds in 1908 and the successful exploitation of copper rapidly changed the economic configuration of the region and turned it from an agricultural state into a producer of minerals.

At the same time the character of German exports to the colonies altered greatly; instead of guns, gin, and beads, they included an ever-increasing variety of textiles, machinery, vehicles, and other more complex merchandise. By 1910 German South-West Africa was importing commodities to the value of 14.275 million marks compared to 2.653 million marks twenty-five years earlier. The bulk of colonial imports, including textiles, provisions, and other commodities, was destined for the African trade, reflecting a small rise in African consumption and, to some extent, a modest and sporadic rise in African living standards.

During the German era, the first feeble beginnings of a secondary industry in the colonies were finally seen. Manufacturing hinged largely on South-West Africa, where skilled white labor was available, and the initial ventures were concerned mainly with the processing of agricultural products and the supply of building materials, electric power, and repair facilities for mines and railways. In 1914 South-West

TABLE 21
Farm Animals in South-West Africa, 1907 and 1913

Farm animals	Number in 1907	Number in 1913
Cattle	52,531	205,643
Horses	3,119	15,916
Sheep bred for meat	204,954	957,986
Goats and sheep bred for wool	3,526	53,691
Angora goats	3,696	31,400
Pigs	1,202	7,772
Ostriches	0	1,507

SOURCE: Oskar Hintrager, *Südwestafrika in der deutschen Zeit* (Munich, 1955), p. 175.

Africa had four machine works, two railway depots, a wagon-building shop, two electricity works, three quarries, a cannery, two breweries, two distilleries, two tanning works, and an ice-making factory. In addition there were numerous small workshops belonging to individual artisans. World War I impelled the Germans to set up some short-lived ersatz industries in East Africa. On a very small scale, the Germans manufactured textiles, pharmaceutical supplies, and a substitute for gasoline made from copra, as well as rubber products, medicaments, and footwear.

In East Africa, European immigrants had to cope with conditions of a somewhat different kind. But like their countrymen in South-West Africa, they performed a valuable economic function as experimenters and as pioneers. They also acquired, in many cases, a curious love-hate relationship to the land of which their Arab predecessors had said that he who drinks of its waters will never forget. They were oppressed by droughts and locusts, by unsuspected deficiencies of the soil, by sickness of man and beast, by boredom, and by the harsh glare of the midday sun over the bush. They were enthralled by the scent of woodsmoke in the air, by the sense of boundless space, by swift and improbably purple sunsets, and by the blue-tinged horizons stretching into infinity.

They experienced all manner of economic difficulties. They had to contend with the supposed "idleness" of Africans and with the government's "failure" to mobilize enough labor. Frontier economy depended on an extensive labor force—all the more so since the settlers could only obtain migrant laborers willing to work for short periods. The bulk of the African population retained their stake in the land, and the majority of settlers called for compulsion to remedy the situation. By 1914 the colony's estimated wage labor force amounted to about 165,000 out of an indigenous population of several millions.

The settlers' attitude toward the colonial authorities was ambivalent. In theory the settlers looked upon themselves as representatives of Kaiser and Reich. Within Germany itself they were considered by right-wingers as an imperial elite destined to carry the imperial eagle to the most distant quarters of the globe; in practice they were the first local pressure group to impose curbs on the power of officials. They were relatively well-educated; they were well-connected to imperial lobbies such as the Kolonialgesellschaft; they had influential spokesmen within the right-wing parties. They secured representation in local advisory councils, where they managed to influence local policy, both in South-West and in East Africa.

South-West Africa was soon accepted as a settler colony par excellence. In East Africa, however, the German authorities could never quite make up their minds, and official policy continued to vacillate to the end of the German regime. Europeans were kept out of African "sultanates" like Ruanda and Urundi; yet few civil servants wanted to exclude German settlers, even though the colonists were apt to challenge the officials' social pretensions and to create a variety of administrative problems.

The settlers tended to look upon Africans with disdain at best and with hatred at worst. To some extent these attitudes grew out of the harsh realities of pioneer farming in a tropical climate; they were also shaped to a degree by the racist ideology so widespread in Europe at the end of the nineteenth century. The colonists felt themselves menaced by the land and by the people they supplanted; they dreaded a repetition of the Maji-Maji uprising. As for the officials, the mere presence of European entrepreneurs presented them with a variety of new administrative problems concerning the health, recruitment, and logistics of a migrant labor force—problems that diminished the glamour of governing "unspoiled" people in the bush.

The settlers' views and their increasing hostility to the officials were reflected in the backwoods press.[14] A private paper was first started in Dar es Salaam in 1899—the *Deutsche-Ostafrikanische Zeitung*. The editor was a hot-tempered, venomous colonial named Willy von Roy, who was far from deferential; he was briefly jailed for suggesting that the governor, Albrecht von Rechenberg, habitually indulged in sodomy. Rechenberg, in turn, tried to curb the sheet by refusing it official advertisements; when this boycott failed the governor started a semi-official paper in 1908, the *Deutsche-Ostafrikanische Rundschau*. He had more luck in silencing the *Usambara Post* by ordering the government school at Tanga not to print it. But these were only minor issues. There were more basic disagreements between government and settlers than the governor's sexual habits.

Fundamentally, the settlers considered that they should be masters of the colony. They believed themselves to be racially superior to the blacks—as did the officials. They commonly believed that blacks had few needs and that they were too lazy to work—an illusion heightened by the fact that the Africans' agricultural peak season coincided with the settlers'; as the colonists saw it, the government should put pressure on Africans to work for wages temporarily. An even more fundamental issue was the future of the colony as a whole. The settlers thought that their own interests should be paramount. They argued that employers should be allowed to beat "their" Africans as they thought fit, a custom of the landowners in the more backward parts of Mecklenburg or Pomerania. White farmers made plentiful use of this presumed privilege—more so than the toughest bailiff in Germany. When Dernburg visited East Africa in 1907 he deplored the ubiquitous presence of the whip on the tables of farmers and employers. Another German visitor, Dr. Karl Weule, commented on "the furious fits of rage to which every white man who has lived long in the country appears to be subject."[15]

Dernburg intended to abolish the employers' right to inflict corporal punishment, but the intended ordinance was never issued. Some slight restrictions were imposed on the use of the whip, but flogging continued to be the rule in East Africa. Iliffe cites figures of 5,944 sentences of corporal punishment in native courts in 1911–12.[16] Rechenberg was unable to stop the practice of beating, but he tried to limit the employers' control over labor and to improve the laborers' conditions. Even though Europeans might be convicted of brutality by the courts —twenty-seven were found guilty in the Dar es Salaam court alone in thirty months—punishment was usually slight.

The less prosperous whites, as distinct from substantial merchants, were inclined to dislike Indians even more than blacks, considering them—especially the small trader—to be dirty, diseased, dishonest, and guilty of sending their profits to India. The whites feared their growth in numbers and their land purchases; the Indians were tough competitors with European merchants and traders. Settler groups regularly demanded that the Indians' rights to enter the colony and to buy land be limited. Rechenberg protected them, but Heinrich Schnee, his successor, largely yielded to European pressure in this matter.

The government did, however, issue a variety of regulations designed to lighten the lot of migrant laborers and to improve their conditions of work. No one can be sure how the relations between government and settlers would have developed had Germany been allowed to hold her East African colony. According to John Iliffe's analysis, the balance of power was beginning to swing toward the settlers by the outbreak of World War I. Schnee was more favorably disposed toward them than Rechenberg, believing that the government should try to strike a balance between white and black interests—a policy that also appealed to Solf, Germany's last colonial secretary.

The East African settlers continued to wield considerable influence at home through right-wing groups in the Reichstag, but they suffered from serious internal disabilities. The settler community was split into different regional lobbies with opposing interests regarding the provision of rail transport. They lacked national cohesion: of 5,336 whites in the colony in 1913, only 4,107 (77 percent) were German nationals. Collectively they were not a wealthy group. The representation obtained by whites on the Gouvernementsrat—a mere advisory body—was much less effective than that obtained by British colonists on well-established legislative councils. Accordingly, they were unable to prevent Africans from growing crops such as coffee that competed with plantation products.

The settlers were never quite sure of their ultimate social objectives. Farmers jeered at Hosennigger (Africans who wore European clothes), but had no compunction about employing mission-trained artisans or storekeepers; townsmen might mutter at the "black peril," but saw nothing wrong in purchasing African-grown food. The wealthier or more efficient employers found that they could live with government

regulations concerning labor conditions that incensed their less prosperous competitors. German soldiers, including reserve officers, might
make pessimistic forecasts concerning the danger of future rebellions
but they did their best to train African soldiers in the use of arms. The
easy camaraderie between conscripted German settlers and African askaris during World War I suggests, moreover, that race relations were
not universally as bad in the backveld as they appeared to humanitarians in the Reichstag. Basically, however, the Germans never resolved
the issue of how they should shape East Africa's future. They continued to vacillate until a world war removed the decision from their
hands.

Attitudes toward Africans

Literary notions did not much resemble the grim realities of life in
the colonies. Neither did they play much of a part in modifying administrative practices. These were shaped primarily by the varying situa-
tions in which administrators found themselves, by the demands made
upon the administrators by their superiors, by changing economic circumstances, and by the varying responses of the indigenous peoples.
There was no such thing as a colonial ethos. There was not even a specifically military or a specifically civilian ethos with regard to the Africans. There is no evidence, for instance, that civilians as a group were
more friendly or less coercive in their relations to Africans than were
military men. Count von Zech, an enlightened administrator who tried
to develop Togo by means of existing peasant cultivation, had a fairly
good opinion of the indigenous Ewe. Jesco von Puttkamer, his gubernatorial colleague in Cameroun, favored German plantation agriculture; hence he found little to praise in the social institutions of the
coastal Africans.

The settlers were apt to be the most harsh in their criticism of Africans. Their attitudes were not necessarily shaped by racist notions, but
by their position in society. A farmer or a trader trying to eke out a
precarious living in the South-West African veld or an East African
planter struggling with loneliness and disease—with unknown
climatological and ecological conditions, troubled by lack of market
and lack of transport—led a grim and difficult life. Unlike an officer or a
civil servant, he could not rely on a guaranteed income at the tax-

payer's expense. If his estate or his shop did not yield a profit, he and his family would starve.

The pioneer settler was apt to be harsh in his attitudes, much harsher than his descendant who was able to live under much easier conditions with schools, hospitals, veterinary posts, shops, railway stations, airfields, repair depots, and other modern facilities within reach. Sickness and a sense of isolation were widespread among the pioneers, whose lives were very different from the image conjured up by colonial publicity brochures. East African settlers, wrote a visitor, were inclined to be excessively irritable; they were overly sensitive and were often consumed by hatred of their neighbor. Conflicts inherent in the metropolitan social structure became more bitter when transplanted to the African interior, where "vanity, arrogance and intense striving for success" continued to trouble the expatriates.[17]

Civilian administrators were far from united in their attitudes toward black people or toward their fellow whites in other walks of life. The average East African official, reported the head of the East African Naval Station around the turn of the century, was honest and industrious. But the run-of-the-mill civil servants had little respect for merchants, whom they regarded as petty hucksters and with whom they failed to consult even on technical questions connected with customs, taxes, and port facilities. Many of the older Bezirksamtmänner, the German naval commander continued, had become "linked in an overly close fashion to non-European elements." Instead of insisting on the use of German, the officials would learn Swahili and would get into the habit of treating Muslim dignitaries like Europeans, especially when these Muslims were descended from distinguished families or were related to the Sultan of Zanzibar.[18] The German respect for nobility was extended to so-called aristocratic nations such as the Fulani and the Tutsi. More realistic officials, such as Heinrich Schnee, who placed special emphasis on the economic development of East Africa, soon became convinced that people like the Nyamwezi—though less picturesque than Tutsi or Masai—were in fact the mainstay of the colony's cash economy.

Professional soldiers differed as widely in their attitudes toward Africans as did the civilians. Officers who had drilled askaris and led them in action were often least subject to pejorative stereotypes concerning

black people. "Once you have got used to the language and local conditions," wrote Captain Fonck, an East African Schutztruppenoffizier,

much the same things go on among black privates as among our German soldiers at home. The men are really much the same, with their good and bad
qualities. There are always a few outstanding men with whom it is a pleasure to
work. In addition, each company has a few incorrigibles and misfits who always
get into trouble or get drunk . . . [but then] the best fighting soldiers were
often men who resorted to pranks and other forms of idiotic behavior while on
garrison duty.[19]

Fonck would have found many German officers who sharply dis-
agreed with him. Captain Kurt Schwabe, a South-West African Schutztruppenoffizier, described the Herero in precisely the same terms
applied by many Allied journalists to Germans in the course of two
world wars. The Herero, he wrote, is "distrustful, arrogant, proud,
and, again, inclined to whine . . ., mendacious, treacherous, thievish
and—when they are numerically superior—brutal and cruel. . . . The
only virtue that they do not lack is courage in war." In this respect,
Schwabe added, the Herero were no better than any other blacks
or—for that matter—the Chinese.[20] Wilhelm von Estorff, a committed
Lutheran, came back from South-West Africa with a very different
impression. The Herero, he argued, were "a proud, gifted and promising people." Germany's duty had been to educate rather than to destroy them, and he felt that his country had sinned grievously by the
cruelty and treachery of her conduct.[21]

Given the great differences of peoples and areas as well as the variety of policies followed in each part of the African empire, African
reactions to their German overlords differed just as widely as German
attitudes regarding the native peoples. The Herero never attempted to
pursue a policy of adaptation to German encroachment, or only did so
in a superficial fashion. A pastoral people with a strong warlike tradition, they preferred to follow conservative leaders like Samuel Maher-
ero and Assa Riarua, who were determined to fight for their land and
for the ways of their ancestors. German conquest created immense bitterness, and the Germans were never forgiven for what they did. "Go
back to your home country and tell your minister that you have erred
and strayed from the path and lost your reason," a settler was told by an
exasperated Herero. "The missionary says that we are the children of

God like our white brothers," said another, "but just look at us. Dogs, slaves, worse than the baboons on the rocks . . . that is how you treat us."[22]

At the opposite end of the spectrum were the Duala, a coastal people in Cameroun who had engaged in overseas commerce since the seventeenth century and had established a local monopoly over the transit trade to the interior. The Germans generally disliked the Duala and broke their monopolistic position as middlemen, yet the Duala's general position probably improved during the period of German colonialism. Their independence as traders were greatly reduced, but not necessarily their net income, and many Duala—especially chiefs like Rudolf Duala Manga Bell—became successful planters of cocoa and commercial food crops, a development supported by the Germans through technical assistance from officials and loans from private companies.

The Duala thus profited from the new order, but they came into conflict with their rulers when the Germans introduced a plan for residental segregation in the city of Duala. The German design involved the removal of some twenty thousand Duala from their existing accommodations into new quarters where they would be provided with public services by the government and furnished with canoe harbors and ultimately a tramway. The German plan ran counter to German economic interests; it derived from preoccupation with racial stereotypes and from concern for administrative neatness and sanitation that also shaped official thinking in many British possessions. In addition, German authorities disliked the manner in which the Duala supposedly "exploited" the value of their land, which continued to rise as the European sector within the economy expanded.

The huge scope of the German plan meant that African landowners would have to be compensated at prices below the level of official estimates. The Duala responded to this economic threat by attempting to manipulate the machinery of German law and politics. They sought to bypass the colonial establishment by appealing for the support of radical groups within the Reichstag—a strategy that failed, even though Duala grievances were fully debated within the German legislature.

In 1914 war broke out, and the German position in Cameroun soon became desperate. Suspecting that Duala Manga Bell was engaged in clandestine contacts with the Allies, the Germans had him arrested, tried, and hanged. Yet in retrospect present-day Duala informants speak of a "golden age" of German rule. Many view the era as the great period in their past, and blame the expropriation crises upon the personalities of individual officials immediately responsible—in particular, Governor Karl Ebermeier and Hermann Röhm, the local district commissioner.

Aged informants of all nations often remember their own past in a golden light. Also, the Duala quite naturally used the notion of the "good German" as a foil to set off the real and assumed vices of the successor French mandatory government. Nevertheless, countries as far afield as Togo and Tanzania at least provide evidence for the complexity of Afro-German relationships and help to explain a measure of respect for the Germans that continues to linger to this day in some parts of Africa.[23]

EIGHT

Economic Development, 1884-1906

During the mid-1880's Germany had established a far-flung network of colonial claims in Africa, and German cartographers proceeded to paint large patches of the continent in Prussian blue. Eventually the German colonial territory in African was much larger than the Reich itself and required a considerable time to conquer.

The development of the German empire in Africa was a vast undertaking requiring much expertise and large outlays of cash, but during the first two decades of colonization there was little capital to spare for such ventures. The pace of foreign and colonial lending picked up after the turn of the century, but only one-tenth of current savings in Germany between 1900 and 1914 went abroad, and the bulk of this was invested elsewhere in Europe. The Austro-Hungarian empire alone absorbed as much German capital as the combined African and Asian continents, and in Africa the capital from Germany invested outside the German colonies—especially in South Africa and Egypt—exceeded the sums invested within the German possessions. By 1914 something like 23.5 billion marks had been invested abroad; of this, 12.5 billion marks went to Europe, two billion went to Africa, and one billion went to Asia.[1]

German investors remained chary of putting their savings into the colonies despite the exertions of the government and despite the tremendously powerful position held in the German money market by a few great banks. Colonial development was slow and hesitant, and within the framework of German capitalism as a whole, colonial capitalists like Woermann and Lüderitz were without significance.

The Traders' Frontier

In the earliest days of African colonization, economic development hinged on the Hanseatic ports—especially on Hamburg, whose original center of activities was Lagos in West Africa, where Hamburg merchants had begun to operate in 1848. The firms of A. Woermann and of Jantzen and Thormählen set up chains of "factories" in many parts of the West African coast from Liberia to Gabon, and German commerce assumed such importance in Cameroun that in 1882 Woermann instituted a regular shipping line to West Africa—a major departure in the history of German maritime enterprise. Woermann and others realized that the future of German shipping lay with the steamship—not with the sailing vessel.

There was an air of romance to the business in Kolonialwaren, but in terms of total traffic, colonial business transactions were insignificant. In 1891, of a total of 3.504 billion marks in export trade, Germany's exports to all her colonies amounted to only 6 million marks. Her commerce with colonial Africa was small even by comparison with traffic to and from South Africa, where German mine owners, wine growers, merino sheep breeders, and businessmen had acquired substantial fortunes under the protection of the Union Jack or the Transvaaler Vierkleur.

German colonial commerce was channeled through only a few cities. Bremen merchants such as Lüderitz had staked out claims in South-West Africa, but the bulk of Germany's African trade passed through Hamburg. Even in Hamburg African commerce was very limited. A good deal of money was made by transshipping British-made goods, a dependence which lessened only during the latter part of the nineteenth century when German factories began to compete with increasing success against British rivals and the inscription "Made in Germany" became a badge of honor rather than a mark of inferior craftsmanship. The Hamburgers were reluctant to tie up large sums in African ventures over long periods and thus had less interest in permanent colonization than in preserving informal influence.

German exports such as guns and liquor were extremely unpopular with the later imperialists, but the Hamburg pioneers had little desire for official supervision that might interfere with their traffic in rifles and

Schnapps. These merchants, like those of Liverpool, felt quite capable of maintaining good relations with African rulers without the help of colonial civil servants. Their relations were strictly egalitarian: if anything, the advantage lay with the indigenous chiefs, whom the Hamburgers learned to humor. They defended the sovereignty of the Zanzibari sultanate, which looked with favor on German traders. Thus colonial annexation was opposed by a majority of the Hamburg senate even in 1890, several years after the formal German empire in Africa had been established.

From the traders' standpoint, Togo was the Musterkolonie. German occupation there had been preceded by a long period of missionary work with the Ewe, and the Norddeutsche Missionsgesellschaft (commonly known as the Bremen Mission) had become so popular that Protestants are still known as Brema in many Togolese tongues. These missionaries—many of them from Switzerland and southern Germany —had little desire to spread German culture: they evangelized in the Ewe tongue, they taught English (the lingua franca of the littoral) in their schools, they ordained Ewe clergymen from an early period. As Robert Cornevin points out in his studies on German colonization, the missionaries' long-term objective was to set up an independent church, Protestant in faith but Ewe in complexion and governance. Many members of the political and literary elite that achieved prominence during the French era following the German occupation of Togo had been educated by German Protestant preceptors.

The Bremen missionaries had been commercially linked first to Great Britain. When the British temporarily abandoned their station at Keta in 1865, the mission turned for its supplies to the Bremen firm of Vietor und Söhne. This choice was natural in that Bremen merchants supported the mission financially and Rudolf Vietor, the son of a former owner of the company, was a prominent missionary. In 1874 the British reoccupied Keta, and German traders established themselves further east—between Lomé (then known as Bey Beach) and Anécho (Little Popo). This region was a haven of free trade set between the African monarchy of Dahomey, which rigidly controlled commerce in the interests of the great magnates, and the British-controlled Gold Coast, whose government had imposed substantial duties to pay for the cost of fighting the Ashanti. In eastern Togo powerful Afro-Brazilian families had switched from traffic in slaves to commerce in palm oil and to plantation agriculture; in addition, a variety of European firms had set up branches along the Togolese littoral.

The Germans took control of this narrow coastal stretch in 1884. In establishing their power they benefited from a far-flung system of local trade geared, above all, to the export of palm produce. Their only serious opposition was in northern Togo, and they subdued opponents like the Konkomba and Kabure by forming alliances with small local Muslim kingdoms such as Kotokoli (Sokode). The Germans considered Islam to be their "natural" ally in the north; accordingly they closed that area to their missionaries and traders. As far as colonization was concerned, the "useful" part of Togo did not extend beyond the southern district (Bezirk) of Atakpamé. Germany's armed forces on the spot were limited; from the military standpoint the wars in northern Togo were small-scale affairs, but their social consequences were far-reaching.

The missionaries and traders together were strong enough to exclude colonizing and plantation companies from Togo, and by 1914 the total number of German plantations occupied less than 12,000 hectares. The country relied on the enterprise of African cultivators and managed to balance its budget by keeping governmental expenditure to the irreducible minimum. The total number of Europeans employed in the central administration in 1913—from governor to gardeners, and including forestry officials, builders, and secretaries—was only twenty. The district staff numbered less than thirty persons, and the colony's armed forces consisted of only a few hundred men.

Togo, a territory considerably larger than Holland and Belgium, produced a revenue less than half that raised in a tiny German principality like Lippe, a survival from the era of feudal lordships. A determined effort was made to expand the economy of southern Togo by providing port and railway facilities; the Germans also employed some professional agronomists and forestry officials in an attempt to diversify the colony's production. At a time when German industrialists were paying ever-increasing amounts for American cotton imports, the Kolonialwirstschaftliche Komitee set out to encourage Africans to grow cotton. Six Afro-Americans trained at Tuskegee Institute were engaged in 1900 to set up an experimental farm; they had to overcome locusts, ants, chiggers, and plant disease, but in the end a useful hybrid was developed. Cotton production increased rapidly from almost none in 1901 to more than 500,000 kilos in 1911. The early Togolese cotton was not competitive in the world market, but during the French period production in the central plateau was expanded.

Palm oil and palm oil kernels remained the colony's main export crops, along with rubber and a limited amount of cocoa—all of them developed by indigenous cultivators at a time when rising world prices seemed to justify promoters of the traders' frontier. In metropolitan terms, Togo's commerce was insignificant: the value of the colony's imports in 1912 was about 11.4 million marks compared to Germany's total export share of 9,827 million marks. But the territory balanced its budget, its military expenditure was negligible, it enjoyed a good press among merchants and humanitarians, and it kept its reputation as Germany's "model colony."

The Economics of Coercion

Cameroun was one of the larger of the new colonies—a land of extraordinary variety, consisting of tropical rain forest, bushland, and a great open savanna belt in the north, whose indigenous peoples had acquired tenuous links with the West through slave trade with the New World. During the nineteenth century, Western merchants gradually shifted to "legitimate trade," and palm oil became an important export product. German influence, at first confined to the shores and creeks along the Gulf of Guinea, remained dependent on the goodwill of the coastal Duala, who acquired a dominant position in the local traffic.

So long as business went well the German coastal traders—who did not at first have permanent stations on land—were content with local protection exercised through German consular courts and warships. Expansion of the African palm oil trade, however, led to a drop in world prices—part of a much wider recession afflicting the world economy between the 1870's and 1890's. As the recession deepened, the traders began to call for inland expansion to enable them to break the Duala mercantile monopoly and deal directly with the producers in the interior. Between 1884 and 1895 the Germans established their rule over the littoral; later, backed by Schutztruppen commandos, they pushed inland, where they dealt in palm products, in ivory, and above all in wild rubber.

From the economic standpoint the Cameroun share in the German trade balance was infinitesimal: by 1898 the colony's exports were worth little more than 4.5 million marks, considerably less than one-thousandth of the total merchandise value imported by Germany at the time (nearly 6 billion marks). But opportunities offered by the development of the automobile and the electrical industries, and the profits made in the Congo Free State by the exploitation of rubber, persuaded German speculators that Cameroun could be squeezed in a similar fashion. In 1898 Julius Scharlach, a Hamburg financier, and other investors—backed by German banks and by Belgian Congo concerns—created the Gesellschaft für Südkamerun (GSK), which received an enormous concession comprising some 5 million hectares. Another major concessionnaire was the Gesellschaft für Nordwest-Kamerun, which also obtained a princely stake in the colony.

Concessionary capitalism was strongly supported by Jesco von Puttkamer, governor of Cameroun (1895–1907) and the son of an ultra-conservative cabinet minister. He respected aristocratic rulers, such as the Muslim lords of Adamawa. According to Puttkamer, Africans were naturally idle and African forest-farming was incompatible with economic progress, tending merely to devastate the land; hence if the country were not to continue to vegetate in a state of "un-culture," capitalists would have to be encouraged to invest their money in plantations.[2] Puttkamer was deeply impressed by the cocoa and coffee plantations he had seen on the Portuguese island of São Tomé and resolved to introduce agricultural enterprise of a similar kind in Cameroun, making the required land grants to German pioneers. He was equally optimistic with regard to rubber. But his views were based on a lack of understanding not merely of indigenous method of African farming, but also of the difficulties faced by plantation companies in many other countries such as Sumatra, where Bremen entrepreneurs had lost a great deal of money.

Despite Puttkamer's endeavors the Germans were unable to transform Cameroun into a plantation economy. The bulk of her exports continued to derive from trade; indeed the plantation companies themselves engaged in commerce as well as in agriculture. The impact of the new rubber economy was fraught with disastrous consequences for many African communities, and the indigenous subsistence economies were subjected to heavy strain. The Germans needed an ever-increasing number of laborers to work on plantations, tap wild rubber, carry loads, construct railways, and perform a host of allied tasks.

Work on the plantations was at first bitterly unpopular. Among Africans the mortality of the hired hands was high, their pay was poor, and their treatment bad—though some companies, such as the Westafrikanische Pflanzungsgesellschaft Viktoria, made serious attempts to improve conditions. Since plantations were unable to secure sufficient voluntary workers, the government began to recruit labor by force. German exactions—sometimes accompanied by vicious cruelty—led to widespread resistance; between 1904 and 1907 there was armed resistance in many parts of southern Cameroun. Armed repression resulted in loss of lives in battle, and even more died through disease and famine.

The growth of a money economy was double-edged in its effects. Some enterprising coastmen joined trading caravans into the interior, where literate Africans—often immigrants from Gabon or the Gold Coast—set up branch factories to collect rubber in exchange for merchandise. Hausa merchants benefited from the German *Pax* by extending their operations from the north to the forest region and the coast; here the northerners exchanged meat for rubber, which they then sold to the Germans. German plantations also began to grow new experimental crops such as cocoa. (In the post-German era Africans discovered the value of cocoa and developed it on their own initiative as a peasant cash crop.)

The Germans discovered that coercion entailed severe economic costs; moreover, their ability to govern by naked force was strictly limited. By the turn of the century there were only forty etatsmässige Beamten (permanent civil servants) in the whole of Cameroun, including the governor, three Bezirksamtmänner, and their respective staffs; the white establishment as a whole—including gardeners, technicians, and supervisors—numbered seventy-seven persons. German military strength at the end of the Puttkamer regime was little more impressive: the armed forces comprised only nine companies of askaris commanded by a handful of German commissioned and noncommissioned officers—a force expected to control a territory six times the size of England with totally inadequate communications and in which they confronted extraordinary climatic, topographical, and medical difficulties.

German abuses in Cameroun never approached those committed in the Congo Free State. The concessionaires, unlike those in the

Congo, had no recognized sovereign powers. Throughout its history German Cameroun incurred heavy annual budget deficits, a condition that gave the Reichstag whatever excuse it may have needed to intervene in the affairs of the colony. Hence the "Scharlach system" met with a wide range of opposition. Critics included the Basel Mission Society, which condemned the concessions, while the Catholic Pallotine Mission tended to defend Puttkamer. German merchants bitterly censured concessionary monopolies as did British traders like John Holt, whom the German authorities did not wish to alienate lest the British interfere with German commerce in British possessions. Parliamentary opposition came from the Social Democrats and the center as well as from various conservatives, including the Pan-Germans, who objected to the stake held by foreign capitalists in German concessionary companies.

In the long run Raubwirtschaft (exploitation) was not profitable. Many companies suffered serious losses, and forced labor was inefficient. Puttkamer noted that chiefs were reluctant to send their best men to work in European employment and often dispatched the weakest they could find. When the Gesellschaft für Südkamerun ran into financial trouble, after making huge initial gains, the size of its concession was substantially reduced. Raubwirtschaft, dependent on the tapping of wild trees, led to widespread destruction; in time, wild-grown produce from Cameroun had to compete with superior rubber obtained from well-run plantations in South-east Asia. The company was forced gradually to introduce a more efficient kind of cultivation. The Gesellschaft für Nordwest-Kamerun failed to adjust its methods, incurred heavy losses, and finally lost its territorial stake in the colony. Between 1900 and 1909 the Gesellschaft für Nordwest-Kamerun paid no dividends whatever. The Gesellschaft für Südkamerun paid no dividends between 1899 and 1902; between 1903 and 1909 its annual dividends (in percent) were as follows: 5.0, 0, 10.0, 0, 0, 0, 8.0.

An economy of coercion also produced widespread inter-white dissensions; plantation managers, merchants, and officials competed for the available supplies of manpower, and sometimes censured one another in unmeasured terms. At the same time, the widespread African unrest and the scandals and abuses associated with the Puttkamer regime combined with metropolitan criticism to produce demands for a more rational form of colonization. Governmental exactions, though still onerous, ceased to be arbitrary and were strictly regulated, and Africans at last came to be looked upon as economic men rather than as merely savages.

In the German colonial hierarchy, Cameroun was a backwater. East Africa, on the other hand, was regarded as a prize possession. With its ancient links to the Orient and India, it had an air of romance that no other colony could rival, and for a long time its image dominated popular imagination concerning the colonies. German scientists and scholars devoted more attention to it than to any other colony. Until 1904, when South-West Africa moved into first place, East Africa's annual trade was generally larger than that of any other German-dominated territory.

The economic realities of East Africa, however, were far different from what was popularity imagined. The colony was a meeting-ground of many different cultures, a land where indigenous people such as the Chagga had developed flourishing agricultural systems and where communities like the Nyamwezi had come to play an important part as porters and traders. But East Africa was also riddled by internecine strife; Ruanda and Urundi in the far interior were warlike kingdoms dominated by the Tutsi pastoral conquerors. In addition, East Africa was the extreme northern frontier of Ngoni expansion. During the nineteenth century, raiding states resembling those of the Ndebele and Zulu in their constitution and plundering habits were set up in parts of what are now southern and eastern Tanzania. The coastal regions and part of the hinterland were dominated by Swahili-speaking Muslim merchants often backed by Arab and Indian financiers and by indigenous African allies. Pre-colonial export trade hinged on ivory and slaves, as well as on such tropical products as spices, sesame, and palm oil.

During the 1880's and 1890's, however, the Germans, British, and Belgians together crushed the Muslim slave trade, and widespread destruction of the elephant herds largely eliminated the traffic in ivory. The Muslims ceased to be a ruling class, though they continued to play an important part in such minor positions of authority as guides, foremen, leaders of caravans, and subordinate officials within the German colonial hierarchy.

In the commercial field Arabs could not easily compete with Indians, who were the country's traders, moneylenders, and clerks. By 1909 the Indian community numbered no more than 4,300, yet they were indispensable as middlemen in the African trade; German opinion was divided with regard to their value. Most administrators and many colonial theoreticians such as Hans Meyer and Kurt Hassert branded them exploiters and usurers, the "Jews of Africa," whose activities helped to guide a considerable part of the colony's export trade to India and Great Britain. But German entrepreneurs in Zanzibar and other coastal cities who dealt with Indian merchants felt that the country could not prosper without the aid of Asian middlemen. This was also the view of Governor Rechenberg.

Initially the Germans thought of placing white peasants on the land, but Count von Götzen as governor (1901–6) took a more cautious attitude toward white settlement than had his predecessor, von Liebert (1896–1901). In addition to Indian immigrants, a few thousand Europeans entered the country, including Greeks and Afrikaners who lacked political influence in the metropolis. Colonists recruited from among German settlers in Russia and Palestine failed to make good in East Africa, where conditions were totally unlike those in their home countries, where sickness was rife, and where they lacked markets for their produce. The area of European settlement was relatively dispersed, with no gigantic land alienations on the scale of South-West Africa or Cameroun. The Germans became convinced that only well-capitalized plantations producing specialized crops such as sisal could succeed financially, and that African cash farmers would have to play a major part in the economic development of East Africa.

The German settlers, often underestimated, made a real contribution to the colony's economic life. Conditions were difficult. There were no developed ports and no railway system, no repair shops and no supply depots, no hospitals, no schools; the infrastructure that farmers take for granted in more developed countries was almost wholly lacking. Markets were scarce or nonexistent. The settler and his family suffered from tropical diseases; his cattle died from little-understood afflictions; crops failed either from too little or too much rainfall, from locusts or from unidentified plant diseases. There was little information concerning soils and ecological conditions: farmers had to experiment.

Nevertheless, Europeans introduced new cash crops such as cotton, sisal, and coffee, as well as new machinery (including steam plows); they were economic pioneers.

In East Africa as elsewhere, European settlement was double-edged in its effect upon the indigenous people. White immigrants competed with black people for the land, but their number was too small to produce more than local shortages. German settlers called for compulsory labor, a serious matter since the agricultural peak seasons of white and black cultivators coincided. Yet European farming—for instance, the cultivation of coffee—had valuable demonstration effects, and Africans learned new methods from European farmers just as the Europeans profited from black farming experience. The Germans encouraged production of African food crops for the market, especially ground nuts, because sisal planters and other employers wanted cheap food for their workmen.

The commercial cultivation of cotton promoted by the Kolonialwirtschaftliche Komitee—the semi-official corporation set up in 1896 under the chairmanship of Karl Supf, a manufacturer, which had engaged the black Americans from Tuskegee Institute in 1900 to pioneer its cultivation in Togo—started production in East Africa in 1902. An experimental station and a cotton inspectorate were set up to improve the quality of the crop. However, the Germans proceeded on the assumption that Africans were insensitive to economic considerations—that they were congenital idlers who would not work except under the threat of compulsion. Africans were therefore forced to devote a month a year to cotton cultivation; of the proceeds of their labor, one-third went into the treasury of the local government, one-third was paid to Swahili foremen, and one-third went to the producers.

The Germans made themselves hated by levying heavy taxes, by impressing labor for the use of private employers, by interfering with elephant hunting, and by similar repressive measures; their colonial policy created widespread discontent. Rebellious activity centered not on the areas of white settlement, however, but on the southern parts of the colony—geographically the most remote and economically among the more backward portions of East Africa. Not until the Maji-Maji uprising had been crushed in 1907 did the Germans end native resistance.

The Pastoral Frontier

South-West Africa at first seemed a worthless acquisition, useless to all but wilderness specialists skilled in wresting a living from a harsh natural environment, to Nama herdsmen, or to Boer trekkers. The Germans' only initial economic stake was a petty traffic in dried beef, hides, ostrich feathers, Schnapps, and trinkets. Even this did not amount to much because the main cattle market was in South Africa, whence itinerant traders came to buy beasts for the markets of Kimberley and other centers; missionaries of the Rhenish (or Barmen) Missionary Society supported a concern that carried out legitimate trade in cattle purchased from the pastoral Herero and sold in South Africa. Such was the land which German policymakers sought to turn into a settlement colony capable of competing on the world markets with pastoral countries such as Australia and the Argentine; this was to be a new German fatherland in the antipodes.

The colonizing task was given to the Deutsche Kolonialgesellschaft für Deutsch-Südwestafrika,[3] but the real pioneering was done primarily by trekboers or more substantial settlers from South Africa and by ambitious German farmers willing to take risks. Also important was a host of amateurs, ex-officers, technicians, demobilized German soldiers, and German navvies and artisans brought to the country to build the railway. These would-be farmers usually had little capital, and opportunities for obtaining agricultural credit were scant; the Landwirtschaftsbank, the first major body providing loans to farmers, began operations only in 1913. Markets were scarce, communications were inadequate, and transport riding was an important subsidiary industry. A pioneering existence was harsh, entailing great risks and limited profits. Concessionary lands thus tended to be out of the reach of these frontiersmen, who soon began to call for the appropriation of African pastures.

While contending with Africans for grazing grounds, the frontiersmen were also dependent on their African neighbors. The most important part of a farmer's capital was his cattle—especially his breeding stock, which no intelligent pioneer would have thought of selling—but this was at first in short supply because the German authorities had neither the means nor the inclination to import beasts from abroad. German colonists therefore had to purchase animals from Africans, who also put a high value on quality breeding cows. The average German pioneer often began his career as a bush-trader—a hard and risky occupation that grew more profitable as Herero in the vicinity of white settlements became accustomed to imported products such as clothes, coffee, sugar, and tobacco.

A major turning-point came with the outbreak of the great rinderpest epidemic of 1896–97 that swept through the whole of southern Africa. The Germans were able to save a substantial portion of their herds by inoculating their beasts, but the Herero herds were decimated. For the first time the settlers could compete successfully with the Herero in selling cattle; at the same time their labor costs fell as impoverished Herero were forced to hire themselves out as workmen. The epidemic also occasioned widespread destruction of draught animals, and the Germans decided to build a railway inland from Swakopmund—a development that increased the size of the internal market.

Europeans began to make a very real contribution to the economy of their adopted land. Immigrant farmers, under conditions of enormous difficulty, gradually learned how to cope with droughts and cattle disease; they improved the indigenous Damara breed by crossing beasts with Simmental, Pinzgau, and Shorthorn bulls; they introduced a variety of new crops; they built cattle-dips and dams, fenced pastureland, and sunk boreholes, along with many other improvements. But economic success increased the demand for cheap land and the appropriation of African grazing grounds. German authorities preferred to incur the hostility of African tribesmen—whose fighting skills were greatly underestimated—than to meddle with powerful concession companies with influence in Berlin. The result was disaster. The ravages of the rinderpest, brutalities inflicted on Africans by individual Germans, a pervasive sense of insecurity, the forfeiture of land, and the fear of future deprivations—all combined to produce an explosion. In 1904 the Herero rose and were soon joined by their erstwhile enemies, the Nama.

Many German settlers were killed; outlying farms were burnt; for a time economic life almost came to a standstill. The Germans struck back in ruthless fashion. Lothar von Trotha, the commander of the German troops during 1904–5, carried out a campaign designed to annihilate the rebels in a classic battle of encirclement, and a large portion of the Herero nation perished miserably in the desert. Trotha and his associates failed to understand that seizure of the enemy's cattle was the key to victory and the conclusion of a profitable peace, an axiom known to every frontier fighter in southern Africa. Nothing was done to save the Herero cattle; the Germans did not even bother to loot the beasts but simply left them to die.

The war against the Nama, who put their trust in mounted guerrilla tactics, was fought with great bitterness. Scattered partisan operations continued in the southern part of the colony as late as 1909. In the end the Germans won, but their colony was impoverished. After protracted fighting in which more than 17,000 white troops were engaged, the majority of German settlers were poor, bankrupt, or dead. The Herero nation had been decimated. Outside Ovamboland, which had remained untouched by the conflict, most Africans were in a deplorable condition; war had smashed their social institutions, destroyed their property, and spread epidemics and sickness. South-West Africa lay in ruins.

NINE

Economic Reform and Its Aftermath
1906-1914

By the year 1906 the pessimistic predictions of the anti-colonialists seemed to have come true. Except for Togo and the small Chinese possession of Kiau Tschau—a trading post administered by the navy— the German colonial empire was not paying for itself. The financial means made available by the Reich for colonial purposes were very limited, and the overseas dependencies had been an equal disappointment to private investors, who had placed only some 229 million marks into the German colonies—a paltry sum equalling only the resources of a single major metropolitan enterprise (see Appendix Table E.5). Some colonial ventures did well, but the great majority of them struggled hard to little or no avail; their annual dividends were usually modest and sometimes nonexistent. The colonial empire accounted for less than one percent of Germany's overseas trade, belying the claims of propagandists and stock promoters.

These economic failures became evident at a time when German domestic politics had grown stormy. After a decade of colonization, reformers and would-be reformers called for a variety of changes designed to render German administration more rational and more professional. There was widespread discontent with the organization of the foreign office and with the direction of foreign affairs in general. There was manifest disgust at the way German authorities had handled critical matters. During the Algeciras crisis (1906), Germany had suffered a diplomatic defeat over Morocco. The so-called Eulenburg affair, an unpleasant court scandal, had disgraced members of the Kaiser's immediate entourage. German colonialism with its military involvement, its aristocratic and financial connections, increasingly came under fire. Parliamentary critics of the government, independent-minded missionaries, and some of the German residents in the colonies censured abuses by individual administrators; the expense incurred in suppressing indigenous uprisings in East Africa and South-West Africa occasioned bitter parliamentary opposition; free traders, settlers, socialists, and Pan-Germans alike criticized the concessionary regimes which so often benefited questionable concerns or seemed to give special favors to foreigners.

Public criticism of colonial abuses led to a number of personnel changes. Excesses committed by German officials were not punished with the severity they deserved, but the Germans were at least willing to wash some of their dirty linen in public and to remove some of the worst offenders from office. Within the colonial service itself were many reform-minded administrators determined to pursue a policy of native trusteeship. They were in no sense a united group, but they did not commit themselves to value judgments made by old-timers like Puttkamer, who regarded the Duala of Cameroun, for instance, as "the most treacherous, the laziest and the most contemptible thugs under the sun"[1]—as a people meriting only the harshest treatment.

The reformers also agreed on certain fundamentals. German entrepreneurs should benefit both Africans and their own shareholders by relying less on coercion and more on economic incentives. Africans should be valued as wage workers, as producers of cash crops, and as potential customers capable of buying German goods. Successful colonization, moreover, could not be undertaken on the cheap; the *mise en valeur* of empire required an extensive logistic infrastructure, including the creation of ports and railways; scientific research was needed by the businessman and the planter. At the same time, German administration should become more professional and more efficient; a district commissioner should be a specialist in African administration, not just an expert in "law and order" or a labor recruiter for local German entrepreneurs.

The old colonial regime was weakened by political dissension within the metropolitan power structure. In the Reichstag Prince Bernhard von Bülow's political position became increasingly unstable as the Catholic Center Party came under control of Matthias Erzberger (1875–1921), who tried to steer a leftist course. Bülow regarded the Social Democrats as well as the minor ethnic splinter groups—including

Poles, Alsatians, and Danes—as irreconcilable opponents. His right-center coalition could not endure without support from the Catholics unless he found new allies, and the most likely choice was the Freisinnige—the left-wing liberals who, between 1904 and 1906, had become increasingly accommodating in their position toward the government. (The "Freisinnige" were divided among the Freisinnige Volkspartei, essentially pro-colonial in its attitude, and the Freisinnige Vereinigung; in 1910 the various left-liberal groups fused into the Fortschrittliche Volkspartei.) Bülow decided to appoint Bernhard Dernburg, a member of the Freisinnige faction and a recognized financial expert, as Kolonialdirektor in 1906. A year later the Kolonialdirektor's office became an independent ministry—the Reichskolonialamt—and Dernburg was assisted by Friedrich von Lindequist, previously governor of South-West Africa as Unterstattssekretär.

The Dernburg Administration

Dernburg was to some extent an outsider in his own country; in the army reserve he never advanced beyond the rank of sergeant. In this he resembled Britain's Joseph Chamberlain, with whom he had certain other features in common. The latter was a Unitarian by faith and a manufacturer by background, while Dernburg had made his way in banking and—though a Lutheran by upbringing—was half-Jewish and was universally referred to as Jew. Like Chamberlain he believed in the application of scientific research to colonialism, and like Chamberlain he was a progressive businessman—not a patrician but a tough entrepreneur famed for his "American" manners, his abrasive disregard for conventions, his brusque self-confidence, and his determination to purge his office of incompetents. Together with luminaries like Rudolf Virchow and Gerhard Hauptmann, he was a member of the German Peace Society, a body regarded with disdain both by the German Establishment and the Social Democrats. He was an anglophile—a proclivity shared by Paul Kayser, Germany's first Kolonialdirektor,[2] and by most German-Jewish bankers—and he admired British methods of colonial governance. He worked for a worldwide Anglo-German understanding, and believed that a policy of reform in the African colonies would promote good relations between the Reich and the British Empire. According to Dernburg—or to firms such as Max M. Warburg

und Kompanie, or to the Reichskolonialamt, or to colonial administra-
tor-politicians like Wilhelm Solf—additional German colonies or
spheres of influence in Africa could be acquired only in collaboration
with Great Britain. Dernburg was in no wise an original thinker. He
was profoundly indebted to senior civil servants, and many of the reforms attributed to him had been initiated before he assumed office.
However he had courage, determination, and a sense of publicity; he
also had excellent financial connections—advantages that helped him
to accelerate the difficult task of ameliorating conditions in Germany's
neglected empire.

Under his new policies the Germans were the first to give practical
training to some of their settlers going to Africa. Students received instruction in agriculture and related subjects at the Deutsche Kolonialschule at Witzenhausen, founded in 1899, and at the Kolonialakademie
at Halle, where there was also a natural sciences institute; linguistic
and ethnographic instruction was given at Berlin University's Seminar
für Orientalische Sprachen, established in 1887. The Kolonialinstitut
was established at Hamburg in 1908 with monetary support from
Alfred Beit, an ally of Cecil Rhodes and—like Dernburg—a financier
of Jewish origin and Lutheran faith. Beit promoted railway development and education in Africa and the expansion of technical training in
Great Britain, and he shared a philosophy of development similar to
that of Dernburg and his economic advisor, Walther Rathenau.[3]

"Scientific" colonialism required improved medical training, which
was provided by the Institut für Schiffs-und-Tropenkrankheiten,
opened in Hamburg in 1899 to serve as a center of research and advanced medical training. All doctors going to the colonies, whether in a
civilian or a military capacity, had to complete a course at the institute
where they learned to conduct independent research into tropical diseases and acquired some familiarity with the kinds of sickness they
were likely to encounter. The institute benefited by continuity of direction under Bernhard Nocht, who remained in charge of its operations from 1900 to 1930. German medical services in the colonies also
were able to draw on experts trained in the Reichsgesundheitsminis-
terium, the Robert Koch Institut, and similar institutions. Robert
Koch, founder of modern bacteriological research, a pioneer in the
treatment of tuberculosis, cholera, and other infectious diseases, exercised a dominant influence on colonial medicine. Physicians such as

Friedrich Karl Kleine, Max Traute, and Emil Steudel were all students of Koch's; their training enabled them not only to work in applied medicine and medical administration but also to carry out original research.

The vast majority of German medical doctors were of bourgeois origin—the sons of merchants, civil servants, and professional men. Friedrich Kleine's father, for instance, was a government medical officer in Stralsund. His son followed in the family tradition, studied medicine at the University of Halle, and later worked for a time in the pharmacological department of the university as an assistant—research he was allowed to continue after obtaining a regular medical commission in the German army. The decisive point in his career came in 1900 when, at thirty-one, he was attached to Robert Koch's headquarters at the Preussische Institut für Infektionskrankheiten in Berlin. He accompanied Koch on a visit to Southern Rhodesia at the government's invitation to carry out investigations into veterinary problems besetting southern Africa. Sharing Koch's work strengthened his resolve to specialize in tropical medicine. From 1906 to 1907 he was Koch's assistant in an expedition to investigate sleeping sickness—a fly-borne disease and a major health threat—and later was placed in charge of operations against this scourge. (He made a number of valuable discoveries in the field of epidemiology and succeeded in transmitting the *Trypanasoma brucei* through *Glossina palpalis*, the tsetse fly.) The Germans had made substantial advances in chemotherapy, and began to treat sleeping sickness with "Atoxyl," a preparation discovered by Paul Ehrlich; they later used "Bayer 205," a more effective remedy. Between 1914 and 1916 Kleine served as chief medical officer in Cameroun, and he continued his work in Africa after the war until he retired because of age.

Dernburg considered good medical training and research essential both for humanitarian and for economic purposes. Africa could not develop unless its manpower was safeguarded and its population allowed to grow. He felt strongly that Africans were "economic men" capable of business foresight and enterprise. Often attacked as a negrophile, he was not anti-European in outlook; in his view South-West Africa could accommodate a hundred thousand Europeans, a remarkably accurate prediction. Like missionary imperialists such as David Livingstone and

John Mackenzie, he believed that Europeans had an essential part to play in Africa. They should go to the colonies as capitalists, entrepreneurs, managers, specialists, and technicians; there were also opportunities for planters and farmers with adequate capital and specialized agronomic skills capable of starting new agricultural industries. But there was no room for unskilled white workmen or peasant farmers. Dernburg's views were shaped not only by his belief in imperial trusteeship for Africans, but also by a profound conviction that the colonial settlers were too few in number and too lacking in experience and financial resources to run a colony. When diamonds were found in South-West Africa in 1908 and settler interests clashed with those of metropolitan investors, he opposed the colonists who believed that overseas capitalists were improperly favored and inadequately taxed.

Dernburg's main interest centered on the Africans as the colonies' chief economic asset. His views were molded to some extent by the demographic predilections of the time. Colonial theoreticians did not worry about African unemployment but about an anticipated lack of industrial manpower; they were not concerned about a future population explosion because they assumed that Africa lacked a sufficient number of people—that the population might remain stationary or even be declining. According to the respective observer's preconceptions, these supposed deficiencies were to be blamed on the evils of colonial capitalism or on the Africans' idleness and immorality. The demographic realities probably differed greatly from these assumptions. The pacification of the colonies, for all its violence, had done away with the slave trade and internecine African wars; moreover, the effects of rinderpest and the spread of the tsetse fly caused demographic shifts which were not connected with German employment practices but rather with the inadequacy of contemporary medical services. There are no reliable demographic data for the period prior to World War I, and most figures depend on guesswork, but it seems probable that in some areas observers confused the dispersal of the African population with depopulation.

Dernburg was determined to pursue a negererhaltend policy (designed to safeguard Africans); as economic men, black people were not lazy savages: "Speculations concerning the Negro's invincible idleness should be consigned to the realm of fables. . . . Given wages commensurate with the value of his labor, the Negro will work at least as hard as a European. Indeed, of all the Negro's instincts, his impulse for acquiring wealth and holding property is perhaps the strongest."[4]

A rational native policy, he believed, would combine philanthropy with profit. Once African producers became more prosperous they would produce more goods for the world market and would buy more German merchandise. Instead of having to fight costly and unpopular campaigns against African rebels, the Reich would be able to count on the loyalty of contested African subjects; well-to-do peasant farmers would be in a position to pay higher imposts into local exchequers; the colonies would become financially self-sufficient and a weight would be taken off the German taxpayer. Economic advance would in turn lead to cultural progress, and German rule could then be morally justified on the grounds of reciprocal benefits as expressed in the Latin tag *do ut des* (I give in order that thou mayest give).

Dernburg's policies entailed a new, less punitive approach in labor relations. Corporal punishment was limited, and tighter labor regulations were adopted to protect labor migrants. Dernburg vigorously defended before the Reichstag a paternalistic policy of safeguarding Africans by providing them with decent housing, better food, improved medical care, and properly supervised labor contracts; Africans, he contended, should not be treated only as a resource but also as human beings. In East Africa a law was passed prohibiting the alienation of land already occupied by Africans. Firmly believing in promoting African peasant cultivation, Dernburg refused to comply with settler demands for the prohibition of Indian immigration; according to both Dernburg and Walther Rathenau, the Indian trader—far from restricting production—encouraged economic expansion by extending marketing facilities into the interior.

These policies were not original; they owed a great deal to the work of bodies such as the Kolonialwirtschaftliche Komitee and to senior German colonial officials. But Dernburg's views were far from those of Scharlach or of Gerhard von Buchka, an admirer of Scharlach and head of the Kolonialabteilung between 1898 and 1900. They were formulated at a time when the conquest of the colonies had been largely completed and the era of open violence was ending. Colonial scandals had been aired in the Reichstag and in the press, and men like Waldemar Horn, governor of Togo from 1902 to 1905, and von Puttkamer had been driven from office.

Economic reform now had considerable support within the ranks of the German colonial establishment. Administrators such as Rechenberg in East Africa, Seitz, governor of Cameroun from 1907 to 1910 and of South-West Africa from 1910 to 1915, and Zech, governor of Togo from 1905 to 1910, displayed a more enlightened outlook than their predecessors. Seitz was convinced that Africans should take a limited part in the local self-government of Cameroun; education, he argued, should not be designed merely to turn blacks into "tools" of the white man. He believed that the future of the Cameroun economy rested on the cultivation of indigenous food crops rather than on the production of rubber for an unstable world market. Despite their various disagreements regarding colonial matters, these men were in accord that Africans must play a more active part in the economic development of their respective countries. Germany could not afford to rule through coercion alone.

The Logistic Infrastructure

Dernburg's logistic program emphasized the construction of railways and port facilities, projects which appealed to soldiers and administrators and also served the interests of heavy industry. More capital flowed into the colonies, where the big banks began to set up a network of branches. "Economic reform" met the wishes of merchants like Vietor who regarded Africans as producers and as actual or potential customers. In Dernburg's day—and long afterward—many missionaries, administrators, and settlers were in the habit of denouncing the popularity of "luxuries" among Africans, who supposedly spent their hard-earned cash on "useless" merchandise. Dernburg and others realized that the increasing sale of clothes, tools, utensils, and consumption goods such as tea, matches, or salt indicated a rise in the customers' living standards and rational economic choices.

The settler communities who accused Dernburg of "negrophilism" were riddled by economic contradictions. Consider, for example, the competition for African labor: an East African labor commissioner observed that "the planters were heaping up trouble on their own heads by outbidding one another with regard to wages and work quotas." Whether they realized it or not, "economic reform" was in the interest of the more efficient employers who could attract workmen by providing better conditions, and who could see no reason why the government should subsidize their competitors by supplying them with forced labor below market cost. The value of conscripts diminished when German plantation companies began to use steam plows— expensive and complex machinery that could not be entrusted to unwilling and unskilled draftees.

Dernburg's "new course" did not mean a totally new departure. Togo, where access to navigable waterways had favored commerce in tropical crops, owed its prosperity to African farmers who sold palm oil, palm kernels, and similar products. Taxation remained relatively low; in the southern districts Africans were expected to work for twelve days a year on public works, but could obtain exemption in return for a small payment. Dernburg and his associates were able to build on existing foundations, and the new economic policy, despite its many limitations, exerted considerable impact on the empire.

The effect of metropolitan reforms on colonial practice was limited. Dernburg preferred market incentives to the compulsory cultivation of crops, but at a distant outstation such as Mwanza in the northwestern part of East Africa, the local administrator had little difficulty disregarding instructions. Though he was censured by Dernburg and Rechenberg for his rough treatment of Africans, official reprimands did not prevent Theodor Gunzert from initiating a coercive system of village agricultural quotas in the Mwanza district that differed little from the system previously established by Governor Götzen.[5] Gunzert's career is discussed in chapter 5. Forced labor continued under various guises, as did brutal beatings. As a rule, German officials had been beaten as children in Lateinschulen and Kadettenanstalten, where teachers were regarded as the students' natural enemies; as adults, these former students often made a habit of beating Africans for disciplinary reasons. In 1912, 8,057 floggings were administered in German East African courts—48 percent of a total of 18,868 sentences; in *British* East African courts, on the other hand, of 9,113 persons convicted, 380 were flogged—4.2 percent of the total.[6]

The general difference in character between British and German colonial administration was apparent to many observers. In 1909 a German naval officer forwarding a confidential report to the Kaiser expressed outrage concerning British administrative practices in West Africa. The British, he contended, were a lax lot. As a result, Africans dwelling along the littoral of the Gold Coast and Nigeria regarded themselves as the equals of white men, rarely saluting even provincial commissioners. Local whites favored the unification of Southern Nigeria with Northern Nigeria, where the natives were not as yet so "insolent" and were treated in a more rigorous fashion. The German officer saw the British example as having an evil influence on Togo, where the indigenous people were impressed by school facilities provided by the British and where exaggerated tales were spread concerning the privileges to which black men were entitled under the Union Jack.[7]

Nevertheless, there was a gradual shift in German values and some abuses were eliminated. Dernburg carried more political and financial weight than any civil servant, however well-born. His reforms led to a substantial increase in private investments in the colonies, and trade expanded dramatically (see Appendix Table E.6). The Reichstag for the first time was willing to spend substantial funds to improve internal communications in the colonies. A fairly extensive transport system was completed; telegraph lines connecting the German colonies with a worldwide system of cable communications were built; shipping services were improved. Just prior to World War I a major wireless station was installed at Kamina in Togo; it was the largest in Africa and was intended to be the chief reception and distribution center for all other German colonial stations. Ironically, the announcement concerning the declaration of war in 1914 was probably the last important message received from Berlin before the station was taken over by Allied troops.

Most important, the Germans began to build railways at a furious pace. Largely because of his business background and his influential connections, Dernburg managed to circumvent the reluctance of the Reichsschatzamt to make loans for railway development and succeeded in mobilizing the required capital, which came mainly from the leading German banks and other large enterprises. During his administration the Reichstag voted a total of 265 million marks ($63.4 million) for building railroads or for guaranteeing private loans. Eight years after Dernburg took office as Kolonialdirektor, the German colonial empire could boast an operating railway system with some 4,500 kilometers of track —a noteworthy achievement, far exceeding the 2,000 kilometers in French West Africa, the 1,200 kilometers in the Belgian Congo (1912), and even the approximately 3,200 kilometers in working order in British Rhodesia.

The construction of this rail network, often under the most difficult climatic and topographic conditions, brought profound changes at every level in the colonies. Infinitely cheaper than porterage, rail transport was indispensable to agricultural development. Kurt Hassert, an economic geographer, calculated that a single railway car could carry as much as ten ox-wagons or 300 carriers; a caravan would require about two months to reach Lake Victoria from the Indian Ocean while the Uganda railway could traverse the same distance in two days. The major part of the railroad systems in the African colonies once under the Kaiser's sway were pioneered during the Wilhelmian period.

The railway network was supplemented by the building of feeder roads—a construction program which was especially successful in Togo, providing a grid of routes and rest houses covering the entire country. Some roads were built with an eye to future motor transport, but the most common vehicle was the bicycle, which—in Togo at least—was already in wide use by Africans during the first decade of this century. As previously noted, the Germans also strung telegraph lines and improved port facilities in various parts of their empire. These innovations changed the logistics of governance beyond recognition. Men, merchandise, and munitions could move much more rapidly; remote areas became more accessible; administrators in distant stations could be supervised more effectively from the center, and in turn could draw more easily on outside help.

In building this new infrastructure the Germans relied primarily on public initiative. Nearly all colonial railways were publicly owned. One of the few exceptions to state capitalism was the so-called Nordbahn line in Cameroun, which went inland a distance of about 160 kilometers from the port of Bonaberri, providing transportation through the difficult forest zone and enabling the Germans to reach the savannah belt. The Nordbahn was owned by the Kamerun Eisenbahn und Betriebsgesellschaft, founded in 1905 with a capital of 17 million marks. This company, which received an imperial guarantee of 3 percent interest on a maximum of 11 million marks, was so successful that dividends were paid one year after the line began to operate in 1911. In 1908 the Reichstag voted funds to guarantee a loan of some 40 million marks for a state-owned line, the Mittellandbahn, which would proceed from the port of Duala to the Njong River, whence transportation would continue by water. Further extensions were planned but not completed. In addition the Germans created new port facilities, especially at Duala, where a dry dock was opened in 1905. In Togo the transport system centered on Lome; three railway lines were built to promote trade, to unify the country logistically, and to further reduce the need for outlets in British territory.

The East African interior at first depended to a considerable extent on the British Uganda railway, whose transport facilities stimulated African cash-crop cultivation in the Lake Victoria region, with the result that the Germany colony became the foremost producer of ground nuts in eastern Africa. Planners such as Rathenau were impressed by what they considered the bold concept of the British, who at great initial expense and risk built the Uganda line in advance of economic development. Despite considerable opposition, Dernburg and Rechenberg decided to extend the existing line from Dar es Salaam to Morogoro through to the Great Lakes. The most powerful of the settler groups would have preferred to extend the northern railway in East Africa, but the central line was to become the spinal column of an extensive system which would open the entire territory. Its construction entailed a commitment to develop African agriculture, and was also helpful to the army. Strategic considerations were always present in the minds of staff officers who during the Maji-Maji uprising had had to rely on the goodwill of their British neighbors to rush a detachment to Lake Victoria by means of the Uganda railway in order to abort a threatened revolt among the Sukuma and the Nyamwezi.

By 1912, when the line had been completed to Tabora, plans were approved for its extension to Lake Tanganyika; construction was also begun to extend the northern line which went from Tanga inland and which was designed to facilitate European settlement and to compete with the Uganda railway. These railways were the making of the ports of Tanga and Dar es Salaam, though the Germans never had an opportunity to fully utilize the economic potential of the new railways. To open the southern part of the colony they considered running a track from Kilwa to Lake Nyasa, but they lacked the time to bring the project to fruition.

These extensive building projects were linked to prevailing misconceptions of Africa's supposed fertility and untapped wealth.[8] Few officials or promoters realized that the colony of East Africa had neither the people nor the goods to support three major railroads even if the Germans had had the money to build them. The proposed Tanga line extension paralleled the Uganda railway and would have served the same area, but the Uganda line—running through two colonies and tapping other colonies on Lake Victoria—at first could not support itself. (A similar lack of realism led to two major railways being built to serve the Belgian Congo.) In the end, the Germans wrecked their own handiwork. In World War I, Commonwealth troops under General Smuts invaded East Africa, fighting down the Tanga and central lines. The Germans destroyed the lines to deny their use to invading Allied forces, taking out bridges and rails and blowing up most of the rolling stock, but they were soon restored by the Allies.[9]

Of the railway systems in all the German colonies, the most extensive was that of South-West Africa. By 1912—when the main part had been completed—the territory was covered by some 2,100 miles of track. The oldest line, which opened in 1902 and ran from Swakopmund to Windhuk, had been put in by the German military and played an essential part in the conquest of the colony. In its construction the Germans pursued a labor policy exceptional in southern Africa: they imported numbers of white workmen to do rough navvying as well as skilled and supervisory work. By 1902 the employed whites numbered 370. Swakopmund, despite its many deficiencies as a port, served as the outlet for a line running northward to Tsumeb which principally served the needs of the mining industry. This track was laid by the private enterprise of the Otavi Minen und Eisenbahngesellschaft, formed to exploit copper deposits in the northern part of the colony. In addition to using African prisoners of war, the Germans hired a number of Italian laborers, but these immigrants were apt to strike and were sufficiently sophisticated to sue their employer in local courts over the terms of their engagement. The Germans therefore relied mainly on Africans to build and run the line, which required the creation of a special training school for African personnel.

Research and Development

The Germans paid a great deal of attention to scientific research and to agricultural instruction in promoting their colonial estates. During the last decade of their colonization in Africa they began to take pride in their success as "scientific colonizers," a claim largely justified by the extent and scope of experiment and research. The transfer of agricultural skill was effected both by private and public enterprise. Officially sponsored research had its origin with the Kolonialwirtschaftliche Komitee, which aimed at combining scientific research with practical experimental work and colonial propaganda, and which issued technical publications such as *Der Tropenpflanzer* (an agricultural journal) as well as specialized monographs. Its work was supported by the Botanische Zentralstelle in Berlin, an organization that functioned as a clearing house for botanical and related studies and received information from various newly established colonial institutions.

These institutions included the Biologisch-Landwirtschaftliche Institut in Amani, East Africa, created in 1902 to study the flora and fauna of the territory, to carry out agricultural experiments, to investigate and improve existing agricultural practices, and to disseminate information by means of publications and a program of instruction. The institute contained botanical and chemical laboratories, and did research on the raising of tropical plants, manuring, and other agricultural matters. Research on a large scale was carried out at a botanical gardens at Victoria in Cameroun, and experimental gardens were set up in the more important administrative stations to furnish additional data.

The Germans paid special attention to the cultivation of cotton because experts feared that the textile industries of the Reich might be faced with severe price fluctuations in cotton or even a worldwide scarcity of this vital raw material. British and French colonizers also stressed cotton-growing in order to become independent of American suppliers. As previously noted (chapter 6), in 1900 the Kolonialwirtschaftliche Komitee began to promote cotton farming as far afield as Togo, Cameroun, and East Africa, and the work was soon intensified. Between 1910 and 1914 the Germans set up six additional cotton research stations and three general experimental stations. Coercion of the kind used before the Maji-Maji rebellion was not resorted to, and economic incentives and persuasion were relied upon. African agricultural demonstrators provided expert advice, and the government furnished seed free of charge, with the result that cotton became an important cash crop. At the same time it was realized that for technical reasons and to increase general productivity the cultivation of cotton would have to be integrated with other agricultural activities, and experimental stations devoted to cotton were expanded to help with various other forms of farming.

By 1910 development had progressed to such an extent that an administrative division of labor became indispensable. The Kolonialwirtschaftliche Komitee was charged with the technical aspects of cotton cultivation, the construction of ginning stations, the purchase of cotton at guaranteed prices, the distribution of prizes, the provision of loans, the control and inspection of cotton quality, and similar functions. The colonial administration was responsible for establishing experimental stations, for conducting campaigns against plant disease, and for the organization of meteorological and related services. Separate agricultural departments were set up in each of the colonies, and by 1914 the agricultural staff of Togo, for example, consisted of fifteen officers of various grades, five assistant agriculturists, and a number of subordinate instructors.

To broaden the base of this program the Germans provided instruction at a number of technical institutions such as the agricultural school at Nuatjä in Togo, where students were given a three-year course in arable farming, cattle raising, the art of plowing, and similar agricultural techniques. Their training completed, alumni were furnished with agricultural equipment and sent off to farm on their own. Experiments were conducted with many varieties of cotton as well as with maize, beans, ground nuts, and other food crops; pastoral farming and planning techniques were studied. In Cameroun, Africans were trained as plantation managers at an agricultural school attached to the institute at Victoria; the Germans created cattle-breeding stations, a forestry department, and a rubber inspectorate with its own stations.[10] In South-West Africa the government joined private enterprise in drilling boreholes for wells and in building dams, and a water department was started with two geologists providing technical advice—considerably extending the area suitable for settlement. The government carried out large-scale research, and by 1914 was operating an experimental station for arable farming, a tobacco station, an experimental horse ranch, a sheep ranch, and an ostrich farm, as well as five experimental stations for truck farming.

The Germans were among the first to give technical educations to some of their emigrants to Africa. These emigrants went to the prestigious Kolonialinstitut at Hamburg, the Seminar für Orientalische Sprachen at the University of Berlin, the Deutsche Kolonialschule at Witzenhausen, and the Kolonialakademie at Halle (see chapter 3). A medical man anxious to serve in the colonies found facilities for specialized study at institutes in Berlin, Hamburg, and Tübingen.

The Material Achievements of German Colonialism

In 1879 Friedrich Fabri, a former mission inspector, wrote what has since become a famous book in German colonial historiography entitled *Does Germany Need Colonies?* He argued that colonies were necessary to the Reich as a market for its exports, as a source of raw materials, and as a place where German emigrants might find new homes under German rule, thus saving the fatherland from the menace of overpopulation. Fabri believed also that colonization would provide a social safety valve and would impede the revolutionary aspirations of the Social Democrats. Within the colonies the Germans would help to civilize and to Christianize the indigenous peoples. Fabri's study was therefore an essay both in political advocacy and in futurology.

However, none of his predictions came true. German colonization helped to spread the gospel in Africa, but the Germans did not "civilize" their dependencies in the sense intended by Fabri. German enterprise played a part in creating a new African elite—a thin stratum of literate craftsmen, junior civil servants, teachers, and cash farmers —but these men were never regarded as part of German society overseas, and few Germans bothered to accord to Africans even the polite address of *Sie* as distinct from the familiar *Du*.

In terms of trade and investment, the importance of the colonies to the German metropolitan economy was negligible (see Appendix Table E.7). The structure of exports altered as consumption goods like gin and beads increasingly gave way to sophisticated merchandise such as mining equipment and rolling-stock, a change reflecting the wider transformation of the German economy. German businessmen, however, had only a marginal interest overseas, and British trade occupied an important position throughout the German colonial empire. German entrepreneurs failed to create a colonial economy for themselves, although the volume and the proportionate share of the Reich in colonial commerce increased during the Dernburg era.

Some colonial propagandists such as Gustav Schmoller, the social historian, had assumed that Germany's external empire would help to solve her internal problems. The colonies, for examples, might ease academic unemployment by supplying jobs for surplus university graduates. In practice, however, the colonies were too insignificant to function as a social safety-valve; they continued to be ruled and policed by a tiny elite whose numbers were too small to affect the employment situation at home. Moreover, the colonies were far from the El Dorado pictured by chauvinist propaganda and by the more dishonest kind of stock-exchange prospectuses. The dependencies failed to yield substantial public revenues and had to be subsidized by the German taxpayers (see Appendix Table E.8).

The colonies raised revenues through taxation, customs, and other imposts, but the Reich had to cover their deficits through a variety of subventions. After 1908 a number of major items relating to colonial expenditure were covered by loans guaranteed by the Reich. Togo, East Africa, and Cameroun raised loans of their own, and exceptional expenditures in South-West Africa—e.g., railways and major public works projects—were financed directly through Reich loans. While some colonial entrepreneurs made a great deal of money, the majority of these enterprises failed to meet their founders' expectations. The colonial reality was far different from the dream world of superprofits depicted by stock exchange prospectuses and by subsequent socialist polemics, and imperialism did not resolve the real or supposed contradictions of German capitalism. By 1913 the total number of firms in all German colonies, including those in the South Seas, was 399; their capital amounted to 506.08 million marks (see Appendix Table E.9).

During the 1906–14 period, the rate of colonial profits slowly increased, but a good deal of money continued to be lost (see Appendix Table E.10). Selected dividends earned annually by firms in different sectors of the colonial economy before World War I are shown in Appendix Table E.11, indicating that much colonial investment remained highly speculative in nature. In African terms, however, a major change occurred. The Germans laid the foundations of infrastructures of roads, ports, and railways for Cameroun, Togo, Tanganyika (East Africa), and South-West Africa; they pioneered modern health, educational, and agricultural services—albeit on a small scale; during the last decade of their rule each colony achieved a miniature Wirtschafts-wunder (economic miracle), and the export of tropical crops expanded considerably (see Appendix Table E.12). But in metropolitan terms the empire remained of marginal importance both for the nation's economy and for German society.

TEN

The Social Impact of Conquest

The overall social impact of German colonization on the African territories was extremely varied. Conditions differed greatly between different colonies such as Togo and South-West Africa, and even within the borders of the same territory; in South-West Africa, for example, German colonialism shattered the fabric of Herero life while leaving the Ovambo people almost unaffected. A social history of the several German colonies would fill a volume; a brief case study of East Africa —the most important German colony—will have to suffice here.

Like all colonial creations, East Africa is an artificial unit. Geographically the coastal region has nothing in common with the lake country of the interior or with the magnificent snow-capped splendor of Mount Kilimanjaro; the ethnographic map is also immensely varied, as is the cultural configuration. Many of the pre-colonial societies of eastern Africa seem to have had one feature in common, however: they were all affected by a widespread crisis occasioned in large part by the inland advance of the slave trade and of the gunpowder frontier.

Slave Trade and Ivory

Long before the arrival of the Germans, the Swahili-speaking peoples of Zanzibar and along the East African coast had developed their own civilization based on plantation agriculture, handicraft production, and maritime commerce, but technical skills were scarce and as a whole eastern Africa suffered from serious economic disabilities. Traders on the coast did some business in palm oil, but the most profitable merchandise was cloves, widely used in cookery and confectionery. Clove cultivation required a good deal of cheap, unskilled labor. Until white farmers introduced such new crops as coffee, sisal, and pyrethrum, and until white entrepreneurs constructed railways, most of East Africa lacked export crops that did not require slave labor for their cultivation.

Inland traders made profits by exporting goods of small bulk and high value such as ivory, a product of exceptional worth, or by trading in slaves, who were capable of traveling on foot. The Zanzibaris lacked sufficient manpower to perform their required agricultural tasks, and they did not command the financial or administrative resources to organize a system of free labor migration. Hence they employed slaves—men and women whose work was not paid for but coerced. Slaves were also exported to the markets of southern Arabia, Persia, and the islands of Réunion—a traffic which continued until it was disrupted and finally eliminated by Western men-of-war.

Muslim slavery, as practiced in the plantations and townhouses of the coast, was usually a tolerable form of servitude. There were many social gradations among slaves. Some slaves acquired wealth of their own; some were placed in authority over free labor; a few even rose to high office. Even the plantation laborers, the most poorly treated of all, did not necessarily lead lives of misery. Sir Harry Johnston, an experienced British administrator, thought that an African bondsman usually led a better life than a convert at a mission station with its regular hours of work, its plain diet, its compulsory charity, and its strict ban on "exhilarating orgies."[1]

The trade in slaves was a different matter. From an economist's point of view, the commerce in captives might be described as Africa's primary labor migration. The slavers brought new goods to the interior—weapons, cloth, bangles—but in human terms the cost of the traffic was heavy. In its pursuit, homes were broken, villages burnt, grain stores looted, crops ravaged. Many slaves perished on the road to captivity; many died through associated famine or disease. According to Wissmann, between four and five persons perished for every slave who reached the coast. Some native states such as the warlike Hehe in the south and the Gogo in the north succeeded in repelling the slavers, but the long-term effects of the traffic on the area as a whole were deleterious.

The incidence and severity of slavery differed widely from district to district in East Africa. In Tabora about 67 percent of the population were slaves; in Lindi about 50 percent; in Kilwa 40 to 50 percent. The economic importance of slave labor sharply diminished in the interior and played little part in the highlands; the Chagga had only a mild form of debt slavery, and the Konde had no slaves at all. It is hard to estimate the total number of slaves in the territory as a whole, but it was probably between 165,000 and 200,000.

There were also variations from district to district in the amount of labor extracted from the slaves. On the coast in Kilwa and on the great estates at Pangani and Tanga, slaves were expected to labor five days a week, in Bagamoyo and Lindi, estate-owners were satisfied with three days' labor a week. Working hours varied from seven hours a day in leisurely run plantations to ten hours in establishments such as those of Pemba, which operated more rigorously. Some slaves were employed as independent laborers or as traders, and were obliged to hand over only part of their earnings to their masters—the lord's share ranging from one-half of the slave's income in Zanzibar to one third in Dar es Salaam and Tabora and to as little as one-fifth in Kilwa.[2] Working conditions were best in the city and worst in the countryside. In general the Muslim slave-owners were accounted better employers than the Europeans because the masters themselves were lethargic and made fewer demands on themselves and their workmen than did the Germans.

More significant than the commerce in slaves was the traffic in ivory. The uses of ivory in the nineteenth century were many and novel; in some ways it played the same part as plastics do in the twentieth century, and as European luxury industries expanded, the demand for ivory steadily increased. It was fashioned into billiard balls, piano keys, cutlery handles, and the wide variety of knicknacks with which Victorians crammed their parlors. India, known to merchants as the "backbone of the trade," purchased enormous quantities of ivory rings left over from the turning of billiard balls and sold them in bazaars as women's bangles; Indian craftsmen used the material for carving toys and ornaments. All producers of ivory goods preferred African to Indian elephant tusks, and by 1870 Africa was estimated to supply some 85 percent of the world's ivory.

The first hunters and traders concentrated on elephant herds along the coast; as these herds were gradually decimated, the traders sought tusks farther and farther inland. Africans who wanted to buy goods but had no ivory to exchange would pay for their purchases with slaves. Thus the slave trade became a symptom of a balance-of-payments problem facing a backward tribel economy anxious to acquire such manufactured goods as cloth and muskets. Thugs lacking salable merchandise would abduct prisoners for sale abroad or to be used as ransom for ivory, making up for lack of capital by the use of violence. As commerce in ivory grew more competitive and as more and more African communities acquired firearms, violence increased, and the effects of the traffic became more serious.

Guns became new instruments of warfare, changed the techniques of hunting, and accelerated the destruction of the elephant herds. Firearms became a prestige symbol, a potent implement that could not be fashioned by customary modes of production. Their importation increased the rate of casualties in war; they exalted the power of chiefs and warlords who commanded advanced weapons or who acquired local monopolies in them; they hastened the consolidation of indigenous states, great and small; and they provided the native people with a host of new goods. In all they had a profound effect upon the development of African culture.

The long-term economic effects of the East African slave and ivory trade are hard to assess. Harsh as it was, the commerce promoted the importation of new products—textiles, guns, knives, pots and pans, beads and trinkets—thereby increasing local consumption by linking backward tribesmen to a wider world economy. But a hunting and man-catching economy ultimately depended on wasting assets; it could not provide the basis for lasting prosperity. The promoters of the ivory trade rarely built up large fortunes, and the stories told by many European explorers concerning the east coast Arabs' luxury were heavily overdrawn. Gross profits of the ivory trade may have been high, but against these the entrepreneur had to set the expense of porterage, the usurious interest on borrowed capital (sometimes as high as 100 percent) the wasted time, and the risk of total loss.

The commerce in ivory also contributed to the creation of a free labor force working for wages. The Nyamwezi people on the high plateau of what is now central Tanzania came to occupy an important position in pre-colonial commerce: they hired themselves out as caravan porters and grew expert in a skilled and relatively well-remunerated occupation. After helping their wives prepare the fields for planting, the men would leave their villages to work as porters for six months. Those who were successful gained prestige and positions of leadership. The number of porters was large—an estimated 100,000 of them passed through Bagamoyo each year in the early 1890's. While not lost to their tribal society, caravan porters tended to become detribalized by their travels and their exposure to new forces outside their village and clan. On their return the porters were undoubtedly a disturbing influence to tribal authorities and to local mores because they had experienced much freedom and had seen new ways unknown to those who had stayed at home. The Nyamwezi people later made an important contribution to the East African economy as plantation workers and askaris.

Caravan leaders intermarried with indigenous people, producing the Swahili language, which became the lingua franca throughout much of what is now Tanzania and through parts of the territories now comprised within Malawi, Kenya, and Uganda. The Arabs spread the religion of Islam in the interior, helping to free many East African communities from their intellectual isolation. Islam remained a minority religion, but it helped to modify many of the traditional societies. Its practice required no great investment, no elaborate network of churches and training institutions, and it was tolerant of African polygamy. Conversion to Islam entailed a variety of social benefits: proselytes joined the fraternity of the faithful and became heirs to a great literate civilization. There was even an element of class distinction in acceptance of the faith: the askari garrison at Bukoba insisted on being circumcised because the Arabized prostitutes would not sleep with uncircumcised men.[3] Religious conversion, trade, and cash crops were all to change indigenous customs.

Governance, Labor, and Life Styles

The German conquest of East Africa was a long drawn-out process which may have intensified pre-colonial violence in many areas, but in the end the Germans acquired a monopoly in the use of armed force. Militarized communities such as the Ngoni and the Hehe ceased to prey on their neighbors' women and cattle, and there was an end to heroic life styles that stressed courage in battle and linked a man's status as a warrior with his right to marry and his kinship obligations. The Germans used corporal punishment widely, but they did away with the more lurid sanctions imposed by various forms of indigenous law on convicted adulterers, murderers, witches, and traitors. The traffic in slaves was liquidated; the age of great armed migrations ended; independent African armies were shattered; pre-colonial "restraints on trade" disappeared. The Ngoni of East Africa, for example, had set up a conquering state—one of many Ngoni kingdoms ultimately derived from South Africa. Within this warlike monarchy, warriors of true Ngoni birth had held all positions of real power. Once the Germans had conquered the land, the Ngoni ceased to prey on their neighbors. The Ngoni ruling group lost its accustomed privileges— tributes, a regular supply of captives, profits derived from trade in slaves and ivory, the notion of absolute Ngoni superiority. The subordinate *sutu*, on the other hand, benefited in certain respects from the *Pax Germanica*. The sutu could now freely sell their labor and keep their earnings, being no longer obliged to yield their wealth to their erstwhile masters; they were able to participate in commerce by collecting wild rubber, a commodity then much in demand; they could freely till the land and dispose of its fruits as they wished. The German appearance probably brought about a gradual diffusion of wealth in Ngoni society. Not surprisingly, Ngoni resistance to the Germans during the Maji-Maji uprising was far from united, as many sutu refused to take up arms against the whites, or did so only under duress.[4]

The colonial administration reorganized the pre-colonial power structure. The Hehe dynasty was broken up, and district chiefs were declared independent; Masai and Arabs could no longer attack villages to steal their women and cattle or to seek slaves. Because villagers had no further need to live close together for protection, they spread out more readily, and areas once left uncultivated as protective zones between tribes were now farmed. Unpopular rulers grew less secure in their power when dissidents could pack up and leave their chief or call on the colonial government to replace him. Before the Germans arrived, the death of a chief often produced violence and a struggle for power; after they came, rival candidates for a chieftainship could not kill their opponents, and opposition to the government's candidate had to be muted. To escape decisions they did not like in their own courts or to avoid traditional obligations, Africans sometimes appealed to the Europeans; porters frequently ignored or defied tribal authorities, claiming that they now would obey only white men.

Under the new dispensation, tribal leaders tended to divide into two factions: those who opposed the colonial system and those who accepted it. The chief stood between the colonists and his people, and few could have found it easy to reconcile the competing interests of the two groups. Minor government officials—askaris, police, and messengers—could make life miserable for the chief and his people by petty tyrannies and demands for food, drink, women, huts, or bribes. Many Africans believed that the Europeans possessed evil powers. Prophets and religious leaders called for the expulsion of the Germans; an uprising of the Gaya of Kavirondo was caused by a magician who told them to drive out the whites. (The Maji-Maji were only the most famous of many tribal insurgents.)

Gradually popular confidence in the German administration of East Africa increased. The district court was an important agent of white penetration. It was an appeals court based on customary law; a judge and assessors heard the cases, and the latter were frequently Arabs and Swahilis. Native interpreters were usually needed; with so many clans, tribes, and nations living together, no one knew all the laws involved. New types of cases came before the courts, and new laws had to be made. Cases between inland Africans and whites usually involved cattle theft or cattle disease carriers, the treatment of African laborers, or game protection; theft and assault, whoring and drinking cases were more common on the coast.[5]

Different traditions made it difficult to determine the truth in many cases. Arabs in a court of law took the Western-style formal oath seriously; Africans did not. Names were confusing, and Africans hid their identity whenever possible. The colonial courts were easily deceived, especially by the more sophisticated Africans, who worked with the court orderlies and interpreters to exploit the Germans' ignorance of African law, customs, and languages. Meanwhile, traditional tribal courts still sat and their procedures continued—illegally. Poison, hot metal, or boiling water ordeals were still used to determine guilt or innocence—usually in cases of adultery, theft, treason, or witchcraft. It was difficult to reconcile European and African laws and create new statutes to serve the colonial conditions.

The East African economic systems had to meet a variety of new challenges. Modes of shifting agriculture required the existence of plentiful land reserves so that exhausted soils could be abandoned; land allotments were made to cultivators by the community. In backward areas the division of labor was largely along sexual lines—the men were warriors, herders, and hunters while the women cultivated the fields; the only farm tools were simple hoes and knives. Changes were attempted by the Germans, but these were not always successful. Thus veld-burning continued, as did the constant movement of villages and farms; the spade failed to replace the hoe. The plow, a major improvement in farming, was not widely accepted because it upset the traditional division of labor and necessitated a radical change in agricultural sex roles; moreover, plows cost a great deal of money, and cattle were not trained to pull them.

Africans initially knew more about farming in tropical conditions than did the Europeans, and they resisted such ill-planned innovations as the introduction of rice, which attracted locusts and required more labor than traditional crops. Resistance to change often derived from economic realities—lack of markets and deficiencies of transport; when the road and rail systems improved, the farmers took more readily to cash cropping. They also began to earn money by collecting wild rubber, ivory, and copal, apparently without any great pressure of the kind that caused scandal in the Congo Free State and French Equatorial Africa. By 1905 the value of exported rubber from East Africa was 2.5 million marks.

Government agronomists and district officers helped with advice, with seeds, seedlings, planting, pest control—and with pressure. East Africans took quickly to planting coco-palms and copra, less readily to cotton. Technically cotton was the most difficult crop to grow and harvest, and was subject to rapid price changes on the world market; government pressure and a guaranteed minimum price, however, saved cotton-growing so that by 1912 the colony exported 1.881 million kg. Coffee was successfully produced near Mount Kilimanjaro, and in 1912 its export value was 749,079 marks.

Economic change could have been faster had the colonial government provided African farmers with more support—transport, agricultural experiment stations, and credit. But although Dernburg and Rechenberg thought of East Africa as a colony to be developed by African peasant farmers, European settlers kept arriving. These settlers demanded and received increasing government attention; more important, they absorbed a great deal of African labor.

By 1913 the German demand for African labor in East Africa was considerable (see Table 22). Of an estimated total of 165,000 African wage-earners, 139,500 worked for Europeans; another 6,000 were askaris. Raum estimates that 70 percent of the total East African labor force was employed by Europeans on plantations, as porters, or as laborers.[6] The implications of this were far-reaching. Linked to the development of a wage economy was the imposition of taxes designed to raise revenue, which induced African cultivators to take up paid employment. By 1910 Africans had become accustomed to paying their taxes in cash rather than in labor or in kind, as they had done formerly. Sanctions against non-payment were severe—huts were burnt and cattle confiscated—so tax defaulters were not numerous. Between 1910–11 and 1912–13 the tax yield from all sources rose from 3,708,745 to 5,096,173 marks. By 1910 the value of European agricultural production in Africa began to overtake that of the Africans, and by 1912 European production reached a value of 19 million marks compared to African production valued at only 12 million marks—though these figures, like most early colonial statistics, are somewhat speculative.[7]

In East Africa, wage labor conflicted with indigenous slavery, which was abolished more slowly and cautiously in the German colonies than in British possessions. German antislavery forces were not as vocal and well-organized as those in Great Britain, and the system of governance of slaves depended to a considerable extent on a partnership with Swahili-speaking people whom the Germans did not want to alienate. Moreover, the Germans were concerned by the rising rate of urban crime in Zanzibar, where slavery had been ended abruptly. In 1901 a Verordnung by the Reichskanzler permitted slaves to work for two days on their own account; in addition, they could no longer be sold without their own consent, and aged slaves, whether bondsmen or freed, had to be cared for by their masters. The administration subsequently issued an ever-increasing number of letters of manumission to individuals—48,079 in all. Finally, in 1904 a new Verfügung provided that all children born after the end of the year should be freed.

The ex-slave who entered wage employment was paid in cash, which enabled him to purchase more goods, including imported merchandise

TABLE 22
Estimated African Employment in East Africa, 1913

Type of employment	Number	Type of employment	Number
Plantations	91,892	Porterage	20,000
Mines	3,000	Mission stations	3,000
Railway construction	13,000	Servants	19,000
Railway employees	4,000	Sailors	1,200
Railway maintenance	3,000	Total African wage earners	172,000[a]
Government service	5,000	Total African wage earners	
Business	2,500	employed by whites	139,500

SOURCE: O. F. Raum, "German East Africa: Changes in African Tribal Life under German Administration, 1892–1914," in *History of East Africa*, ed. Vincent Harlow et al. (Oxford, 1965), 2:191–92.
[a] Includes approximately 6,000 askaris.

such as textiles. Local weavers faced stiff competition from machine-made imports, with the result that cloth became cheaper. Many African groups resisted wearing European dress, but in time familiarity with European fashion became a mark of prestige. The importation of European cloth had unanticipated indirect consequences: because imported apparel had to be washed regularly with soap (unlike local cloth, which was smeared with ochre), cheap textiles probably did more to improve standards of health and cleanliness than the pioneer doctors' medical efforts.

The availability of new goods made more Africans willing to work for money, but their chiefs often imposed additional labor demands on them in order to acquire new symbols of power such as uniforms and stone houses. These required money and outside artisans, which strained tribal budgets. The shape of the traditional round hut was influenced by colonial rule: the escape door in the huts in Usambara was eliminated because it was no longer needed to provide an escape in the event of a surprise attack by hostile warriors; the central fireplace was often replaced by a lamp and by blankets to keep the sleepers warm; with the spread of reading and writing, tables and chairs were introduced. Eventually, with the addition of windows and Western furniture, the round hut was converted into a rectangular house divided into livingroom, bedroom, and kitchen.

As roads and railways were built in East Africa, new markets selling many new goods sprang up along them. Villagers were able to sell more of their cattle, fish, grain, and vegetables; sewing machines and bicycles, tailors and repair shops appeared; markets grew as the purchasing power of the Africans increased and their wants became more varied. Rail transportation opened the colony to inland travel—by 1908 the Usambara railroad was carrying over 200,000 passengers per year. Towns and cities grew: the combined urban population of the ten largest cities in East Africa was 100,000 in 1905. Throughout the colony government buildings, rail depots, churches, hotels, barracks, bomas, stores, and farmhouses became common sights.

The total demographic impact of these innovations is hard to assess, given the inadequacy of surviving statistics. The effect of German conquest on the health of the people was double-edged. Warfare and conquest brought not only battle casualties but also hunger, sickness, and venereal disease; particularly before the era of reform, Africans succumbed to a wide variety of illnesses, especially disorders of the lungs and nutritional deficiencies. In Cameroun, for instance, the death rate of plantation laborers in 1905–6 has been estimated at 10 percent per annum. Labor migration entailed innumerable afflictions until the Germans began to take measures to license recruiters and to better the migrants' lot by providing rest houses along the roads to work and insisting on better food, better accommodations, and sanitary facilities.

Because of wide variations in the conditions prevalent in a single colony, the total effect of these reform measures is difficult to assess. The 1912 official report for East Africa complained that the planters in the Morogoro district continued to resist health measures that had long been accepted by employers in the north of the colony: water supplies, sanitation facilities, and medical treatment for workers remained inadequate. This state of affairs, said the report, was due to the fact that the Morogoro plantations were still being developed and as yet had failed to yield profits. Conditions on the more established plantations in the Arusha district were far superior, largely because employers were able to hire local rather than migrant workers.

The Germans made efforts to ameliorate health conditions by inoculating Africans against smallpox, isolating lepers in special villages, attempting to treat sleeping-sickness, and setting up hospitals. By 1913 there were 120 German doctors at work in the colonies, and the number of Africans treated in government institutions had increased from 4,516 in 1904 to 100,348.[8] The first beneficiaries of the new medical services were probably members of the African elite, soldiers, and junior civil servants, while those in more remote areas were little affected. It seems likely, however, that the demographic expansion which has characterized the former German territories over the past half-century began during the end of the German era.[9]

Urban Life

Like other European colonialists, the Germans were townbuilders par excellence. In South-West Africa, for example, there had been no cities before their arrival; primitive economies such as those of the Nama, the Ovambo, and the Herero were unable to sustain urban life. An inland center like Windhuk or a port like Swakopmund owed its existence to German colonial enterprise. In East Africa the Germans to some extent built upon existing foundations. Sultan Seyyid Majid, the ruler of Zanzibar, had planned to develop a major port and trading center at Dar es Salaam on the shore of the Indian Ocean, but he died in 1870 before his palace and the city were finished. The Germans took over the decaying town by agreement with the successor sultan in 1886, and an early German visitor described it in 1887 as follows:

Dar es Salaam had sunk as quickly as it had risen under Seyyid Majid. When we set foot on its soil, it was a town of ruins. The place and its port were desolate. . . . All the streets were overgrown with grass and bush and the individual groups of houses were joined by narrow native paths only. The town, therefore, teemed with snakes, scorpions, centipedes, mosquitoes and other pests. . . . In the halls of the Sultan's palace lived bats and castor-oil plants were rampant in its walled gardens.[10]

Dar es Salaam became the capital of East Africa in 1892; the Germans tried to develop its port facilities, but Bagamoyo remained the major port in the colony until after 1905. A town plan was drafted in 1891, and two houses each for senior and junior colonial officials were erected. The four buildings were well-made—stone for the ground floor, steel and wooden frame for the upper stories—and were still occupied as government offices fifty years later. These houses for officials were joined to the officers' mess. All quarters on the ground floor served as offices and messes; living quarters, with common bathrooms and lavatories, were on the upper floors. In these spartan arrangements of 1893 the governor's deputy and the chief justice were given suites of three rooms; the director of public works, the treasurer, and the commander of troops were assigned two rooms each; all others had one.

By 1913 there were 3,536 white men, 1,075 white women, and 725 white children in the colony. Housing arrangements in Dar es Salaam did not satisfy the German wives who began to arrive around 1900 and who transformed the tone of white society. African mistresses were concealed or banished; stiff collars became de rigueur in the capital. The beer garden—conveniently near the brewery—became the town's social center for ordinary citizens, but a club was opened early in the 1900's restricted to officials of higher grade and to the upper class of non-official society, and messes reproduced the caste system prevalent in metropolitan Germany. A few low-quality hotels were run by Syrians and Greeks.

In this little colonial town, rickshas were the usual mode of transportation; only high officials had horse-drawn vehicles. The Germans, however, were indefatigable experimenters, and the military made an effort to train zebras for riding and driving. One lieutenant with a ten-year-old zebra mare rode her on safari. Another officer was not so successful and terrorized the city whenever he tried to drive his zebra "four-in-hand" through the streets; even his heavy club did not curb the team's wildness as townsmen fled from its path.

From 1905 on, Dar es Salaam grew rapidly because of the German railroad construction to Lake Tanganyika; by 1914 it had some 20,000 inhabitants, about 1,000 of whom were Europeans. A lighterage port was developed with quay and customs sheds, modern cranes and transporters, and a road; a building boom began—new roads, government offices, a new hotel, schools, banks, and churches appeared. The offiicial part of town had become an attractive colonial city with pleasant tree-lined streets and substantial houses whose red-tiled roofs blended into the background. Architecturally the Germans had produced a pleasing variation on the late Wilhelmian style—simplified, well-adapted to the tropical environment, quite different from the ugly spread of corrugated iron-roofed bungalows that disfigured so many new colonial towns. Dr. Franz Stuhlmann, director of agriculture in the colony from 1893 until 1903, when he became the first director of Amani, planned the public gardens, including the experimental area, using ornamental trees and flowers and long seedbeds planted with trees and shrubs of potential commercial value such as coffee, teak, and rubber.

There was also a very different Dar es Salaam. Squeezed in between the European residential quarters in the east, the commercial section in the southwest, and the well-planned new "native" township in the west was a labyrinthine jungle where Indian shops and dwellings mixed with Arab and African huts, defying all efforts at proper municipal administration and sanitation. German officials trained in the jurisprudential tradition of the Referendar and the Assessor were ill-equipped to cope with these conditions or to administer the transient population of the new city. Even worse were the adjacent swamps infected by mosquitoes whose presence made life both unpleasant and unhealthy.

But even the society of Dar es Salaam was changing. The town-dwellers' chief occupations formerly had been trade in ivory and slaves and agricultural enterprise. Land had been freely available, and profits were used to expand plantations by buying more slaves. There was an indigenous class of artisans, both slave and free. Under the new administration, life was changed by the railway and by expansion of the cash economy. The old-style artisans found their methods too leisurely and cumbersome; many were forced to learn their trades afresh and to work with new tools. Hereditary apprenticeship declined as new occupations required that the young men acquire skills from aliens. Parental control was weakened. The traditional classes were widely supplanted by Indians even though Schnee—yielding to settler pressure—restricted Indian immigration. The laboring classes and the ex-slaves became accustomed to better-paid wage labor in the service of whites. Immigrants flocked into the town as workmen and domestic servants, as hawkers, and as thugs, pimps, and whores. Westernization had come to stay.

Education in the Colonies

German rule in Africa lasted three decades. Much of this time was spent in conquest, and some years were wasted because the Germans—like their neighbors—lacked both the will and the resources to spend money where it was needed. Yet German officials and missionaries made important contributions to colonial development:

they laid the foundations of modern educational and medical services in the territories under their control.

Colonial educators faced problems that far transcended those of imparting literacy. The pioneer school teacher, whether missionary or layman, saw himself as the representative of a new way of life: he stood for a creed of individual economic effort and for European methods of production, and he represented the values of the monogamous Western family as opposed to the ideals of extended kinship groups practicing polygamy. Western education had a social message, necessitating the creation of printing presses and workshops as adjuncts to church and school. Education was seen only as a means to an end. The missionaries considered it an instrument of their ministry and a device for the creation of a new class of literate Africans—teachers, pastors, and evangelists. Western pedagogues, government officials, and entrepreneurs wanted it to be used for the training of clerks, foreman artisans, telegraphists, interpreters, printers, and such—the noncommissioned officers of administration and of a new industrial labor force.

Missionary enterprise exerted an impact on the economy as well as on religion and education. Its representatives created new wants and spread a wide range of new skills, marketable only in a Western economy, with the result that the great majority of mission alumni became wage or salary earners. By 1911 graduates of mission schools in Togo were being employed as interpreters, clerks, and supervisors in government service, as telegraphists and assistants in the post office, as engine drivers, conductors, and station masters on the railway, as salesmen, buyers, and cashiers with commercial firms, and as teachers and evangelists in missionary employ.

In East Africa mission-trained Africans were hired as supervisors on plantations; some of them became successful cotton farmers, while others joined the police or even the military signalling units of the Schutztruppe. Other alumni were printers, painters, builders, shoemakers, and artisans in other fields. The use of the printed word increased; mission schools turned out literate Africans, and newspapers and journals began to cater to their tastes. Letter-writing increased—in East Africa 673,000 letters were carried in 1900. Modern communications spread throughout the territory, and people could communicate over the entire colony.

Missionary linguistic policies were responsible for converting a considerable number of African languages into written form and for spreading their use as languages of scholastic instruction. In East Africa, printing was done in German, Swahili, Sambaa, Zaramo, Chagga, Bondei, and Gogo; in Cameroun the Basel Mission Society would have liked to use Bali or Duala in its schools—a policy rejected by Governor Seitz, who in 1910 enforced a comprehensive system of regulating schools, provided government subsidies to approved institutions, and insisted that German be taught wherever schools put a second language in the curriculum.

The colonial governments established Regierungsschulen of their own, designed to fill the growing demand for junior officials and craftsmen; they also employed government schools as a policy instrument. In Cameroun the Germans deliberately placed a Regierungsschule at Garua to provide instruction for the local Muslims, thus preventing an undue preponderance of coastal people in the literate professions. In East Africa government schools served to consolidate the tacit alliance between the Germans and the Muslim Swahili-speakers whom the Germans used as junior partners in government. This policy led to a virtual Kulturkampf between government officials and missionaries, who objected to the administration's reliance on an alien Muslim elite, but the government was unchecked.[11] In 1891 Governor von Soden decided to start schools to train minor officials in the coastal areas. As a result of the Bushiri uprising of 1889–90, Soden was careful to respect Islam, and Muslims were favored as students, much to the irritation of the missionaries. The first school was established in Tanga in 1892, and lessons were given in Swahili by teachers trained at the Oriental Seminar in Berlin.[12]

The curriculum reflected the administration's need for clerks, interpreters, customs officials, akidas, and jumbas. Pupils had to memorize "The Laws Governing the Action of Native Magistrates"; even small boys had to recite those that dealt with the powers of the *Majumbe* (chief) or of village magistrates. On certain days the school would attend the government court, listen to the cases, and observe punishment by flogging.[13]

The headmaster of Tanga school after 1895 was Paul Blank, a gifted man who established the basic system for government schools. He came to East Africa after military service and training as a primary school teacher in Germany, and was fluent in Swahili when he arrived.

During his career in the colony he kept pushing for educational expansion but was usually told there was not enough money. He did what he could and aimed at educating the few—not the many—by modifying the German Volkschule to produce minor colonial officials needed to work for the government. The courses covered accounting, official forms, and typing tasks that the jumba and the akida had to perform. According to Dr. Heinke, the training program in 1900 included

seven consecutive courses lasting two years. During the first year, the pupil acquires sufficient knowledge of reading and writing and arithmetic. During the second year . . . importance is attached to training suitable people to help with the country's administration.

The aims are to develop character towards obedience, tidyness, punctuality, conscientiousness and a sense of duty. The curriculum of the second year also includes drafting letters, short reports, receipts, and so on. Important forms and documents are shown, also tax procedure and simple accountacy. . . . Important government regulations and the basic principles of German Law are the final subjects of study. A systematic study of the German language has so far not been done. . . . An extension of the course beyond two years was not possible because of the urgent need for trained men in the administration.

The demand for clerks, teachers, translators and tax officials is so high that even Tanga School with its high number of pupils cannot satisfy it. . . . A former student of Tanga School at present employed as a scribe in the Secretariat can do half the work of a European. His salary is 36 R. A European gets 150 R and housing etc. hence the government saves money.[14]

In its approach the government was more empirical than the missions. At Tanga the coastal people, backed by the local Koran teachers, were reluctant to send their children to the new establishment lest the administration try to convert the youngsters to Christianity. These suspicions were dispelled by appointing a government Koranic teacher, a move that led to bitter and sustained opposition from the mission societies. The authorities provided boarding facilities at Tanga; they persuaded jumbas and village headmen to send their children to the school, working initially with rural pupils who responded more easily to German discipline than did town-bred students. As trained men from the interior managed to get good jobs in the administration, Tanga's urban population became interested, and in 1899 the Germans were able to make education compulsory.

The curriculum now corresponded roughly to that of a German elementary school, but instruction was added in subjects like bookkeeping and agriculture. A small crafts school was opened, headed by a

Syrian and expressly designed to break the local monopoly held by Indian carpenters and builders. Blank also formed a teachers' training college whose graduates later opened village schools inland. In addition he started a printing press; by 1899 the government had resolved that Swahili must be written in Latin characters.

The missionaries had opposed the spread of Swahili—it was the language of Islam and the slave trade. But German officialdom remained firm that Swahili and German were the official languages of the colony and refused to recognize letters in other languages sent to officials. The Germans did not use the African elite from St. Andrews College in Zanzibar because the men were trained in English rather than in German and Swahili; the St. Andrews graduates taught in mission schools and worked in commerce.[15]

African education was the primary concern of the government, and European education was ignored until 1905, when schools for the children of Boer settlers were established. By 1902 there were three main schools for indigenous students at Bagamoyo, Dar es Salaam, and Tanga, and four inland schools run by the Bezirksamtmann—a total enrollment of about 4,000 students; four years later the main government schools had increased to six and inland schools to twenty-seven. This network satisfied the government's need for minor officials, and the system was expanded little thereafter. East Africa in 1913 had a government education structure of five European schools, nineteen African main schools, and sixty feeder schools; one Rektor and sixteen European teachers ran the system. Even after twenty-five years their purpose was limited to providing primary schooling for children of officials, traders, and farmers, and to producing minor African officials for the administration.

The mission schools did far more educating than the government schools, and without official financial aid or advice. The extent of their work remains hard to assess because the available statistics vary in accuracy. It is certain that by 1913 there were something like 150,000 baptized Africans in the various German colonies—men and women who were in some measure affected by Western missionaries (see Table 23). By 1911 more than 120,000 Africans in the German colonial empire attended school of some kind, most of them at the elementary or sub-elementary level (see Table 24).

The quality of pioneer education varied greatly. Money and trained

TABLE 23
Missionaries and African Converts in the German Colonies, 1912–1917

Colony and religion	European clergymen, lay workers, sisters	Baptized Africans	Colony and religion	European clergymen, lay workers, sisters	Baptized Africans
Togo:			East Africa:		
Catholics	80	14,657	Catholics	696	62,124
Protestants	11	17,000	Protestants	190	10,605
TOTAL	91	31,657	TOTAL	886	72,729
Cameroun:			South-West Africa:		
Catholics	103	28,000	Catholics	90	5,028
Protestants	41	18,236	Protestants	59	23,375
TOTAL	144	46,236	TOTAL	149	28,403
			GRAND TOTAL	1,270	179,025

SOURCE: Anton Mayer, ed., *Das Buch der deutschen Kolonien* (Potsdam, 1933), pp. 356–57.

TABLE 24
Education for Africans in the German Colonies, 1911

Type of school/students	Number	Type of school/students	Number
Togo:		South-West Africa:	
Primary schools		Primary schools	54
(incl. 2 govt. schools)	315	Post-primary schools	1
Post-primary schools		Trade schools	5
(incl. 1 govt. school)	5	Total students	4,359
Trade schools		East Africa:	
(incl. 2 govt. schools)	4	Elementary schools	
Total students	13,746	(incl. 78 govt. schools)	955
Post-primary and		Higher-level schools	
technical students	395	(incl. 2 govt. schools)	48
Cameroun:		Trade schools	
Primary schools		(incl. 3 govt. schools)	17
(incl. 4 govt. schools)	499	Total students	66,647
Post-primary schools		Post-primary and	
(incl. 2 govt. schools)	21	technical students	2,163
Trade schools		Grand total of students	118,869
(incl. 2 govt. schools)	11	Grand total of post-primary	
Total students	34,117	and technical students	4,583
Post-primary students	2,061		

SOURCE: Martin Schlunk, *Die Schulen für Eingeborene in den deutschen Schutzgebieten am 1. July 1911: auf grund einer statistischen Erhebung der Zentralstelle des Hamburgischen Kolonialinstituts dargestellt* (Hamburg, 1914), *passim.*

instructors were always scarce. Africans did not take readily to the
new schools and to discipline. Punishments were harsh—flogging for
teachers and pupils in both mission and government schools. Severe
and brutal punishment was not uncommon; in one reported case a boy
was flogged to death. The government felt called upon to issue the following order in 1911:

> In the case of pupils under sixteen only moderate strokes with the cane are
> permissible up to a maximum of ten strokes on the bottom only. The use of the
> kiboko (a whip made of hide) on pupils under sixteen is forbidden. In the case
> of Arab and Indian pupils and black teachers no punishment with the Kiboko is
> to be given. . . . Corporal punishment of black teachers is unsuitable; their
> prestige with pupils and the local population is bound to suffer.[16]

The impact of the schools was uneven, confined to a few regions, and
hard to assess in educational terms. Compared with their competitors
the Germans did not do badly. East Africa, which absorbed more European workers than all the other colonies, was the main focus of Germany's missionary effort; by 1921 British reports stated that literacy
was widespread there:

> It must be admitted that the degree of usefulness to the administration of the
> natives of the Tanganyika territory is in advance of that which one has been
> accustomed to associate with the British African Protectorates. Whereas the
> British official may often have had to risk the mutilation of his instructions to a
> chief by having to send them verbally, the late German system made it
> possible to communicate in writing with every *Akida* and village headman, and
> in turn to receive from him reports written in Swahili.[17]

Fürsorge as a Colonial Doctrine

No one can predict how German colonialism would have developed
had the Reich been permitted to keep its overseas dependencies. All
that can be said is that reformist sentiments voiced by missionaries,
merchants, secular pedagogues, and the more enlightened officials
were on the increase before World War I put an end to the German
colonial empire. Dernburg, it is true, lost the support of his right-wing
allies and resigned from office in 1910—still a coming man in German
politics, but one who never arrived. He was succeeded briefly by Dr.
Friedrich von Lindequist, a former governor of South-West Africa who
sympathized with settler interests; Lindequist, however, left office in
1911. Solf, the last incumbent at the Reichskolonialamt, followed in the

Dernburg tradition. As governor of Samoa he had defended the interests of the indigenous people against German planters; he was a firm believer in developing the colonies through indigenous agriculture; he disliked Arbeitszwang (coercive labor) and was a confirmed admirer of the principles of indirect rule enunciated by Lord Lugard.

The Deutsche Gesellschaft für Eingeborenenschutz (DGES) played an important part in popularizing reformist notions, which were also aired in liberal newspapers. The budget commission of the Reichstag prepared a set of far-reaching reform resolutions that were opposed by the right-wing parties, but the resolutions passed, and the Reichstag committed itself to a doctrine of Fürsorge (trusteeship) that essentially accorded with the views of the DGES, and also with the older traditions of Bismarckian paternalism.[18]

By the terms of the new policy, the Reichstag demanded that the chancellor "safeguard life, liberty, and property of the natives in the colonies." Forced labor was to be eliminated in every form; African workmen were not to be separated from their wives; African workers on European plantations were to be entitled to work and to own their own plots, to receive an adequate amount of land for the purpose, and to live in villages of their own. Steps were to be taken to reduce African mortality by improving medical services and by prohibiting recruitment in areas where climatic conditions differed greatly from those prevalent in the new place of work. The government was to promote the settlement of workers' families at or near the breadwinner's location, and laborers were not to be recruited in such numbers as to lead to the destruction of indigenous economies and family life. Legislation was to be enacted to improve conditions for both white and black workers in industry and in farming; the government was to regulate working hours and to impose minimum wages; the number and size of plantations were to "correspond correctly to the existing number of the African population."

The realities of German colonialism contrasted sharply with the intent of the Reichstag resolutions. Settlers continued to obtain concessions in both South-West and East Africa, and a rigorous system of discipline pervaded the German labor regime. On paper the Reichstag by 1914 had committed itself to a doctrine of social imperialism whose trusteeship provisions went beyond those as yet accepted by any other European colonial power in Africa. The French concept of development of colonial estates for the mutual benefit of the colonizers and the colonized did not develop until the 1920's; *mise en valeur* as advocated by Mangin was the equivalent of what the Germans had been doing since 1906. Contemporary Belgian notions of *moralisation* were concerned primarily with the elimination of abuses entailed by King Leopold's tyrannical regime in the Congo Free State. British doctrines of "native trusteeship" placed more emphasis on the formal use of African political institutions and less on government intervention for social purposes than the new German concept of Fürsorge.

ELEVEN

End of Empire

The Kolonialreich at War

War broke out in Europe in 1914, but the German colonial empire was ill-equipped to participate in hostilities. The Kaiser's colonial dependencies were scattered and geographically isolated; the German navy could not assure their supplies; the German colonial forces were numerically too weak to threaten any of their rivals. The troops in German colonies in Africa numbered about 7,000 in 1912 compared with 12,000 in British West Africa, East Africa, and Northern Rhodesia, 14,000 in the Portuguese colonies, and 18,000 in the Belgian possessions. German rule, though widely unpopular, was sufficiently well-established to preclude the resurgence of large-scale African uprisings, but the Germans were in no position to use their colonies as bases for offensive enterprise. Not surprisingly, the Germans would have liked to keep the war away from Africa, but the Allies felt that the continent's neutralization would only benefit the Kaiser. They were determined to conquer the German overseas empire, if only to acquire bargaining chips for the peace conference to come.

Togo was the first German colony to fall; within a fortnight the small German police force surrendered unconditionally. The Cameroun campaign lasted a good deal longer. The French and British forces had the advantage of numbers and superior artillery, but the Germans held the inner lines, had superior leadership and tactics, and knew the country in a way the invaders did not. The Germans also had unity of organization and command while the Allies had to coordinate a medley of convergent forces from British, French, and Belgian territories.

The most important Allied base was Nigeria, which supplied the largest Allied contingent—a force of 4,000 Africans and 350 British officers; of these, 1,000 became casualties. In the southern forest the invaders faced extraordinary physical difficulties—heat, disease, and an inhospitable terrain ideal for ambush. An initial assault on Cameroun from Nigeria proved disastrous, and the Allies made a direct attack on Duala. The Germans blocked the channel leading from the estuary of the Duala river by sinking ships and freight cars, some of them filled with concrete, but the Allies penetrated the barrier, captured Duala, and pushed the Germans inland. The defenders then turned Jaunde (Yaunde) into their main adminstrative center and continued to fight. By the end of the campaign the British communications ran some four hundred miles; their advance guard was as far from its bases as London is from Edinburgh, with supplies brought by carrier columns strung out along seemingly endless bush tracks. Even the most hardened African troops found the going almost impossible; conditions were so grim that when the fighting ended some 40 percent of the Nigerian soldiers were lame.

Eventually the Allied forces prevailed. The Germans ran short of ammunition, while their opponents maintained supplies by command of the sea lanes. German retreats diminished the area from which they could draw askaris and reserves. The Allies had a large reservoir of African soldiers and porters; the northern province of Nigeria alone supplied some 25,000 carriers. German resistance finally disintegrated. A considerable portion of the German colonial forces, followed by many askari families, entered Spanish territory, where they were interned. The rest surrendered, and by 1916 Cameroun was once more at peace.

Hostilities in South-West Africa were of a different kind. This was essentially a white man's war, with the Germans arrayed on one side and the South Africans on the other. On paper the Allies had an easy task; the total German military establishment, including professional Schutztruppen and European reservists, amounted to only 3,000 men—mostly mounted troopers—against a South African force of some 67,000 whites and more than 33,000 African laborers.[1] But the campaign was far from popular among the Afrikaners. A serious uprising broke out in South Africa headed by Colonel Maritz, who rallied the most irreconcilable Afrikaner nationalists under his banner and initially hampered Allied operations.

The Germans were assisted by geography. On the west the arid coast was flanked by shallows and threatened by storms and fog; an invading force had to carry with it all its supplies, including drinking water. Once the intruders had surmounted the difficulties of landing, they faced a second line of defense consisting of sand and almost impassable rock. The Orange River was a formidable obstacle with its deep gorge and infrequent, easily defended fords or "drifts," and beyond the Orange lay another thirst belt. In the east the frontier ran through the parched and uncharted Kalahari desert.

Here also the Allied offensive began with some initial reverses. South African soldiers made a successful landing at the port of Lüderitz in South-West Africa, but a force invading from the south suffered great hardships: one column was cut off and forced to surrender at Sandfontein. The Germans, however, could not prevail against superior manpower, supplies, and ammunition. Allied strategy depended to a considerable extent upon securing control of the railway system, and the South Africans rebuilt the tracks destroyed by the retreating Germans—a task entrusted to Sir George Farrar, head of a great mining concern, who was killed when his trolley collided with a locomotive. Using enveloping tactics, the South Africans captured Windhuk; they then pushed the Germans farther inland, capturing the townships of Namutoni and Tsumeb and thus preventing their opponents from retreating farther north. In 1915 the Germans finally surrendered on terms designed to secure the future of German settlers in the territory.

The most interesting campaign was fought in East Africa, the only region where German troops held out until the end of hostilities in Europe. Again the German forces were numerically far inferior to the enemy's. At the outbreak of the war they amounted to little more than 5,000 men, including askaris, police, and white conscripts, and during the war about 11,000 askaris and 3,000 settlers were mobilized—a force which tied down some 114,000 British troops as well as substantial Belgian and Portuguese forces.

The East African campaign was full of picturesque details. For example, the British employed a professional white hunter to track down a German cruiser hidden in the Rufiji delta, where her crew had so skillfully camouflaged the vessel that it looked just like one more clump in the tangled, dark-green undergrowth. In another episode the Germans sent out a zeppelin with supplies to their beleaguered army;

the airship got as far as Khartoum, where the British, having broken the German wireless code, sent it back to its base in Bulgaria by forged signals.

Above all it was a war of extreme hardship in a country where nature and disease conspired to turn whole armies into walking hospitals. The war was fought on the backs of sweating porters. Both sides requisitioned supplies and conscripted great hosts of African porters whose sacrifice and suffering probably exceeded that of the soldiers.[2] The armies performed remarkable feats of footslogging. Paul von Lettow-Vorbeck, the German commander, and his multi-ethnic force covered well over 2,300 miles—a distance greater than that from East Prussia to the Ural mountains—traversing some of the world's most inhospitable country.

The campaign was full of military "firsts": the first use in the tropics of mechanized armor, observation planes, bombers, and airborne ambulances—all pioneered by the British. The Germans were devoid of such military transport. The askaris' standard weapon, the Mauser M71, was a museum piece; these single-shot .450–caliber rifles fired black-powder cartridges that gave off thundering reports and emitted clouds of black smoke which immediately revealed the rifleman's position. But the Germans made excellent use of their machine guns, and they had unity of command against the heterogeneous forces arrayed against them, which included Indians, Belgians, Portuguese, whites from South Africa, Great Britain, and Rhodesia, as well as black fighting men from Nigeria, the Gold Coast, Nyasaland, and Northern Rhodesia.

The Schutztruppe was trained as a single unit. In addition to Africans such as Hehe and Nyamwezi, the Germans conscripted their own settlers—most of them well-adjusted to the country, inured to local conditions and to tropical disease. Originally these whites were formed into separate Schützen companies comparable to British settler units like the Northern Rhodesia Rifles, but to achieve greater cohesion Lettow-Vorbeck gradually assigned European enlisted men to African companies and placed blacks into Schützen groups. In time the two became virtually indistinguishable. From military necessity rather than conviction, Lettow-Vorbeck, a Prussian Junker whose political predilections seemed reactionary even to many of his colleagues, thus created the first racially integrated force in modern colonial warfare.

There were many reasons for the cohesiveness of the Schutztruppe. It was an elite force. The proportion between officers and soldiers was high, and the soldier's confidence in his superiors was seldom misplaced. The Germans shared the discomforts of campaigning with their African troops, and their strong personal leadership won the loyalty and respect of the askaris. Black draftees and press-ganged carriers might desert, but the bulk of the askaris remained loyal to their commanders—even in the last stages of the war when the morale of many German units began to give way on the Western front. Lettow-Vorbeck, in his book *My Reminiscences of East Africa*, tells of a German officer exhausted by a long march collapsing on his return to camp; one of his askaris rushed over, took off a sock that he had been wearing for six days, and wiped the face of the astonished German. "This is our custom," he said; "we only do it to our friends."

As a body the askaris were a relatively privileged group, well-paid by African standards.[3] Above all they were professionals, and for many a veteran the army was the only home he had ever known. Many long-serving soldiers had begun their military careers as youngsters—orphans, runaway slaves, or youths bereft of family ties—who had attached themselves to a grown-up soldier as a servant. Once old enough, they would sign on as askaris and in turn employ a "boy" of their own who himself might later choose the profession of arms. For all of them discipline was harsh; serious offenses might be punished by as many as fifty lashes, though during the East African campaign this brutal system was greatly relaxed. Training was exacting, but no more so than in the German army; German instructors were apt to be impressed by the little difference between an African and a German soldier.

In East Africa the tactical unit was the field company, a self-contained body equipped with two machine guns and with its own carriers—almost an army in miniature; more mobile than British colonial battalions, it was in appearance more like a band previously raised by a Swahili warlord than the Prussian formation in which Lettow-Vorbeck had been trained. The companies were followed by the soldiers' own servants, porters, and the soldiers' wives, who cooked their husbands' meals and looked after the sick—their presence adding a touch of gaudy color to the bedraggled-looking troops. In the last stages of the war, Lettow-Vorbeck relied entirely on captured enemy supplies, and when an important depot had been looted, a German convoy looked like a carnival procession.

Arriving at a bivouac at the end of a day's march, the porters and soldiers' servants cut branches to make frames for tents or grass-roofed huts, the women crushed corn and started campfires, and hunting patrols brought in game. Interior lines enabled the Schutztruppe to fall back on food depots set up earlier along strategic routes where the villagers grew food in advance of the army's need. If neighboring cultivators thus had less to eat, it mattered little to Lettow-Vorbeck, who gained increased mobility and denuded the countryside ahead of the pursuing British.

The industrial war effort was also adapted to local conditions. The Germans created tropical ersatz industries; they manufactured a gasoline substitute from copra and dye stuffs from indigenous barks; they wove army blankets, made boots, minted gold coins, and distilled Schnapps. From local plant life they produced such things as a disinfectant, a quinine substitute, digitalis, and a benzine substitute; ointment bases were made from hippopotamus and elephant fat. Thus the German army, though badly stricken by disease, suffered less from malaria than its opponents, and the incidence of gangrene and tetanus remained extraordinarily low despite open wounds and the ravages of a climate that encouraged putrefaction.

With respect to East African civil-military relations, Governor Heinrich Schnee and Lettow-Vorbeck were an ill-assorted pair. The latter considered Schnee an interfering bureaucratic busybody, while Schnee's comments, recorded in his private papers preserved at the Geheime Staatsarchiv in West Berlin, portray Lettow-Vorbeck as a brilliant soldier but also a ruthless egocentric and a "psychological sadist" who took pleasure in bullying his immediate subordinates.

The rift between these two men went far beyond a clash of personalities. Schnee was a liberal according to the standards of Wilhelmian Germany, whereas Lettow-Vorbeck was a conservative. Lettow-Vorbeck regarded East Africa as no more than a military preserve to be used to tie down the maximum number of Allied troops; Schnee would have liked to keep the colony neutral and preserve its hard-gained prosperity. Lettow-Vorbeck was willing to ride roughshod over the rights of Africans in the matter of press-ganging carriers and in requisitioning food and other supplies; Schnee observed the bureaucratic niceties to an extraordinary, sometimes ridiculous degree, but he was not simply a pettifogging bureaucrat: he was convinced that unless the Germans trod softly they would provoke another Maji-Maji revolt. To some extent Schnee succeeded. There was no major uprising, although in the Lindi district to the extreme south British intelligence agents were able to raise African irregulars recruited from local villages and organize them into quasi-military units that operated behind the enemy lines.

In the end, Allied superiority in men, materiel, and seapower told. By 1917 the British had managed to conquer the richest and most important German colony—a welcome success in a war as yet singularly devoid of major British victories. Lettow-Vorbeck, having been forced to abandon the colony, embarked upon a guerrilla campaign. He attacked northern Mozambique and then marched into what is now northeastern Zambia, where he finally laid down his arms at Abercorn on learning of the German capitulation in Europe. Insignificant in the number of his troops, his feat of arms made his reputation as the ablest colonial soldier of World War I; it also created a legend for those German colonial revisionists who subsequently challenged the Versailles peace settlement and whose activities helped to place a heavy political mortgage on the Weimar Republic.

African Reflux

Under the terms of the peace treaty of Versailles, the Germans surrendered all claims to their former colonial empire. The peace settlement prevented the emergence of a Germanophone Africa linked to central Europe by ties of language, commerce, and administration, and deprived the Germans of a substantial number of their colonial assets under the guise of reparations. Many settlers lost all their wealth, and the colonial officials lost their jobs and returned to Germany, disappointed or embittered men. Some of them, like Theodor Seitz and Heinrich Schnee, turned to politics; others went into business or into publicity ventures. One such was Erich Schultz-Ewerth, co-author of a classic study on African law, who directed an expedition—well-publicized in postwar Germany—in which one Count Luckner circumnavigated the world in a sailing boat. Still others took up academic careers: Eduard Haber, originally trained as a mining engineer and then a senior official in East Africa and later in Samoa, became professor of colonial sciences and economics at Tübingen University.

The German ex-officials who returned to the fatherland after World War I had a more difficult time than did their British and French confrères who were forced to abandon their colonial careers in the 1950's and 1960's, when Western Europe was relatively prosperous and qualified men had little difficulty in getting jobs. In 1918 the Schutztruppen veterans found a defeated and impoverished Germany which appeared to them to be a humiliated country. Under the concept of the mandates system, the Germans were considered less suited than other colonizers to govern backward races, an assumption referred to by the Germans as the Kolonialschuldlüge. The appropriation by the Allies of the German colonies under the guise of mandates was more offensive to nationalistic Germans than outright annexation on the part of victors claiming the spoils of war.

The war of bullets was followed by a war of books. German nationalists defended their country's record and levelled accusations against their former enemies, making a formidable though unintentional contribution to the critique of imperialism in general. (The debates concerning the German colonies entered a new era after World War II; historians then looked back on the history of imperialism from a fresh perspective based on the realities of a postwar world which saw the liquidation of the French, British, and Belgian empires in Africa and the rise of African nationalism.)

A minority of historians continued to stress the more positive achievements of imperialism and its capacity for reform. Defenders of the German record could point to the obvious economic development that had taken place in the German colonies in Africa, buttressing their case by emphasizing the reformist element. By 1914 the German colonial service was more or less on a par with that of Great Britain, and in its professionalism was superior to that of France. This does not mean that there was no ill treatment of Africans in German colonies; injustices continued, but they no longer derived from the idiosyncrasies of individual administrators, and some attempts were made to punish abuses. As a result of these and other reforms, Germany's colonial prestige began to rise rapidly in Europe just prior to World War I—an ascent reflected in numerous unsolicited testimonials furnished by contemporary British observers, including convinced imperialists like Sir

Harry Johnston and critics of colonial abuse like H. R. Fox Bourne and E. D. Morel. These men agreed that the Germans had made an effort at colonial housecleaning, that abuses had greatly diminished after Dernburg took office, that the best type of German official was efficient, hardworking, and well-trained, and that the Germans had made major advances in developing their colonial empire and in applying scientific methods to their task.

In the employment of military force the Germans had shown themselves capable of considerably greater ruthlessness than the British. Cecil Rhodes, taking his life in his hands in order to negotiate personally a peace treaty with angry and despairing Ndebele chiefs in the rebel stronghold in the Matopos in Southern Rhodesia in 1896, is a vastly more attractive figure than von Trotha in pursuit of his Vernichtungsstrategie against the Herero. British rule at its best was preferable to German governance. In a confidential report to the Kaiser in 1909, a German gunboat commander wrote:

I was astounded to see the egalitarian manner in which the British run the Gold Coast. The British are hesitant about levying taxes; they dither over instituting forced public works. The Africans believe themselves to be the equals of the whites; even Provincial Commissioners are rarely saluted. The coastal Africans are loyal to the British; they look upon the inland Ashanti as their enemies and they are willing to serve in black volunteer units commanded by British officers.[4]

The treatment of Africans, continued the German officer, was equally "lax" in Southern Nigeria, where the chief of police was "pro-native" and would not fire on African rioters. Not surprisingly, the Togolese Africans were impressed by British rule, and exaggerated tales were current in the colony with regard to the liberties granted to Africans in British colonies.

German rule, however, was not more authoritarian than French or Belgian governance, and once the process of reform had started, the Germans overall did not compare unfavorably with their colonial rivals. Certainly the difference between them was not of sufficient magnitude to justify Western notions during World War I to the effect that the Germans, of all whites, were peculiarly unfit to govern colonies. An administrator like Zech would have found himself at home with a fellow Catholic and fellow aristocrat like Sir Hugh Clifford in the British service, and a district officer like Gunzert would not have differed

TABLE 25
Reichstag Representation by Party, Selected Years, 1884–1912

Political party	1884	1893	1907	1912
Right-of-center parties:				
Conservatives	78	72	62	45
Free Conservatives (incl.				
Deutsche Reichspartei, etc.)	28	28	24	14
Anti-Semites	—	16	1	—
National Liberals	51	53	55	45
TOTAL	157	169	142	104
Center and left-of-center parties:				
Left-Liberals (Freisinnige, etc.)	67	37	42	42
Center party (Zentrum)	99	06	104	91
Social Democrats	24	44	43	110
Miscellaneous (incl. ethnic minorities)	50	51	66	50
TOTAL	240	228	255	293

SOURCE: Hans-Helmuth Röhring and Kurth Sontheimer, *Handbuch des deutschen Parlamentarismus* (Munich, 1970), p. 432.

greatly from his British successors in what became known as the Tanganyika territory.

In all probability, the piecemeal reforms made in German colonial policy during the decade preceding World War I reflected a cautiously progressive evolution of contemporary Wilhelmian society. This development found expression, for instance, in the constitutional advances made within the Reich in 1911 by Alsace-Lorraine, the discontented Reichsland acquired from France in 1871. The change was also revealed in the growing majority obtained by the "anti-Establishment" parties (Left-Liberals, Center, and Social Democrats) over the right-of-center parties (Conservatives, Free Conservatives, and National Liberals) and in the demise of the anti-Semitic parties within the Wilhelmian Reichstag during the period 1884–1912 (see Table 25). This process was cut short by World War I, a political and social disaster whose consequences the Reich was never able to surmount.

After World War II the climate of opinion changed radically. By the 1950's the very term *colonialism* had become a word of abuse to many intellectuals. To ascribe a moral superiority to one colonial power over another seemed a trivial endeavor; colonialism was condemned in toto. Its more positive aspects were played down or denied altogether in terms that would have been incomprehensible not only to Rhodes and Lugard but also to Marx and Engels. Empire-building overseas supposedly had helped to promote war between the colonialists; despite many disputes, however, the European powers had managed to carve up Africa without coming to blows. Anglo-German relations in the colonies were tolerable and even the most annexationist Germans did not go to war in 1914 simply to aggrandize Germany's African empire. Critics, including scholars of the stature of Henry A. Turner and Hans-Ulrich Wehler, argued that Germany's colonial endeavors contributed to agitation for a battle fleet, thereby helping to lead Germany into a disastrous Weltpolitik and ultimately to war with Great Britain; in truth, however, there were only very tenuous links between the German navy and the African colonies. Moreover, navalism did not necessarily depend on the existence of an overseas empire; the Austro-Hungarian and Italian navies were substantial, measured by the resources of the societies that sustained them, yet the Habsburgs had no colonies, and Italy's overseas empire was modest.

Writers such as Hannah Arendt went further still and argued that the seeds of totalitarian terror were contained within the policies pursued by the Europeans in Africa.[5] This interpretation was a curious reversal of the doctrine current in the 1930's that sought to explain the relative immunity from fascism of such Western powers as Great Britain and France by the fact that they possessed great colonial empires whose wealth had enabled the British and French bourgeoisie to stay in power without fascist excesses.

Arendt's interpretation has some merit. Colonial right-wingers such as Peters shared many of the ideas that later inspired Nazism. Early supporters of the Nazi Party like Liebert or the Duke of Mecklenburg, founder of the ultra-nationalist Vaterlandspartei, believed in German superiority. They supported a policy of territorial expansion and of German settlement in both Africa and—more important—eastern Europe, where the Slavs were to be pushed back and Germany's *Lebensraum* was to be expanded. These men romanticized rural life; they professed to despise cities and industrial civilization in general; they were anti-democratic by conviction and often—though not always—bitterly anti-Semitic. There were direct organizational links between members of the colonial movement and a great variety of rightist groups; the Flottenverein (Navy League), for instance, with its

anti-British proclivities, was an outgrowth of the Deutsche Kolonialgesellschaft.

There are some parallels between Wilhelmian and Hitlerian notions
of racial purity. German settlers in her Pacific possessions, like Dutch
settlers in Indonesia, had no hesitation about marrying local girls: no
legal or ecclesiastical obstacles stood in the way of such alliances. In
Africa, the situation was substantially different. In South-West Africa
white women were at first greatly outnumbered by white men: in 1901
the ratio stood at 19 women to 100 men. Leutwein therefore asked the
Deutsche Kolonialgesellschaft to send out more white women, but
the DKG could not keep up with the demand, especially when demobilized German soldiers began to settle in South-West Africa in considerable numbers after the Herero-Nama uprising had been crushed.
White veterans therefore contracted marriages with Baster girls, many
of whom proved to be attractive matches for German workingmen; the
girls were generally pretty and well-spoken, and some of them provided their husbands with substantial cattle dowries. There were also
cases of white women who crossed the color line: Paul Rohrbach tells
the story of a German woman whose husband, a farmer, was killed by
the Herero; she became the wife of a Herero captain until—much
against her will—she was freed by a German mounted detachment.

Such proceedings met with the intense disapproval of the local
German authorities. Leutwein himself believed the racial lore that the
bad qualities of the partners in mixed marriages were more easily
transmitted than their good qualities; hence the mixed breeds of Latin
America and South-West Africa were supposedly inferior to their
European ancestors. Practical considerations also were influential.
Such slogans as "Cuba for the Cubans," a rallying cry then current,
frightened Leutwein by implication. Under German law the children
of mixed marriages acquired the nationality of their German fathers;
they were able to serve in the Germany army and to enjoy the
privileges of German citizens. Leutwein feared that these children
with mixed backgrounds would not remain loyal to the fatherland: in
fifty years Germany would be faced with the demand of "South-West
Africa for South-West Africans," and thus might lose her colony.[6]

The Kolonialabteilung refused to commit itself, but allowed local authorities in South-West Africa and East Africa to make policy through
administrative decisions. Settlers in East Africa strongly opposed

mixed marriage. In South-West Africa, Deputy Governor von Tecklenburg instructed registry offices not to register mixed marriages, justifying his policy partly on racial grounds and partly in terms of political considerations. *Mestizos*, he wrote to the Auswärtige Amt, were normally inferior to both their parents; the presence of mixed breeds endowed with full civic rights would prevent German immigration and impede the spread of German civilization. Legislation against mixed marriage was a positive good; it would help to "educate" the settlers and modify their immature concepts of social morality.[7]

Metropolitan legislators, especially the Social Democrats and the Center party, took a more principled position; against strong right-wing opposition, the Reichstag passed a resolution sanctioning interracial marriage. Widespread hostility against mixed unions continued among German settlers, scholars, and administrators, however; the racial nonsense accepted by them as gospel truth was part of the intellectual currency at the time. Von Tecklenburg's belief that "immature" Germans should "learn" from Britons, Boers, and Americans was not peculiarly Wilhelmian; such prejudices continued to have wide acceptance from Britain to Australia without, however, leading to a totalitarian catastrophe.

A more blatant instance of what might be called a proto-Nazi policy was the German treatment of the Herero people. Helmut Bley, the historian of South-West Africa, supports the Arendt thesis; he points to the pervasive racism that animated the colonial settlers, censures the Germans for robbing the Herero and other Africans of their land, exploiting their labor, and creating what he considers to be a legalized state of lawlessness, and condemns the brutality of German military methods against the Herero resistance in South-West Africa.

The interpretation that links colonialism with totalitarianism in Germany, however, has numerous weaknesses. It greatly overemphasizes the importance of colonialism to German life. As has been seen, the colonial empire never played a significant part in the German economy, and in post–World War I Germany the colonial idea did not become popular, much to the chagrin of colonial propagandists. By 1948 the British Overseas Civil Service employed some twenty thousand regular officers, while the regular German colonial establishment had numbered but a few hundred. Ex-colonial administrators were few and lacked political influence. No former colonial governor had managed to carve out a career of national importance for himself; even Dernburg never rose beyond the position of "a man with a future."

The Arendt-Bley school, moreover, takes insufficient account of the ideological and sociological divergencies within German colonialism. Men like Liebert—with their admiration of the Junker and the real or supposed virtues of the German peasant combined with their hatred of democracy and industrial civilization—represented only one of many strands within German colonial thought. The reformist views which appealed to merchants like Vietor had nothing in common with Liebert's views. The supporters of German settlement in the colonies were not necessarily anti-liberal. Paul Rohrbach, a supporter of European settlement and self-government in South-West Africa, considered himself a democrat; he saw German settlement in the colonies as desirable for economic reasons and because German colonists were less submissive to traditional authority and thus more fitted for self-government than were their stay-at-home compatriots. Rightist notions went counter to what might be called the mercantile-industrial school of thought represented by men such as Kayser, Dernburg, Rechenberg, and Solf. Kayser, for example, was a progressive who accepted industry but tried to improve the lot of the working classes; he was also an anglophile who thought that German colonialism would be successful only if carried out in collaboration with Great Britain.

Differences of opinion between the various schools of colonialist thought became especially apparent during World War I—this time over the definition of war aims. The most militant and chauvinist groups, the Pan-Germans and their allies, looked to colonial expansion in Africa, but their principal stress was on the need to acquire more territory in Europe. Their dreams of expansion were as vast as they were unrealistic; they wanted to acquire Belgium—including the Flemish coast—and the French mining districts of Briey and Longwy; they meant to annex huge areas in eastern Europe which were to be settled by racially pure Germans, a most unrealistic program at a time when German peasants were no longer looking for new land but were drifting into the cities in search of jobs. The militant Deutsche Vaterlandspartei, which enjoyed wide backing among industrialists as well as among landowners, glided into a chauvinistic dream world far removed from the Realpolitik to which the party was ostensibly wedded: Germany must expand through Russia to the Pacific; Germany must rule the interior of Africa; Germany must advance to the gates of India.[8]

The moderates, in contrast, were willing to be satisfied with acquisitions in Africa. Scholars such as Hans Delbrück and Hermann Oncken—leading historians of Wilhelmian Germany and both critical of the Pan-German program—looked to Africa as a diplomatic safety valve. German colonial administrators and colonial politicians, the people actually involved in running the overseas empire, tended to support limited annexations in Africa rather than Pan-German aspirations. People of this kind included Heinrich Solf, who was selected in 1918 by Prince Max von Baden to negotiate peace with the Allies. Solf was a member of the Deutsche Gesellschaft, a middle-class body that sought a compromise peace in the West but also looked to the creation of a German Mittelafrika stretching from the Atlantic to the Indian Ocean; this was a cause dear to the officials in the Kolonialamt, who compiled ambitious plans for extending the German empire in Africa at the time when it was being shattered by Allied arms.[9] According to Solf, colonial expansion would serve as a means of cementing Anglo-German friendship, as an engine of colonial reform, and as a substitute policy to that of large-scale expansion in Europe.[10]

Mittelafrika was half forgotten in the Weimar era, but the cause of colonial revisionism remained a live political issue. The colonial-minded began to work for restoration, at least in part, of the German colonies and for the rights of German residents in the former colonies. The Deutsche Kolonialgesellschaft (DKG), headed by Seitz from 1920 to 1930 and by Schnee from 1930 to 1933, played a leading role in promoting this cause. It placed special emphasis on trying to influence the German youth movement through organizations such as the Bund Deutscher Kolonialpfadfinder among boy scouts, the Akademische Kolonialbund among students, and the Bund für Kolonial Erneuerung among workers. It also spread nationalistic propaganda among Germans abroad; its efforts centered on South-West Africa, where a whole network of irredentist schools, clubs, and gymnastic organizations came into being. In 1922 the DKG joined with other pro-colonial organizations to form a united colonial lobby, the Koloniale Reichsarbeitsgemeinschaft (KORAG), which had close links with a variety of German banks and industrial undertakings. Leading officeholders with financial ties included Kurt Weigelt, a director of the Deutsche Bank;

Wilhelm Laverenz, a director of the Deutsche Reichsbahn; Paul Led-
erer of the Deutsche Länderbank; Richard E. Pestel of the Diskontogesellschaft; Wilhelm Tang of the Deutsch-Südamerikanische Bank;
and Ludwig Kastl of the Reichsverband der deutschen Industries.[11]

The cause of German colonial restoration found support among the
right-wingers of the Deutschnationale Volkspartei—above all among
the heirs of the National Liberals. But of ten prominent ex-colonial
governors only two became Nazis—one of them, Schnee, a most unreliable one; one was a member of the Center party; five more or less
followed the National Liberal tradition. The majority of colonial directors and colonial secretaries in charge of the German overseas empire
were drawn mainly from Free Conservative or National Liberal backgrounds (see Appendix B).

Most strongly committed to colonial restoration was the Deutsche
Volkspartei, a moderate right-of-center group composed of members
of the educated middle class—civil servants, industrialists, and professional people. The Catholic Center party also included colonial revisionists such as Johannes Bell, a cabinet minister under Philipp
Scheidemann; there were other revisionists in the ranks of the liberal
Deutsche Demokratische Partei, the successor to the Freisinnige, including Dernburg and Dr. Wilhelm Külz. The latter had made his
reputation before World War I as mayor of Bückeburg in the Land
Lippe, which he provided with the most advanced municipal legislation known at the time; he was Reichskommissar for local self-government in South-West Africa in 1907–8. During the Weimar period
he reached ministerial office, and in 1946 became founder and first
head of the Liberal Democratic party in the Soviet zone of Germany.
The colonial movement additionally had some right-wing Social Democratic sympathizers, among them Dr. Max Cohen-Reuss, a Reichstag
deputy.

During the Weimar era the colonialist movement thus was not
dominated by Free Corps leaders or by racist demagogues, but by
the older bourgeois parties, the heirs of the Wilhelmian colonial
establishment—by bankers, merchants, and ex-bureaucrats like
Schnee. They were colorless men, indistinguishable from the majority
of Weimar politicians, incapable of building up a mass following. Organizations such as the DKG could not mobilize the force of German
chauvinism on behalf of a program of colonial restoration nor could

they appeal to Germany's economic interests. The traffic between the Reich and Africa was small, and with her former African colonies was insignificant (see Appendix Table E.13). In 1927, for instance, Germany exported more than seven times as much to the Grand Duchy of Luxembourg as to South-West Africa, the Camerouns, Togo, and Tanganyika combined.

Not surprisingly, the Weimar variant of colonialism appealed only to small minorities: to former colonial administrators who had lost their jobs, to former German settlers who had lost their property, to dreamers and romantics, and to a few German businessmen who had a share in the trade of the former colonies or who were anxious to acquire a stake in overseas commerce. The mass appeal of German colonialism was among the German settlers of South-West Africa, where the German-speaking community produced its own form of irredentism. In Germany itself indifference to colonial issues was so great—even in the Hamburg mercantile community—that Solf advanced colonial revisionists to drop their emphasis on economic arguments and base their demands on Germany's legal rights and German honor.[12]

The military component of the former German colonial establishment played only a limited part in the new German government because the military factor in the colonies had always been small and the German colonial forces produced no military giants. A possible exception was Paul von Lettow-Vorbeck, whose name became a household word in the Weimar Republic, where undefeated German generals were at a premium. Lettow-Vorbeck threw in his lot with the militant nationalists; he became a prominent member of the Deutschnationale Volkspartie but later joined the Volkskonservative Vereinigung, a more moderate splinter group that seceded from the Deutschnationalen in 1930.

Eduard von Liebert became a Nazi, and some ex-colonials became Freikorps leaders. They included Franz Ritter von Epp (see below) and Ludwig Rudolf Georg Maercker, formerly a Schutztruppenoffizier in East Africa and later in South-West Africa, and a divisional commander in World War I. After Germany's defeat he formed the Freiwillige Landjägerkorps and drew heavily on rural recruits from Westphalia. His Free Corps emphasized the value of mixed formations in which machine gun and artillery units were to cooperate with infantry in street fighting, and in 1922 formed the Deutsche Kolonialkriegerbund. He gained a reputation for ruthlessness in suppressing working-class insurgencies and was responsible for forming Einwohnerwehren (armed middle-class militias) in Leipzig, Halle, Magdeburg, and Braunschweig.

The most important recruiting grounds for the Freikorps—those irregular armies that played such an important part in the genesis of Nazism—were not to be found within the miniscule establishments of the former Schutztruppen but along Germany's eastern border. It was in Silesia and in the Baltic provinces that German irregulars with a self-consciously right-wing orientation continued to fight after World War I. Their outlook was anti-Bolshevik and anti-Polish; their bias was continental more than colonial.

The ex-colonial soldiers were by no means a united group—no more than was the German army. An interesting dissenter with a colonial background was Berthold von Deimling, a Badensian, descendant of a long line of civil servants and clergymen. He joined the German army as a "one-year volunteer," obtained a commission, and subsequently volunteered for service in South-West Africa, where he was regarded as a humane soldier by the standards of the time. He rose to be head of the local Schutztruppe and during the world war commanded the Fifteenth Army Corps on the Western front. According to his memoirs, he became disillusioned with the German "Establishment" because of its blind desire for annexations, the pretensions of the general staff, and the insane strategy of attempting to "bleed" the French into surrender at Verdun.

When the monarchy collapsed, Deimling—now sixty-five—broke with the empire that had ennobled him for his services, severed his links with the officer class, and joined the Deutsche Demokratische Partei, a liberal organization widely lampooned as "die Judenpartei" (the party of the Jews). From the standpoint of his former comrades-in-arms, worse was to come. He became co-founder of the Reichsbanner Schwarz-Rot-Gold in 1924, the political combat formation of the Social Democrats. In 1930 he joined Thomas Mann, Gerhard Hauptmann, and other German luminaries in denouncing anti-Semitism as a "cultural crime." Eventually he was expelled from all German officers' organizations for spreading pacifist propaganda.[13]

Deimling's most bitter opponents were in the ranks of the radical right, but the militant rightists were more concerned with expansion in

Europe than in Africa. Hitler was a product of the old Austro-Hungarian Empire, not of the north German Hanse towns, and his primary ambitions were continental rather than maritime; his first priority was the creation of a great empire to be founded in eastern Europe at the expense of the Russians and of the other "inferior" Slavic peoples. He initially rejected the Wilhelmian policy of colonial expansion, observing that "instead of a healthy policy of acquiring land in Europe, a policy of colonialism and trade was adopted. This course was all the more mistaken because its proponents thereby hoped to escape war." He proposed to build a huge continental bloc freed from all taints of Jewry that, initially at least, would work in alliance with Great Britain, a fellow "Nordic" power. Colonial agitation, Hitler argued, played into Jewish hands:

> Our Jewish press has managed again and again to concentrate [German] hatred above all against England; hence many a German jackass has all too willingly fallen into the Jewish trap, chattered about the revival of Germany's naval power, protested against the robbery of our colonies, demanded their recovery, and has thereby provided the material that a Jew scoundrel could then transmit for practical propagandistic purposes to his fellow-Jews in England.[14]

One of the handful of former colonialists who identified themselves with the Nazi cause was Franz Ritter von Epp (1868–1946), a painter's son from Munich who became a Schutztruppenoffizier in South-West Africa, participated in the Herero campaign as a company commander, was a regimental commander in World War I, and subsequently led the Eppsches Freikorps in Bavaria in 1919 and the Bayrische Schützenbrigade during the fighting in the Ruhr in 1920. In 1924 he became head of the Deutscher Kolonialkriegerbund, a colonial veterans' organization founded in 1922. He retired from the Reichswehr with the rank of lieutenant general, joined the Nazi party, and was elected to the Reichstag in 1928 as a Nazi deputy. Epp played an important part in consolidating Nazi power in Bavaria, where he was named Reich police commissioner in 1933; he also acted as the Nazis' chief colonial expert and served as head of the Kolonialpolitische Amt within the party. His formal position in the Nazi hierarchy was quite high because of his personal faith in the Führer, to whom he had personal access. In the end he was arrested, but survived the demise of the Nazi regime.[15]

As the Nazi party grew stronger, many other ex-colonialists joined the movement, and the Deutsche Kolonialgesellschaft under Schnee increasingly veered to the right. In 1932 the DKG called for closer collaboration with the Nazis; all colonial organizations were unified in 1936 within the Nazi-directed Reichskolonialbund,[16] and colonial propaganda became increasingly strident.* The traditional colonial establishment, however, failed to acquire any real power. Schnee, for instance, shifted his allegiance from the centrist Deutsche Volkspartei to the Nazi party in the mistaken hope, shared by many members of his class, that experience of office would make the Nazis more "responsible." Within a few years, he was disillusioned by Nazi terror, and he and his wife unsuccessfully attempted to give some help to former Jewish or "non-Aryan" friends. The Nazis had little liking for men like Schnee. At first the Führer and his entourage placed little stress on colonial demands, particularly because they wished to establish friendly relations with Britain. Colonial revisionism became much more influential as early hopes for good relations with the British waned. Influential Nazi revisionists included Joachim von Ribbentrop, German foreign minister from 1937 to 1945, and Hjalmar Schacht, president of the Reichsbank from 1930—an early supporter of Hitler who later grew disillusioned with the Nazi regime and was confined to a concentration camp in 1944. Colonial activity reached its peak during the early stages of World War II, when the Nazis devoted great effort and ingenuity to training officials, promoting research, and building a

---

*In more general terms, the "vulnerability" of European settlers to Fascist and National Socialist doctrines in the 1930's remains to be examined. The Germans in South-West Africa were strongly influenced by Nazism, but returned colonials played little part in the Nazi movement in Germany itself. Of the 581 early Nazi respondents studied by Peter H. Merkl (*Political Violence under the Swastika* [Princeton, 1975]), only 1.2 percent had resided in the colonies, mainly South-West Africa. To the best of our knowledge, there is no study concerning the psychological attitudes of German settlers in terms of a "Fascist" personality pattern, but a study concerning the attitudes of white settlers in Southern Rhodesia provides no evidence that white Rhodesian voters are more "hard-minded" than voters in Great Britain. (See Cyril A. Rogers, "The Organization of Political Attitudes in Southern Rhodesia," *Rhodes-Livingstone Journal*, No. 25 [1959], pp. 1–19.) The British whites in Rhodesia were disinclined to vote for the British Union of Fascists. H. H. Beamish was the only avowed Fascist ever to be elected to the Southern Rhodesian legislature, where his career was undistinguished. The bulk of the white Rhodesian electorate reacted to the Great Depression in 1933 by electing a moderate Tory, Dr. Godfrey Huggins (later Lord Malvern), to power. The white settlers in the Portuguese colonies were long treated with suspicion by the Salazar dictatorship, which feared white separatism. Indeed many of the poorer Angolan settlers inclined to Marxism and rallied to the Lisbon government only after the massacres committed by the FLNA forces in northern Angola in 1961.

colonial ministry to administer a nonexistent empire in Africa. The shadow Kolonialreich, collapsed, however, and in 1943 Hitler issued orders to suspend all colonial activities. Germany's dream of reviving its colonial empire came to an ignominious end.

The relationship between colonialism and Nazism raises questions wider than those bearing on the Nazi party's stand regarding the African colonies. Colonialism is charged with familiarizing Europeans with the politics of totalitarian rules—mass enslavement, mass expulsion, and mass extermination. In an embryonic form these methods appeared during the Wilhelmian period, though they reached their full employment only during the "Thousand Years' Reich." A variant to this theme is that colonialism appealed to intellectuals such as Grimm, Kipling, and the French writer Pierre Mille with its martial virtues and its supposed ability to create an integrated society of white colonial rulers. These Herrenmenschen, these expatriate members of a master race, were supposed to display a new spirit of heroism and equality. The colonial experience was praised because of its supposed ability to transcend the class struggles of the West, to overcome its bourgeois spirit, and to regenerate an overly urbanized people. Such assumptions, the argument continues, merged easily with those held by the Fascists and National Socialists of a later era.

But the romantic distaste for a peaceful existence, the glorification of heroism and violence, the search for an integrated society purified by storms of steel are not necessarily linked to the colonial experience. In 1914 almost all Western intellectuals—left, right, or center—welcomed war. There are few exceptions—largely on the left. The bellicose outpourings of 1914 are now seldom mentioned but they were strident enough at the time. Bergson, Scheler, Santayana, Freud, Weber and Durkheim, Tawney and Toynbee all preached war. So did the greatest literary artists of the time, men like Thomas Mann, Rainer Maria Rilke, Anatole France, and H. G. Wells. The avant garde writers—Futurists, Vorticists, and Expressionists—had no wish to be left behind; Isadora Duncan, Maeterlinck, Georg Heym and many others rejoiced that a "rotten peace" had at last come to an end. These intellectuals looked upon the war as a means of redemption, an instrument of destruction, and a way into a new society. Their outpourings, like the pre-colonial literature produced by Grimm, derived from an age of longing for an integrated society in which isolated in-

tellectuals would once more find personal fulfilment.[17] These notions
bore no relation to the realities of the life led by a white plantation
manager at a forlorn station in Cameroun or a white shift-boss on a
South-West African copper mine, and they were not usually shared
by the practitioners of colonialism in the bush.

It was World War I, not the colonial experience, that created the
instruments and institutions for totalitarianism. The imposition of
forced labor on workmen in occupied Belgium during the war had totalitarian connotations, although there is no evidence that ex-
colonialists were involved in this policy. More infamous was a design
worked out in 1915 to annex a strip of Polish territory to the German
empire: the native-born Polish population was to be expelled from the
border zone.[18] Civil servants associated with this project included
Rechenberg, who was a comparative moderate, a man who favored the
creation of a separate Polish state within the German sphere of
influence and an opponent of the large-scale population transfers envisaged by the Pan-Germans and their like.

There is, however, no evidence that European population transfers
were inspired by colonial practice. The policy of expelling minorities
en masse in order to solve ethnic problems in eastern Europe was not
only a German policy but also that of many Balkan peoples innocent of
a colonial past. Turkish groups, for instance, were forced to emigrate
when the Balkan states gained independence from the Ottoman
monarchy; the Turks in turn expelled the Greeks from Asia Minor after
World War I. Following World War II the Poles removed the Germans
from areas taken over from the erstwhile Reich, and the Czechs drove
out the German minorities from Bohemia and Moravia. Colonialism in
no wise influenced their policies—policies that went far beyond anything a governor such as Rechenberg would have considered feasible.

Nor do terror tactics of the kind used by Trotha in South-West Africa
suffice on their own to create a totalitarian state. The Germans in
South-West Africa, for all their ruthlessness, were no more brutal
against the Herero than the Australians had been in their treatment of
the Tasmanians, than the Americans were in their conduct toward the
Indians, or than the Hausa were to be in their dealings with the Ibo in
northern Nigeria. Yet none of these atrocities led to the creation of totalitarian states.

The essence of totalitarian terror does not lie in killings alone but in prophylactic liquidations. Certain groups are killed not because of what they have done but because of what they might do in the future. Such was the rationale in Stalin's destruction of the kulaks. The practitioners of totalitarian terror also believe that mass murder—of the kind practiced in Treblinka and Auschwitz—somehow has a therapeutic value for society, and will help to change the very nature of mankind. The Nazis thus tried to wipe out the Jews and other groups of people not because they feared insurrections but because they wished to create a new type of "Aryan man," whose fate they believed to be threatened by the mere existence of supposedly Satanic peoples.

A totalitarian state requires a coercive state machine much more extensive and elaborate than that available to any colonial power in Africa. In 1910, five years after the battle of the Waterberg, the entire German military and police establishment in South-West Africa amounted to only 2,800 men in small, scattered units which had to control and defend a territory more than six times the size of England. Modern totalitarian governments require a state machinery that differs both quantitatively and qualitatively from the civil and military forces available to the Germans in any of their African colonies. The objectives of a totalitarian state are unlimited; in theory, at least, it wishes to control every aspect of life for the purpose of creating a supposedly new and better world. A pre-World War I colonial administration that comprised no more than a small number of permanent civil servants could not possibly envisage such far-flung objectives. Even at its worst, colonial rule—German or non-German—differed both in its quantity and in its quality from Nazi totalitarianism. To confuse the two not only fudges the issue but also subtly excuses the evils of Nazi tyranny.

TWELVE

Conclusion

The question remains: To what did it all amount—the thirty-years effort made by Germany to conquer and rule her African colonies? To the majority of Germans who thought about such matters two generations ago, the answer seemed simple: German colonialism was a history of glorious deeds. In today's climate of opinion there has been a turn against colonialism in general, and against the Wilhelmian variant in particular. To many, the record of colonialism appears to be no more than a well-documented story of crime and exploitation—oppression for the vanquished and corruption for the victors.

Our own interpretation differs from what has now become conventional wisdom in academe. In terms of German metropolitan society, the African colonies—indeed the entire African continent—played an insignificant role. Germany's trade with Africa was negligible; between 1894 and 1913 the German government spent more in developing and maintaining her colonies (1,002 million marks) than the value of all her commerce with these territories (972 million marks). In 1913 German exports to the African continent had a value of no more than 158.7 million marks, or less than 2 percent of a total national export value of 10,095.6 million marks; German exports to her African colonies had a value of only 57.1 million marks.

Colonialist economic lobbies attained some importance after the empire had been built, but not before. Shipping lines, banks, railway builders, and suppliers profited from colonial rule, as did merchants, traders, and planters, but the colonialists were no more united in their political than in their economic preferences. Their cause lacked mass appeal, especially among the workers and peasants. For the great majority of Germans, places like Little Popo-Land (with its unfortunate German nursery connotation) were distant, slightly comic regions. The relative indifference to colonial issues continued after World War I. The debate concerning the Kolonialschuldlüge was of great concern to retired colonial civil servants incensed at the suggestion that Germany's colonial record had been much worse than that of any other country, but colonial revisionism was a pseudo-grievance; its role in German politics after the war was very limited, and we have found no evidence that would significantly link colonial enterprise to the rise of Nazism.

The German colonies did nothing to solve the demographic problems faced by the Reich. At the outbreak of World War I, the Union of South Africa, a minor recipient of German emigrants in comparison to the other British dominions, had twice as many German settlers as the entire German colonial empire. German colonial society shared certain features with Wilhelmian society in the Reich: respect for rank and precedence, fascination with ceremony and pomp. In social terms, however, the two societies had little in common. The colonial whites were largely adult males: women and children made up but a third of the entire settler population. Something like one-fifth of these whites were foreigners—a much larger share than in Germany. Colonial society was dominated by professional men in official or semi-official employment; of 14,419 adult men, more than one-third—5,067 to be exact—were employed in the army, the police, the administration, and the mission societies (see Table 26). These hierarchically organized elites derived their income not from rents, wages, or profits like the other settlers, but from salaries of a reasonably secure kind. They prided themselves on their tradition of "service," which they commonly—and mistakenly—believed to be ethically superior to the profit motive. The superior status and prestige of the military-administrative salariat, distinguished by diplomas and epaulettes, continued beyond the demise of the white empires, as did the notion of officialdom's moral superiority over men of business.

There was no white unskilled working class. The "lower classes" were made up of artisans, skilled workers, miners, shopkeepers, innkeepers, and such; altogether, the poorer whites numbered less than one-fifth of the white population in the colonies as a whole, though they accounted for a considerably larger proportion in South-West

TABLE 26

Social Categories of Whites in the German Colonies, 1911

Occupation/ sex-age/ nationality	South-West Africa	East Africa	Cameroun	Togo	Pacific colonies	Total
Civil servants	881	401	244	87	121	1,734
Army and police	2,072	195	119	—	—	2,386
Missionaries and clergy	70	428	117	66	266	947
Merchants, shopkeepers, innkeepers	1,035	311	436	64	288	2,134
Artisans, laborers, miners	2,572	293	84	29	98	3,076
Planters and farmers	1,390	683	111	5	208	2,397
Other male inhabitants	895	538	122	50	140	1,745
Women and children	5,047	1,378	222	62	539	7,248
Total German population	11,140	3,113	1,311	327	1,056	16,947
Total white population	13,962	4,227	1,455	363	1,660	21,667

SOURCE: Andrew R. Carlson, *German Foreign Policy, 1890–1914, and Colonial Policy: A Handbook and Annotated Bibliography* (Metuchen, N.J., 1970), p. 57.

Africa. In economic terms, the most influential working-class groups were the planters and farmers, but even they were not very significant either in numbers—less than one-fifth of the adult males—or in wealth.

German capitalists never regarded the colonies as exclusive preserves. Certain shipping companies serving the overseas possessions were subsidized, and railway builders drew their construction materials exclusively from the fatherland, but Germany's colonial tariff policy encouraged foreigners to trade in her dependencies. There was no attempt by Germany to use protective customs duties to secure a monopoly of colonial commerce, as in the French empire; German and foreign merchants paid the same rates. British capitalists and traders played an important part in the development of the German colonies, and soldiers and civil servants on the spot normally enjoyed fairly friendly relations with their British counterparts. German colonialism sometimes had an anglophobe streak, but many German colonizers respected the British and hoped to profit from their experience. The main sources of Anglo-German tension were certainly not to be found in the colonies; no Anglo-German colonial dispute ever attained the intensity of, say, the Anglo-French conflict over Fashoda, a colonial boundary quarrel that had nearly led to war between the two countries in 1898.

Given the size and diversity of her colonial empire, Germany's impact on the many peoples under her sway is hard to assess. Colonialism was not all of a kind; even within the same colony during the same period of time there were many different colonialisms. What appeared an intolerable tyranny to the Herero was no more than a tolerable form of overlordship to the Ovambo. By and large the effect of colonialism— German and non-German alike—was double-edged. European conquest and governance entailed a great deal of violence. During the decades preceding 1914 and continuing on through the Great War, there were numerous small wars in the colonies as well as large-scale rebellions; forced labor and obligatory porterage took heavy tolls of some African peoples; many communities were forcibly subjugated, moved to new settlement areas, or made to grow new crops. To conquer and police their colonies, the Germans employed black troops; to defend their colonies against Allied conquest, they conscripted Africans as soldiers and carriers, and the death and illness rates among these men were high. The German colonists were notoriously ready to inflict corporal punishment on disobedient workmen and criminals. (In the German armed forces, beating as a punishment had been officially abolished only in 1872, but brutal whippings continued to be administered to cabin boys in the navy, and there were many cases of "unofficial" beatings in the army.)

The material well-being of Africans did not improve until after conquest; it once again declined during World War I. This is not to say that pre-colonial Africa had been free of violence and bloodshed. War and famine had been ever-present specters for backward rural communities depending on small and often uncertain agricultural surpluses. But the new colonial powers had more efficient means of destruction than their predecessors, and often made greater and more regular demands for labor and taxes, for crops and services than had traditional rulers.

Colonization, however, also had positive consequences. In this respect the founding fathers of socialism took a more balanced view of the colonial phenomenon than most of their latter-day successors. Marx wrote that British intervention on the Indian subcontinent produced the greatest social revolution ever to have occurred in Asia: the raj imposed unity upon India, broke traditional and oppressive forms of society, and introduced railways, telegraphs, modern means of administration, and a host of other innovations; however selfish and brutal they may have been, the British set in motion a series of revolutionary changes with far-reaching and ultimately beneficent consequences. Engels was even more outspoken: he observed that the French conquest of Algeria was "an important and fortunate fact for the progress of civilization," that nothing would be more dangerous than to idealize pre-colonial raiding economies, and that "after all the modern *bourgeois*, with civilization, industry, order, and at least relative enlightenment following him, is preferable to the feudal lord or to the marauding robber."[1]

The German conquerors performed comparable functions in the territories over which they established temporary control. Like the British in India, they created a new system of unified administration. They developed the political framework for four colonial territories whose configuration had been unknown to pre-colonial Africa. Three of these—Togo, Cameroun, and Tanzania—are now sovereign states; a fourth—South-West Africa (Namibia)—is struggling toward independence.

Colonial conquest may have accelerated indirectly the spread of Christianity in its struggle against rival creeds. But colonization was essentially a secular affair. In the colonies there was no established church; there was no Kirchensteuer, no state-raised taxation to support the churches as there was in Germany. Evangelization was a matter for missionary specialists, and many German empire-builders were themselves sceptics or unbelievers. Colonial conquest, by weakening traditional religious bonds, was in the long run as apt to spread creeds of human autonomy—the conviction that man was wholly master of his own fate, free to shape himself according to his own unfettered will— as the religion of Christ. "Development" became a secular gospel, and Africans for the first time became aware of the notion of "economic progress"—or indeed "progress" in general.

Under the new dispensation, men and merchandise moved more freely, further, faster, and cheaper than ever before. Railways, roads, steamers, and cars opened up even the remotest regions to new ideas and goods. The German administrations imposed unity and new laws over vastly greater units than those that had been dominated by traditional kings. Soldiers, traders, missionaries, officials, and labor recruiters collaborated, wittingly and unwittingly, in building up cash economies based on wage labor which were more productive than the economies they supplanted. They introduced entirely new methods of production, that differed both qualitatively and quantitatively from those employed by earlier conquerors.

In economic terms, the impact of German colonialism was far from insignificant. Within less than one generation the Germans accomplished a great deal—despite the obstacles of distance, climate, disease, and their own ignorance concerning colonial conditions. They introduced modern methods of scientific research; they helped to pioneer the study of African linguistics, ethnography, and related sciences. They built harbors and roads; they set up new industries; they created railway systems. In terms of practical development they began slowly, but progress accelerated after 1905. Overall, the Germans laid some 4,500 km. of railway track; their achievement far exceeded the colonizers' record in French West Africa (just over 2,000 km.), in the Belgian Congo (over 1,200 km.), and even in the British Rhodesias (about 2,300 km.). In turn, the construction of railroads stimulated other forms of transport. Roads and rest houses were built to serve the railways (especially in Togo), and telegraph lines, port facilities, and shipping enterprises were constructed to link the colonies to the metropoplis.

Steampower applied to water and land transportation made African resources more accessible to the world market. As new crops were exported, new goods came in to create new wants among Africans. To the traditional products of African trade such as metalware, liquor, and textiles were added foodstuffs (tea, rice, sugar, dried fish, flour), building materials (cement, corrugated iron, lumber), machinery and tools (bicycles, sewing machines, machetes, hoes). New goods stimulated trade and encouraged Africans to sell their labor or crops on the market in order to satisfy new desires. The impact of colonialism was uneven, but in many parts of the German colonial empire the old ways were abandoned. While some traditional skills were lost, new ones were acquired.

Cheaper transportation stimulated the development of export markets. Steamships were not only faster but also could carry three or four times as much cargo as sailing ships; railways opened up vast areas to cultivation and trade. From the mid–1890's the growing needs of the industrialized West occasioned a rise in the world price of tropical products; the rise in prices stimulated tropical African exports—cocoa, coffee, palm kernels and oil, copra, cotton, groundnuts, sisal, tea, and rubber. African societies, backed by commercial concerns, the colonial administrations, and missionaries, responded to the new demand and expanded their exports.[2] The colonial *pax*, better transportation systems, the introduction of new or better strains of food crops, and the spread of improved agricultural extension work by missionaries and agriculture departments improved the food supply, while crops for export also increased.

The German colonial governments enhanced agronomic productivity by working through the traditional agricultural framework and introducing technological innovations such as plows, manure fertilizer, crop rotation, irrigation, and new crops. A major impetus for substantial economic change in the African regions once controlled by the Germans derived mainly from the colonial period, and the logistical, administrative, and scientific infrastructure for promoting change began in the German era of rule. Wage labor and cash-cropping had a part in transforming the peoples and economies of German Africa, although the receptivity of diverse peoples to economic change varied considerably.

Mining was another engine of development, at least in South-West Africa.[3] A fairly elaborate technology and a variety of skills were required in this field, and it promoted ancillary industries concerned with such operations as the treatment and processing of ores, the production of hydroelectric power, construction, cement plants, and repair shops.[4]

In terms of Germany's metropolitan economy, governmental loans and subsidies to the colonies amounted to little; on the other hand, the German colonies did not carry a heavy burden of debt. According to contemporary German estimates, at the outbreak of World War I Cameroun owed no more than 46 million marks and East Africa owed 56 million marks compared to 154 million marks for French West Africa, 186 million for Nigeria, and 460 million for the Belgian Congo. In African terms, however, the capital, skills, and techniques brought to Africa by colonial governments and companies represented a real transfer of resources and technology. None of the colonial achievements would have been possible without the use of African labor, often under harsh or coercive conditions, but without European capital, skills, and markets African development would have been greatly retarded.

The advances achieved by the Germans were aided by a steady rise in world raw material prices from the 1890's onward. The resultant development was uneven in impact and in extent. By the end of her colonial era, Germany's African colonies as a whole remained economically backward and mainly dependent on fairly simple forms of farming. Yet measured against the material poverty and technological backwardness of the areas before the Germans arrived, the rate of economic change had greatly accelerated. Within thirty years the German colonies moved from the Iron Age into the era of steam power and the internal-combustion engine. Had Marx and Engels been able to examine the colonial record of their own countrymen, they would surely have felt their conclusion confirmed that, for all its evils, colonialism served a progressive function in history.

Reference Matter

Selected List of German Colonial Governors and Their Political Affiliations

Leutwein, Theodor (1849–1921). A supporter of the National Liberals before World War I. Refused to run for the Reichstag except on the basis of a *"bürgerliche Sammelkandidatur,"* that is, a general middle-class coalition. Birthplace: Strümpfelbronn (near Freiburg im Breisgau). Protestant. Landeshauptmann, then Governor of South-West Africa, 1894–1905.

Liebert, Eduard von (1850–1934). Before World War I, an influential member of the Deutsche Kolonialgesellschaft. From 1904 to 1918, president of the Reichsverband gegen die Sozialdemokratie, which aimed at fighting the influence of socialism among workers and the lower middle class; dissolved in 1918. Member of the Reichs- und Freikonservative Partei, 1907–13. Represented the Konservative Partei in the Prussian Landtag, 1917–18. Member of the Alldeutsche Verband. Co-founder of the Deutscher Wehrverein, 1912. Joined the Nationalsozialistische Deutsche Arbeiterpartei (NSDAP) in 1929. Birthplace: Rendsburg, Schleswig-Holstein. Protestant. (See also Appendix C.) Governor of East Africa, 1896–1901.

Lindequist, Friedrich von (1862–1945). Judge in South-West Africa, 1894. Consul general in Cape Town, 1900. Governor of South-West Africa, 1905–7. In 1907 became Unterstaatssekretär, resigned in 1911 because he disapproved of the Franco-German agreement on Morocco. In World War I became an administrator charged with health questions. Vice-President of the Deutsche Kolonialgesellschaft. President of the Deutscher Seeverein (formerly Flottenverein), 1920–34). In 1921, Erster Vorsitzende of the Deutscher Schutzbund (nationalist cartel designed to appeal to Germans abroad for the purpose of promoting German expansion). Member of the executive committee of the Nationalklub (nationalist group slanted to members of the financial, bureaucratic, and military elite). Birthplace: Wosteritz (Rügen). Protestant. Governor of South-West Africa, 1905–7.

Rechenberg, Albrecht von (1861–1935). Zentrum deputy in the Reichstag, 1913–14. Vice president of the Deutsche Kolonialgesellschaft, 1923–25. Member of the executive committee of the Mittwochsgesellschaft (political discussion group founded in 1915 by Ernst Bassermann, a leading National Liberal, and Ludwig Stein, professor of philosophy at Berlin University). Birthplace: Madrid (Spain). Catholic. Governor of East Africa, 1906–7.

Schnee, Heinrich (1871–1949). Member of the Deutsche Volkspartei, which he represented in the Reichstag 1924–33; subsequently represented the NSDAP. President of the Deutsche Kolonialgesellschaft 1931–33; president of the Koloniale Reichsarbeitsgemeinschaft (an association of pro-colonial organizations); president of the Deutsche Weltwirtschaftliche Gesellschaft, 1931–42; president of the Bund der Auslands-Deutschen, 1926–33; member of the Interparlamentarische Union; German delegate of the Weltbund der Völkerbundsgesellschaften, served as president of the Deutsche Gesellschaft für Völkerbundsfragen, later known as Deutsche Gesellschaft für Völkerrecht und Weltpolitik, until 1945. Birthplace: Neuhaldensleben (Sachsen-Anhalt). Protestant. Governor of East Africa, 1912–18.

Schuckmann, Bruno von (1857–?). Prussian estate owner; served in German consular service, later in Reichskolonialamt; Governor of South-West Africa, 1907–10. Member of the Prussian Landtag for the Deutsch-Konservative Partei, 1904–7 and 1912; executive member of the Deutschnationaler Kolonialverein. Birthplace: Rohrbeck. Protestant. Governor of South-West Africa, 1907–10.

Seitz, Theodor (1863–1949). Supporter of the National Liberals before World War I. President of the Deutsche Kolonialgesellschaft, 1920–30; a personal friend of Schnee. Birthplace: Sekenheim (Baden). Protestant. Governor of Cameroun, 1907–10, of South-West Africa, 1910–15.

Soden, Julius von (1846–1921). Between 1900 and 1914, member of various moderate Land government cabinets in the kingdom of Württemberg. Birthplace: Ludwigsburg, Württemberg. Governor of East Africa, 1891–93.

Solf, Wilhelm (1862–1936). Studied Oriental languages in Berlin, London, and Calcutta; in 1894 entered Kolonialabteilung. District judge in Dar es Salaam, 1898. Municipal council chairman in Apia (German Samoa), 1899. Governor of German Samoa, 1900–1911. Staatssekretär in the Reichskolonialamt, 1911–18. During World War I favored a compromise peace designed to create a German Mittelafrika in preference to continental expansion. Staatssekretär in the Auswärtiges Amt, October–December 1918. Wrote Kolonialpolitik (1919). From 1920 to 1928 German ambassador in Tokyo, where he worked for a German-Japanese entente. Member of the "Mittwochabend" discussion circle (group founded in Berlin in 1914 by the National Liberal Eugen Schiffer), and of the Deutsche Gesellschaft (centrist political group founded in 1914). Vice president of the Deutsche Kolonialgesellschaft. Joined the Deutsche Demokratische Partei. In 1932 member of the Arbeitsausschuss für Bürgerliche Sammlung, which attempted to form a united front of the smaller and more moderate middle-class parties during the world crisis. Board member of the Continentale Commerz-Gesellschaft A.G. Birthplace: Berlin, Protestant. (Wife arrested by the Nazis for political reasons in 1944).

Selected List of *Kolonialdirectoren* and *Staatssekretäre* and Their Political Affiliations

Bell, Johannes (1868–1949). Attorney. Represented the (Catholic) Center Party in the Prussian Landtag from 1908, and in the Reichstag from 1912 to 1933. Last German Reichskolonialminister, February 1919 to May 1920. Co-signatory of the Versailles Treaty. Reichsjustizminister in the second Marx Cabinet, 1926–27. Supporter of Christlich-Demokratische Union after World War II. Birthplace: Essen, Rhineland.

Buchka, Gerhard von (1851–1935). Jurist. Oberlandsgerichtsrat in Rostock, 1886. Reichstag deputy for the Konservative Partei, 1893–98. Member of the Commission on the German Judicial Code (*Bürgerliches Gesetzbuch*). Member of the executive committee of the Deutscher Flottenverein, 1897. Kolonialdirektor, 1898–1900. Vice chancellor of Rostock University, 1902. Wrote *Vergleichende Darstellung des Bürgerlichen Gesetzbuchs . . .* (1888). Birthplace: Neustrelitz.

Dernburg, Bernhard (1865–1937). Son of Friedrich Dernburg, a jurist and a National Liberal deputy in the Reichstag. Director of the Darmstädter Bank, and the Deutsche Treuhändergesellschaft, and many other financial organizations. Supporter of the Freisinnige Volkspartei, a liberal party. Appointed Kolonialdirektor in 1905. Staatssekretär in charge of the newly founded colonial ministry, 1906–10. In 1913 admitted to the Herrenhaus (Prussian Upper Chamber). At the beginning of World War I directed German propaganda in the United States. In 1919 co-founded the Deutsche Demokratische Partei, a liberal, middle-class party. Member of the Arbeitsausschuss Deutscher Verbände (designed to oppose the Versailles Treaty). Minister of finance in the Scheidemann cabinet, April-June 1919. From 1916 to 1920, president of the Bund Jungdeutschland (cartel of moderately nationalist youth organizations). Supporter of the Deutsche Liga für den Völkerbund. Birthplace: Darmstadt.

Hohenlohe-Langenburg, (Prince) Ernst zu (1863–1950). Son of Hermann Fürst zu Hohenlohe-Langenburg, a Freikonservativ deputy in the Reichstag and a founder of the Deutsche Kolonialgesellschaft. From 1900–1905 acted as regent on behalf of Duke Eduard Karl, a minor. Kolonialdirektor, 1905–6. Represented the Freikonservative Partei in the Reichstag, 1906–12. In 1915, deputy ambassador in Constantinople; favored a compromise peace. Birthplace: Langenburg.

Kayser, Paul (1845–98). Jurist; an expert in labor law; a protégé of Bismarck's. Transferred from the Reichsjustizministerium to the Auswärtiges Amt. Kolonialdirigent, 1890. Kolonialdirektor, 1894–96. Later Senatspräsident at the Reichsgericht (the highest German court). Birthplace: Oels, Lower Silesia.

Richthofen, Oswald von (1847–1906). Son of a Prussian consul general. Joined Auswärtiges Amt, 1855. Represented Germany in the directorate of the Egyptian Caisse de la Dette. Kolonialdirektor, 1896–98. Unterstaatssekretär, 1898. Staatssekretär in charge of the Auswärtiges Amt, 1900. Prussian Staatsminister, 1905. Birthplace: Jassy.

Selected List of Schutztruppenoffiziere Who Rose to General Officer's Rank

Beaulieu, Martin Charles de (1857–1945). Served as adjutant to General von Schlieffen; later chief of staff of the Schutztruppe in South-West Africa; subsequently promoted to be head of the VI, then of the XIV Army Corps; retired as general of infantry.

Deimling, Berthold von (1853–1944). Fought in the South-West African uprising; Schutztruppe commander in 1906 and 1913, nobilitated 1905; a corps commander on the western front during World War I; later joined the Deutsche Demokratische Partei; in 1924 co-founded the "Reichsbanner," a Social Democratic combat organization.

Estorff, Ludwig von (1859–1943). Commanded a Schutztruppe in South-West Africa, 1907–11; a divisional commander in World War I; later served in the Reichswehr, in which he headed a Reichswehrgruppen Kommando; left the army with the rank of lieutenant-general, having been implicated in the Kapp Putsch; later became closely linked to Friedrich von Bodelschwing, opposed the pro-Nazi Deutsche Christen, and sympathized with Lutheran critics of Nazism.

Franke, Viktor (1865–1936). Served in South-West African Schutztruppe from 1896; commanded a Schutztruppe in World War I and capitulated in 1915; retired as a major general.

Glasenapp, Georg von (1857–1914). Served in South-West African uprising as commander of a marine battalion; held the Oberkommando der Schutztruppe in the Reichskolonialamt, 1908–14; retired from the army as a lieutenant general shortly before World War I.

Lettow-Vorbeck, Paul von (1870–1964). Fought in South-West Africa under von Trotha; commander of the Schutztruppe in East Africa, 1914–18; in 1919 became a divisional commander in the Reichswehr and suppressed a Communist uprising in Hamburg; retired as a major general in 1920; a member of various right-wing organizations, including the Volkskonservative Vereinigung, a splinter group that had seceded from the Deutschnationale Volkspartei in 1930.

Liebert, Eduard von (1850–1934). Served in East Africa from 1890; governor of East Africa from 1896 to 1901; nobilitated in 1900 and later placed in charge of a Generalkommando; joined the Reichs- und Freikonservative Partei; in 1904 became head of the Reichsverband gegen die Sozialdemokratie; during World War I served as divisional commander; left army as an infantry general; joined Nazi party in 1929. (See also Appendix A).

Maercker, Ludwig Rudolf Georg (?–?). Schutztruppenofficier in East Africa and later in South-West Africa; divisional commander in World War I; after the war formed the Freiwillige Landjägerkorps, drawing heavily on rural recruits from Westphalia; in 1922 formed the Deutsche Kolonialkriegerbund; formed armed middle-class militias (Einwohnerwehren) in Leipzig, Halle, Magdeburg, and Braunschweig.

Morgen, Kurt von (1858–1928). An explorer and Schutztruppen officer in Cameroun; nobilitated in 1904; served as a divisional commander and then as a commander of a reserve corps in World War I; retired as infantry general.

Pavel, Kurt von (?–?). Commanded Schutztruppe in Cameroun, 1901–3; retired in 1910 as lieutenant general; nobilitated in 1913.

Quade, Ferdinand (1860–?). Served in South-West Africa as chief of staff of Schutztruppe, 1904; from 1906 headed Oberkommando der Schutztruppe; rose to be major general.

Rümann, Wilhelm (1881–?). Joined the German navy during the 1890's; served in the 4th field company under Ritter von Epp in the Herero campaign, 1904–5; during World War I commanded a torpedo-boat flotilla and retired as rear admiral; joined the Nazi party in 1930 and became Leiter der Marineabteilung in the Wehrpolitische Amt der Nationalsozialistischen Deutschen Arbeiterpartei; when the Reichskolonialbund was formed in 1936, became its senior manager (Hauptgeschäftsführer); an associate (Mitarbeiter) in the Reichsleitung des Kolonialpolitischen Amtes and an S.S. Oberführer.

Scherbening, Walther (1860–1914). Chief of staff in the Schutztruppe, South-West Africa; rose to be major general.

Schmidt, Arthur (1888–1972). Joined the Schutztruppe for South-West Africa in 1912 as lieutenant; after World War I served in the Free Corps Eulenburg in Lithuania and Upper Silesia; in 1920 accepted for service by the Bayrische Landespolizei; rejoined the army in the 1930's, rose to be lieutenant general in World War II; Bavarian Landtag deputy for the National Demokratische Partei after World War II.

Schmidt, Rochus (1860–?) A Schutztruppenoffizier, Bezirkshauptmann in Bagamoyo, East Africa; major general in the Landesgendarmeriekorps; commander of the Landesgendarmeriekorps of the military government, Lithuania, in World War I.

The German Colonial Administration 1899 and 1913

The Auswärtige Amt, 1899

Kolonialabteilung
  HEAD: Direktor. PERSONNEL: 5 Vortragende Räte (senior officials) and 5 Ständige Hilfsarbeiter (junior professional staff).

Ober-Kommando der Kaiserlichen Schutztruppen
  HEAD: Direktor der Kolonialabteilung as deputy for the Reich Chancellor. PERSONNEL: 2 staff officers and a medical officer.

Kolonialrat
  HEAD: Direktor. MEMBERS: drawn from the ranks of business, academia, missionary groups, and other lobbies with colonial interests.

The Reichskolonialamt and Its Senior Officials, 1913

Staatssekretär des Reichskolonialamts (Minister for the Colonies)
  Unterstaatssekretär (Under Secretary of State):
    Abteilung A (Department A). HEAD: Direktor. PERSONNEL: 8 Vortragende Räte and 7 senior technical officers. SCOPE: political affairs, general administration, legal questions, medical and veterinary questions, scientific research, mining, forestry, concessions, schools, transport, banking statistics, reports, etc.
    Abteilung B (Department B). HEAD: Dirigent. PERSONNEL: 3 Vortragende Räte and 3 senior technical officials. SCOPE: financial questions, public works, transport, budgets, currency, railways, ports, customs, etc.
    Abteilung C (Department C). HEAD: Dirigent. PERSONNEL: 3 Vortragende Räte and 7 senior technical officials. SCOPE: personnel matters and disciplinary questions; housekeeping functions (registry, records, finance, etc., for the office as a whole)—Zentralbureau (central office), Geheimes Sekretariat and Geheime Kalkulatur (audit), Geheime Registratur (registry), Koloniale Hauptkasse (treasury), and Geheime Kanzlei (chancellery).

Schutztruppen, also known as Abteilung M. HEAD: Chef des Oberkommando der Schutztruppen. PERSONNEL: 8 military officers, 8 senior technical officers, 3 Vortragende Räte. SCOPE: military operations, supplies, planning, medical and veterinary questions, personnel, etc.; housekeeping functions for the military—Geheimes Sekretariat, Geheime Registratur, and Kassenverwaltung der Schutztruppe (military treasury).

Administration and disciplinary organs: (1) Disziplinarhof assessors. SCOPE: administrative law and disciplinary questions. (2) Disziplinarkammer (Disciplinary Chamber). PERSONNEL: president and 5 assessors. SCOPE: administrative law and disciplinary questions.

Our source for this appendix is *Handbuch für das Deutsche Reich* (Berlin, 1913), pp. 370–76.

Tabulations Showing German Colonial Economy 1880-1927

The thirteen tables in this appendix, arranged in roughly chronological order, are illustrative samples of German trade and economic developments in Africa drawn from published sources.

TABLE E.1
German Foreign Trade, 1880
(Thousand marks)

Area	Exports	Percent of total exports	Imports	Percent of total imports
Europe	2,827,575	91.3%	2,538,723	88.3%
Africa	5,162	0.2	17,115	0.6
Asia	27,148	0.9	66,481	2.3
The Americas	237,660	7.6	236,290	8.2
Australia	1,824	—	7,807	0.3

SOURCE: *Brockhaus Konversations-Lexikon* (Leipzig, 1896), 5:138.

TABLE E.2
Total Subsidies Made by the Reich and Total Capital Invested by German Companies in African Colonies, 1884–1914
(Million marks)

Colony	German Reich	German companies[a]
South-West Africa	278.0	141.0
East Africa	122.0	106.0
Cameroun	48.0	95.0
Togo	3.5	4.0
TOTAL	451.5	346.0

SOURCE: H. Schnee, ed., *Deutsches Kolonial-Lexikon* (3 vols., Leipzig, 1920; entries under "Kapitalanlagen" and "Finanzen," which are themselves important articles).
[a] Not including private individuals and mission societies.

TABLE E.3

German Revenue and Expenditure in South-West Africa, 1898–1913
(Thousand marks)

Year	Expenditure	Revenue	Year	Expenditure	Revenue
1898	5,176	390	1905	162,170	2,560
1897	5,960	840	1906	62,670	3,220
1898	7,380	890	1907	35,070	6,330
1899	9,310	1,280	1908	125,080	6,910
1900	10,880	1,333	1909	34,080	17,620
1901	12,624	1,880	1910	47,260	18,090
1902	9,499	2,240	1911[a]	51,130	17,600
1903	11,170	2,240	1912[a]	45,020	17,610
1904	66,450	2,090	1913[a, b]	54,140	15,800

SOURCE: Alfred Zimmermann, *Geschichte der deutschen Kolonialpolitik* (Berlin, 1914), p. 279.
NOTE: The annual deficits had to be covered by Reich loans and subsidies.
[a] Budgeted estimates.
[b] In 1913, the value of currency, with gold as the standard, and with the value of the monetary unit expressed in U.S. gold dollars, was German mark, 0.23; British pound sterling, 4.86; French franc, 0.19; and Belgian franc, 0.13. Figures from *The New International Yearbook, 1914* (New York, 1915), p. 174.

TABLE E.4

Germany's Colonial Finances, 1892–1893
(Marks)

Colony	Revenue	Expenditure	Reich subsidies
East Africa	1,619,600	7,376,200	5,756,000
Cameroun	504,100	492,200	—
South-West Africa	22,000	771,000	745,800
Togo [1892]	220,400	202,400	143,300
[Berlin University]	2,512,490	2,512,490	—

SOURCE: Alfred Zimmermann, *Geschichte der deutschen Kolonialpolitik* (Berlin, 1914), *passim.*

TABLE E.5

German Colonial Investments: Private Capital versus Reich Capital through 1906
(Marks)

Colony	Private capital	Reich capital
East Africa	92,687,231	15,730,026
South-West Africa	45,848,021	37,877,028
Cameroun	42,661,858	5,489,910[a]
Togo	12,914,000	9,759,723[a]
Pacific colonies	35,020,448	11,114,743
TOTAL	229,131,558	79,971,430

SOURCE: Bernhard Dernburg, *Koloniale Finanzprobleme* (Berlin, 1907).
[a] Including loans.

TABLE E.6
Trade of the German Colonies in Africa, 1903 and 1910
(Thousand marks)

Colony and year	Imports		Exports	
	Total	From Germany	Total	To Germany
East Africa				
1903	11,118	2,969	7,054	2,674
1910	38,659	19,677	20,805	12,585
Cameroun				
1903	9,426	6,702	7,139	4,490
1910	25,480	19,991	19,924	17,248
Togo				
1903	6,105	3,509	3,616	1,668
1910	11,466	6,298	7,222	4,526
South-West Africa				
1903	7,931	6,712	3,443	380
1910	44,344	34,455	34,691	28,674

SOURCE: Otto Mayer, *Die Entwicklung der Handelsbeziehungen* . . . appended table [13].
NOTE: The German mark, like the U.S. dollar and the British pound sterling, was based on the gold standard; in 1914 the comparative values were as follows: mark = $0.23, £ = $4.86.

TABLE E.7
Comparison of Trade in German African Colonies with Total German Trade, 1910
(Thousand marks)

Category	Imports	Exports
African colonies	11,949	82,643
Germany	8,934,100	7,474,700

SOURCE: *Statistisches Jahrbuch für das Deutsche Reich* (Berlin, 1911), and Alfred Zimmermann, *Geschichte der deutschen Kolonialpolitik* (Berlin, 1914), p. 309.

TABLE E.8
Total Expenditure and Revenue Raised in All African Colonies, 1907–1913
(Thousand marks)

Year	Total expenditure	Revenue raised in colonies
1907	73,130	23,580
1908	155,530	24,110
1909	68,200	42,630
1910	82,430	48,720
1911[a]	97,130	47,990
1912[a]	90,100	49,900
1913[a]	92,030	51,900
TOTAL	658,550	288,830

SOURCE: Alfred Zimmermann, *Geschichte der deutschen Kolonialpolitik* (Berlin, 1914), pp. 307–8.
[a] Projected.

TABLE E.9

Number of Firms and Amount of Capital in All German Colonies, 1913

Type of firm	Number	Amount of capital (*million marks*)
Mining:		
Diamonds		29.99
Other		111.91
TOTAL	126	141.90
Trade, industry, etc.	109	133.48
Plantations and pastoral farming	138	117.72
Transport:		
Shipping		41.8
Railways, telegraphs, etc.		60.04
TOTAL	16	101.84
Banking	10	11.14

SOURCE: *Der Grosse Brockhaus* (Leipzig, 1931), 10:328.

TABLE E.10

Dividends of German Colonial Firms as of 1913

Type of firm	Number	Number having paid dividends	Highest rate paid in any year (*percent*)
Diamond mining	48	3	55%
Rubber plantations and trade	58	8	15
Cocoa plantations and trade	22	4	10
Sisal plantations	19	(?)	25

SOURCE: Alfred Zimmermann, *Geschichte der deutschen Kolonialpolitik* (Berlin, 1914), pp. 310–11.

TABLE E.11

*Annual Dividends Earned by Selected Firms in African Colonies
prior to World War I*

Firm and years listed	Dividends (*percent*)
Deutsch-Ostafrikanische Bank, 1905–9	0.5, 8.75, 8.75, 9.75, 10
Deutsch-Westafrikanische Bank, 1905–11	0, 5, 5, 5, 8, 10, 10
Deutsche Afrika-Bank, 1906–10	4, 8, 8, 8, 8
Deutsche Togo Gesellschaft, 1903–10	0, 0, 1, 2, 3, 0, 6, 6
Deutsch-Westafrikanische Handelsgesellschaft, 1900–1911	10, 10, 10, 0, 2, 5, 10, 7, 7, 4, 5, 7
Deutsche Ost-Afrika-Linie, 1895–1911	6, 6, 3, 3, 6, 8, 3, 2.4, 0, 0, 4, 0, 0, 3, 6, 8, 8
Gesellschaft Nordwest-Kamerun, 1900–1909	0
Gesellschaft Süd-Kamerun, 1899–1910	0, 0, 0, 0, 5, 0, 10, 0, 0, 0, 8
Deutsche Kolonialgesellschaft für Süd-west Africa,[a] 1885–1905, 1905–8, 1908–9, 1909–10, 1910–11	0, 20, 25, 64, 51

SOURCE: *Von der Heydt's Kolonialhandbuch. Jahrbuch der deutschen Kolonial- und Überseeunternehmungen* (Berlin, 1907–).
[a] Originally a colonial society, later a holding company with shares in other mining companies (esp. diamonds) and in wool and whaling.

TABLE E.12

*Increase in Exports of Key Commodities in East Africa,
Cameroun, and Togo, 1905–1913*

(Tons)

Commodity	Year	East Africa	Cameroun	Togo	Total
Palm kernels	1905	—	9,518	3,200	9,718
	1913	—	15,999[a]	7,140	23,139
Palm oil	1905	—	2,606	425	3,031
	1913	—	3,595[a]	1,174	4,769
Copra	1905	3,729	—	14	3,743
	1913	5,477	—	163	5,640
Groundnuts	1905	1,422	—	49	1,471
	1913	8,960	—	80	9,040
Sesame	1905	1,111	—	—	1,111
	1913	1,476	—	—	1,476
Rubber	1905	326	1,034	115	1,475
	1913	1,367	2,926	91	4,384
Cocoa	1905	0.2	1,414	13	1,459
	1913	12[a]	5,157	335	5,604
Coffee	1905	641	—	—	641
	1913	1,059	—	—	1,059
Sisal	1905	1,140	—	—	1,140
	1913	20,835	—	18[a]	20,853
Cotton	1905	189	—	134	326
	1913	2,192	—	503	2,695

SOURCE: Heinrich Schnee, ed., *Das Buch der deutschen Kolonien* (Leipzig, 1937), pp. 426–28.
[a] Figures are for the year 1912.

TABLE E.13

German Foreign Trade, 1927

(Million marks)

Area	Imports[a]	Percent of total imports	Exports[a]	Percent of total exports
Europe	7,483.5	52.9%	7,974.6	73.8%
Africa	609.4	4.3	256.9	2.4
Asia	1,412.2	10.0	826.0	7.7
The Americas	4,272.6	30.2	1,649.9	15.2
Australia	356.4	2.5	82.8	0.8
TOTAL	14,134.1	100.0%	10,790.2	100.0%
Belgium	454.8	3.2%	363.1	3.4%
Luxembourg	75.2	0.5	78.0	0.7
Germany's former African colonies	9.7	—	12.1	—

SOURCE: *Der Grosse Brockhaus* (Leipzig, 1929), 4:633.
[a] Trade in commodities (excluding precious metals and other specialized items).

Notes

Chapter One

1. Jürgen Hahn-Butry, ed., *Das Buch vom deutschen Unteroffizier* (Berlin, 1936), pp. 25–26, provides some data concerning the social origins of German noncommissioned officers during one year shortly before 1914. Among 1,700 applicants accepted for the Unteroffizierschulen, there were 1,115 graduates from preparatory Unteroffiziersvorschulen (where young men of sixteen were trained for two years before entering an Unteroffiziersschule) and 548 fusiliers who were permitted to enter the Unteroffiziersschule without a preparatory course. The latter group comprised 153 former students of high, middle, and elementary schools, 149 clerks, 70 artisans, 56 sons of peasants and agricultural workers, 41 servants, 21 traders, 5 gardeners, and 3 waiters, but only 49 industrial workers and one miner.

2. Georg Zivier, *Deutschland und seine Juden* (Hamburg, 1971), p. 168, and Theodor Seitz, *Vom Aufstieg und Niederbruch deutscher Kolonialmacht* (3 vols.; Karlsruhe im Breisgau, 1927–29), 3:126.

3. Manufacturers and merchants rarely got beyond "The Order of the Red Eagle, Fourth Class"—a decoration accessible to a medium-rank bureaucrat. As regards titles, the designation of Regierungsrat would be given to a senior official of some standing—for example, a Bezirksamtmann (district commissioner) in the colonies with a considerable amount of service. A colonial governor might acquire the relatively modest title of Geheimer Regierungsrat, but unlike a governor in a British colony he would never be raised to the nobility for purely civilian achievements.

4. See specially Hans-Ulrich Wehler, *Bismarck und der Imperialismus* (Cologne, 1969), an important work.

5. For a detailed account, see Fritz Ferdinand Müller, *Deutschland-Zanzibar-Ostafrika: Geschichte einer deutschen Kolonialeroberung 1884–1890* ([East] Berlin, 1959), *passim*—written from the Marxist standpoint.

6. Dr. Friedrich Schroeder-Poggelow to Major A. Palézieux-Falconnet, 26 July 1888, Palézieux Papers, no. 7; Bundesarchiv Koblenz.

7. See Bruno Kurtze, *Die Wirtschaftstätigkeit der Deutsch-Ostafrikan-*

ischen Gesellschaft in den Jahren 1887–91 und ihre wichtigsten Vorausset-zungen (Jena, 1913), p. 34.

8. Between 1886 and 1899 the company paid no dividends on its ordinary shares; between 1900 and 1911 the dividends on the ordinary shares went up annually (in percent) as follows: 2.0, 0, 0, 0, 2.5, 3.5, 5.0, 5.0, 5.0, 6.0, 8.0. Alexander Lucas, general representative of the DOAG in Zanzibar and creator of its local organization, became a director of the company and also of the Deutsch-Ostafrikanische Bank, the Handelsbank für Ostafrika, the Gesellschaft Nordwest-Kamerun, and other concerns; he was also a director of the Alldeutscher Verband (the Pan-German League), a militantly chauvinist body. Karl von der Heydt sat on the directorates of numerous companies, including the Handelsbank für Ostafrika and the Deutsch-Ostafrikanische Bank; he was also a leading member of the Reichs- und Freikonservative Partei, a member of the Alldeutsche Verband, and a founder member of the Deutsche Kolonialgesellschaft. (Sources: *Von der Heydt's Kolonialhandbuch* [Berlin: 1912 ed.] and Heinrich Schnee, ed., *Deutsches Kolonial-Lexikon* [Leipzig, 1920].)

9. William Abraham, "The Life and Times of Anton Wilhelm Amo," *Transactions of the Historical Society of Ghana*, 7 (1964):60–81.

10. See Helmut Washausen, *Hamburg und die Kolonialpolitik des deutschen Reiches 1880 bis 1890* (Hamburg, 1968), *passim*.

11. See, for instance, Alfred Zimmermann, *Geschichte der deutschen Kolonialpolitik* (Berlin, 1914).

Chapter Two

1. Schroeder to Palézieux, 27 November 1892, Palézieux Papers, No. 7; Bundesarchiv Koblenz.

2. In 1907 the share capital and reserves of the Dresdner Bank and the Diskontogesellschaft amounted to 231 million and 277 million marks, respectively. Table N.1 shows the sums invested in the African colonies.

TABLE N.1

Colony	Private capital	Capital invested by the Reich (including loans)
East Africa	92,687[a]	15,730[a]
South-West Africa	45,848	37,877
Cameroun	42,661	5,489
Togo	12,914	9,759
TOTAL	194,110	68,855

SOURCE: L. H. Gann, "Economic Development in Germany's African Empire, 1884–1914," in *The Economics of Colonialism*, eds. Peter Duignan and L. H. Gann (Cambridge, Eng., 1975; vol. 4 of *Colonialism in Africa*, eds. Duignan and Gann), p. 217.
[a] Millions of marks.

3. *Deutsche Kolonialzeitung*, vol. 1 Heft 1 (1884): 1–3, esp. the article by Freiherr von der Brüggen, "Das Reich und die Kolonisation."

4. Heinrich Schnee, *Als letzter Gouverneur in Deutsch-Ostafrika: Erinnerungen* (Heidelberg, 1964), pp. 15–17.

5. Schroeder to Palézieux, 24 November 1887, Palézieux Papers, no. 7; Bundesarchiv Koblenz. Schroeder-Poggelow, a physician, later became a leading member of the DKG; He was co-founder of the Deutsch-Ostafrikanische Plantagengesellschaft.

6. Otto Diehn, "Kaufmannschaft und deutsche Eingeborenenpolitik in Togo und Kamerun von der Jahrhundertwende bis zum Ausbruch des Weltkrieges. Dargestellt unter besonderer Berücksichtigung des Bremer Afrikahauses I. K. Vietor" (doctoral dissertation, Hamburg, 1956), *passim*.

7. The original, which Liebert reprints without a trace of embarrassment, contains verse such as this:

> Noch manches Eiland lockt und lauscht
> In Palmen und Bananen
> Der Seewind braust, die Wege rauscht
> Auf! freudige Germanen . . .

Eduard von Liebert, *Aus einem bewegten Leben: Erinnerungen* (Munich, 1925), p. 95.

8. A. H. Kober, *Einst in Berlin* (Gütersloh, 1959), pp. 157–59.

9. See, for instance, Theodor Seitz, *Vom Aufstieg und Niederbruch deutscher Kolonialmacht* (3 vols.; Karlsruhe, 1927–29), 2:112.

Chapter Three

1. In 1907 German private investments in the colonies amounted to 229 million marks; by 1913 the sum had risen to 506.8 million marks. For a detailed assessment of German economic development and a bibliography on the subject see L. H. Gann, "Economic Development in Germany's African Empire, 1884–1914," in *The Economics of Colonialism*, eds. L. H. Gann and Peter Duignan (Cambridge, Eng., 1975; vol. 4 of *Colonialism in Africa*, eds. Duignan and Gann).

2. Colin Newbury, "Partition, Development, Trusteeship: Colonial Secretary Wilhelm Solf's West African Journey, 1913" in, *Britain and Germany in Africa: Imperial Rivalry and Colonial Rule* eds. Prosser Gifford and William Roger Louis (New Haven, 1967), pp. 455–77—an important comparative study.

3. Adolf Wermuth, *Ein Beamtenleben: Erinnerungen* (Berlin, 1922), pp. 276–78.

4. Jake Spidle, "The German Colonial Civil Service: Organization, Selection and Training" (Ph.D. dissertation, Stanford University, 1972).

5. Schnee to Solf, 19 September 1901, Solf Papers, Bundesarchiv Koblenz.

6. Heinrich Schnee, *Als letzter Gouverneur in Deutsch-Ostafrika: Erinnerungen* (Heidelberg, 1964), pp. 9–24.

7. "Karl Helfferich: Kolonialdienst," Seitz Papers, no. 5, Bundesarchiv Koblenz.

8. See Nikolaus von Preradovich, *Die Führungsschichten in Österreich und Preussen, 1804–1918; mit einem Ausblick zum Jahre 1945* (Wiesbaden, 1955), pp. 104–5, for the position of Prussia at large.

9. Department "A" dealt with political, general administrative, and legal questions; Department "B" was concerned with finance, public works, and other technical affairs; Department "C" looked after personnel matters. A separate military department dealt with the Schutztruppen.

10. See Spidle, "The German Colonial Service," pp. 136–37. A Bezirksamtmann started at 8,300 marks per annum and enjoyed free housing, travel expenses, clothing allowances, and so forth.

11. *Ibid.*, pp. 287–88.

12. These included names such as G. Bleichröder, Albert Ballin, Jacob S. Stern, Robert Warschauer, Arthur Fischel, Carl Fürstenberg, Georg Salomonsohn (of the Diskontogesellschaft), Max M. Warburg, and Paul von Schwabach.

13. By 1914 Germany had invested 23.5 billion marks abroad; of this, two billion had been invested in Africa and one billion in Asia. See Herbert Feis, *Europe, The World's Banker, 1870–1914; An Account of European Foreign Investment and the Connection of World Finance with Diplomacy before the War* (New Haven, 1930), pp. 60–78. The capital of the firms in the German colonies amounted to no more than 506.08 million marks by 1913; see *Der grosse Brockhaus* (Leipzig, 1931), 10:328.

Chapter Four

1. Theodor Seitz, *Vom Aufstieg und Niederbruch deutscher Kolonialmacht* (3 vols.; Karlsruhe, 1927–29), 1:110–12.

2. For Rohlfs's diplomatic work in East Africa, see Fritz Ferdinand Müller, *Deutschland-Zanzibar-Ostafrika: Geschichte einer deutschen Kolonialeroberung, 1884–1890* (Berlin, 1959), esp. pp. 196–97. For a biography, see Konrad Guenther, *Gerhard Rohlfs: Lebensbild eines Afrikaforschers* (Freiburg im Breisgau, 1912). Rohlfs's works are numerous, but especially noteworthy is his *Quer durch Afrika: vom Mittelmeer nach dem Tschad-See und zum Golf von Guinea* (2 vols.; Leipzig, 1874–75).

3. There are conflicting accounts concerning Emin's relationship with the pasha's widow. According to the version accepted by Alfred Zimmermann's standard *Geschichte der deutschen Kolonialpolitik* (Berlin, 1914, p. 153), Emin actually married the lady. However, Georg Schweitzer strongly suggests that no marriage ever took place (*Emin Pascha: eine Darstellung seines Lebens und Wirkens* [Berlin, 1898]).

4. Quoted in Roger Jones, *The Rescue of Emin Pasha: The Story of Henry M. Stanley and the Emin Pasha Relief Expedition, 1887–1889* (New York, 1972), p. 394.

5. See Franz Stuhlmann, ed., *Die Tagebücher von Dr. Emin Pascha* (5 vols.; Hamburg, Brunswick, and Berlin, 1916–27).

6. Vita Hassan, *Die Wahrheit über Emin Pascha, die ägyptische Aequatorialprovinz und den Sudan* (Berlin, 1893), p. 17.

7. *The German Army from Within by a British Officer Who Has Served in It* (New York, 1914), pp. 62–63.

8. *Ibid.*, p. 90.

9. See Colonel Donney et al., eds., *L'Art militaire au Congo* (Brussels, 1897), pp. 8–9, 34, 66–68.

10. By 1913 the whole of East Africa contained no more than eleven Bezirksämter and about an equal number of Bezirksnebenstellen; Togo had two Bezirksnebenstellen and four Bezirksstationen; South-West Africa had twelve Bezirksämter; Cameroun had six Bezirksämter and fourteen Stationen and Posten. The total German personnel employed in the district administration in all capacities—including clerks—was thirty-seven in East Africa, twenty-six in Togo, forty-three in South-West Africa, and forty-seven in Cameroun.

11. Theodor Leutwein, *Elf Jahre Gouverneur in Deutsch-Südwestafrika* (3d ed.; Berlin, 1908), pp. 541, 542.

12. Helmut Bley, *South-West Africa under German Rule* (Evanston, Ill., 1968), p. 223.

13. According to published German statistics which probably underestimated the total population of South-West Africa, the colony in 1913 comprised 78,810 Africans and 14,300 whites. The Herero were said to comprise 24 percent of the African population, the Bergdama 24 percent, and the Nama 14 percent. The overall population density of the colony remained extraordinarily low—only 0.22 persons per square kilometer.

14. Governor Schuckmann to Kolonialamt, 12 February 1908, *Abt. L a. Akten betr. der portugiesischen Kolonien*, no. 6 [copy]. Auswärtige Amt, Bonn.

15. Notes concerning a conversation with Chief Ramboule, 16 May 1908, Franke Papers, no. 22, Bundesarchiv Koblenz.

16. Gustaf Adolf Graf von Götzen, *Deutsch-Ostafrika in Aufstand, 1905/6* (Berlin, 1909), pp. 30–35.

17. Gerhard Jacob, "Die deutsche Kulturleistung in Ruanda-Urundi" (n.d.), Kleine Erwerbungen, no. 40, Bundesarchiv Koblenz.

18. R. F. Eberlie, "The German Achievement in East Africa," *Tanganyika Notes and Records*, no. 55 (September 1960), p. 191.

19. See August Full, *Fünfzig Jahre Togo* (Berlin, 1935), p. 103. For a popular Marxist critique, see Manfred Nussbaum, *Togo—eine Musterkolonie?* (Berlin, 1962).

20. See A. Schlettwein, "Togo," in eds. Erich Schultz-Ewerth and Leonhard Adams, *Das Eingeborenenrecht: das Sitten und Gewohnheitsrecht der Eingeborenen der ehemaligen deutschen Kolonien in Afrika und der Südsee* (2 vols.; Stuttgart, 1929–30), 2:5–120.

21. Circular dated 11 February 1907; cited in Full, *Fünfzig Jahre Togo*, pp. 101–2.

22. Solf to Professor Passarge, 29 October 1906, Solf Papers, no. 28, vol. 9, Bundesarchiv Koblenz.

23. Solf to Lugard, 13 October 1913, Solf Papers, no. 41, Bundesarchiv Koblenz.

24. Ludwig von Estorff criticized his German troops in South-West Africa on the grounds that the officer corps contained an excessive proportion of men without the qualities of independent leadership and enterprise. See Estorff, "Die Lehren des grossen Aufstandes" in E. G. Jacob, ed., *Deutsche Kolonialpolitik in Dokumenten* (Leipzig, 1938), pp. 297–99.

25. Robert Cornevin, "The Germans in Africa before 1918" in *The History and Politics of Colonialism, 1870–1914*, eds. L. H. Gann and Peter Duignan (Cambridge, Eng., 1969; vol. 1 of *Colonialism in Africa*, eds. Duignan and Gann), p. 384.

26. Medza (1895–1961) went to a German school in Yaoundé for two years, then served Dominik as a domestic servant; later he was hired by a German merchant and ultimately became chief of the group *Mbid' Ambani nord*. See "Entretien avec M. Paul Bissome Dza, 26 mars 1968", Box 8, Quinn Papers, Hoover Institution Archives.

27. Jesco von Puttkamer, *Gouverneursjahre in Kamerun* (Berlin, 1912), pp. 88–89; Jesco von Puttkamer, *Zwölf Kriegsaufsätze* (Berlin, 1915), p. 56.

28. Bordereau d'Envoi, no. 5, "Territoires occupés . . .", 1917," Box 3, Quinn Papers, Hoover Institution Archives.

29. Lwamgira first served as "Native Adviser"; then from 1926 to 1945 he worked as secretary to the Native Administration-Bakama Council, and in 1932 was a witness at the London Parliamentary hearings on Closer Union in East Africa. See Ralph Austen, *Northwest Tanzania under German and British Rule: Colonial Policy and Tribal Politics, 1889–1939* (New Haven, 1968), pp. 89–91 and *passim*.

Chapter Five

1. Helmut Bley, *South-West Africa under German Rule, 1894–1914* (Evanston, Ill., 1968), pp. 236–37.

2. By 1914 the Höhere Justiz and Verwaltungsbeamten (higher judicial and administrative officials) had to be trained Assessoren or junior judges with good references; senior forestry officials had to be Forstassessoren; medical doctors had to have at least two years of practical experience, preferably specialized training in tropical medicine; agronomists had to be qualified Diplomlandwirte with a knowledge of English.

3. Paul Leutwein, "Das koloniale Beamtentum," in *Die Reform des deutschen Beamtentums*, ed. Adolf Grabowski (Gotha, 1917), p. 115. For a full annotated bibliography on the subject as a whole, see the section on "German Africa" in *A Bibliographical Guide to Colonialism in Sub-Saharan Africa*, eds.

Peter Duignan and L. H. Gann (Cambridge, Eng., 1973; vol. 5 of *Colonialism in Africa*, eds. Duignan and Gann), pp. 386–410.

4. "Georg Lux," MA 95375, Bayrisches Hauptstaatsarchiv, Munich.

5. This account of Gunzert's work as district commissioner in Mwanza is adapted from Theodor Gunzert, "Memoirs of a German District Commissioner in Mwanza, 1907–1916" (trans. Joyce Hutchinson, ed. Ralph A. Austen), *Tanzania Notes and Records*, no. 66 (December 1966), pp. 171–79.

6. Gunzert had an Assessor (deputy), three secretaries, seven to eight assistants such as police corporals, a government doctor, veterinary officer, agricultural officer, post and customs officer, and a public works foreman.

7. When the colonial government withdrew its guaranteed minimum price for the first crop, Gunzert bought it up with money from district funds, stored it, and sold it later at a profit.

8. Ralph A. Austen, *Northwest Tanzania under German and British Rule: Colonial Policy and Tribal Politics, 1889–1939* (New Haven, 1968), p. 83.

9. See Major C. C. Dundas, "Report on German Administration in East Africa: 1919" [copy], Kleine Erwerbungen, no. 555, Bundesarchiv Koblenz.

10. Adalbert Bauer, "Der Arbeitszwang in Deutsch-Ostafrika" (doctoral dissertation, Würzburg, 1919), pp. 48–49. See also Reichskolonialministerium, *Die Behandlung der einheimischen Bevölkerung in den kolonialen Besitzungen Deutschlands und Englands* (Berlin, 1919), pp. 69, 72, for a defense of German colonial practices based partly on the principle of *tu quoque*.

Chapter Six

1. Hans-Ulrich Wehler, "Bismarcks Imperialismus 1862–1890" in Wehler, ed., *Imperialismus* (Cologne, 1970), pp. 258–88. For the German navy, see Holger H. Herwig, *The German Naval Officer Corps, 1890–1918: A Social and Political History* (Oxford, 1973).

2. See Heinrich Fonck, *Deutsch Ost-Afrika: eine Schilderung deutscher Tropen nach zehn Wanderjahren* (Berlin, 1907).

3. Georg Maercker, *Unsere Schutztruppe in Ostafrika* (Berlin, c. 1893), pp. 19–21.

4. Ludwig von Estorff, *Wanderungen und Kämpfe in Südwestafrika, Ostafrika und Südafrika, 1894–1910* (Wiesbaden, 1968), pp. 11–14.

5. Paul Leutwein, *Afrikanerschicksal: Gouverneur Leutwein und seine Zeit* (Stuttgart, 1929), p. 119.

6. Ernst Nigmann, "Die Wissmann-Truppe" in *Deutsche Kolonialpolitik in Dokumenten*, ed. Ernst Gerhard Jacob (Leipzig, 1938), p. 355.

7. Curt von François and Theodor Leutwein in South-West Africa and Eduard von Liebert, Friedrich von Schele, and Adolf Graff von Götzen in East Africa either combined command of the Schutztruppe with a governorship or had served as Schutztruppen commanders before attaining gubernatorial office.

8. Franz Stuhlmann (1863–1928) explored parts of East Africa, served in the

Schutztruppe, joined Emin Pasha in an expedition to the lake country in 1890, did cartographic work, was appointed director of the institute at Amani in 1903, and in 1908 returned to Germany as general secretary of the Weltwirtschaftsarchiv in Hamburg. He edited Emin Pasha's diaries and also wrote extensively on both his own and Emin Pasha's explorations.

9. For a selected listing of Schutztruppenoffiziere who rose to general officer's rank, see Appendix C.

10. Eduard von Liebert, Berthold von Deimling, Hermann von Wissmann, Kurt von Morgen, and Tom von Prince were all enabled to add the prefix "von" to their names by virtue of their military and administrative service in the colonies.

11. Report by Colonel von Schleinitz, 1 June 1907, RM 6035, Bundesarchiv Freiburg.

12. Adolf Rüger, "Der Aufstand der Polizeisoldaten" in Helmuth Stoecker, ed., *Kamerun unter deutscher Kolonialherrschaft* (2 vols.; Berlin, 1960), 1:97–131.

13. Commander Bertram of S.M.S. "Sperber," "Militärpolitischer Bericht," 8 March 1906, RM 5, 6037, Bundesarchiv Freiburg.

14. Information supplied by Major Max Köhn, formerly of the Cameroun Schutztruppe, at Freiburg im Breisgau.

15. By 1905, for instance, East Africa contained a total of twenty-two administrative districts. Of these, eleven were still run by the military; of the remaining eleven, six were in the charge of former soldiers.

16. See Ralph A. Austen, *Northwest Tanzania under German and British Rule: Colonial Policy and Tribal Politics, 1889–1939* (New Haven, 1968), pp. 31–61.

17. The literature on the subject is extensive. See especially John Iliffe's account in *Tanganyika under German Rule, 1905–1912* (London, 1969), and G. C. K. Gwassa and John Iliffe, eds., *Records of the Maji-Maji Rising* (Nairobi, 1967). For local German views, see, for instance, "Äusserungen der Detachement-Führer über die Entstehung des Aufstandes in Ostafrika," F. 7 574, Bundesarchiv Freiburg. For Götzen's view, see "Report on the Causes of the War: 26.12.1905" in Reichstag, *Anlagen*, vol. 4 (1905–6); *ibid.*, vol. 22, no. 194, pp. 3080–84.

18. See, for instance, Report by Colonel von Schleinitz of the Schutztruppe, 1 June 1907, RM 5, 6035, Bundesarchiv Freiburg.

19. Grosser Generalstab. Kriegsgeschichtliche Abteilung, *Die Kämpfe der deutschen Truppen in Südwestafrika* (Berlin, 1906–7), 1:19.

20. "Von der Tätigkeit der 2 Feldkompanie . . ., 1903–1904," Franke Papers, no. 21, Bundesarchiv Koblenz.

21. Kommando der Schutztruppe, "Überblick über die Entsendung von Verstärkungen für die Schutztruppe," 1 November 1908, M 1184 and 08, A 1, RM 5, 6056, Bundesarchiv Freiburg.

22. See, for instance, report by Commander Fuchs of H.M.S. "Panther,"

"Militärpolitischer Bericht," 9 September 1908, RM 4, 5671, Bundesarchiv Freiburg.

23. Ludwig von Estorff, *Wanderungen und Kämpfe in Südwestafrika, Ostafrika und Südafrika, 1894–1910* (ed. Christoph-Friedrich Kutscher; Wiesbaden, 1968), *passim*.

24. A. Haywood and F. A. S. Clarke, *The History of the Royal West African Frontier Force* (Aldershot, 1964), p. 502.

25. See Fr. Vieter, "Erinnerungen aus Kamerun" (typescript), Box 8, Quinn Papers, Hoover Institution Archives.

26. G. C. K. Gwassa, "The German Intervention and African Resistance in Tanzania," in *A History of Tanzania*, eds. I. N. Kimambo and A. J. Temu (Nairobi, 1969), p. 94.

27. "Wer nicht kommt zur rechten Zeit, der muss essen was übrig bleibt"; "Fünf Minuten vor der Zeit, ist des Soldaten Pünktlichkeit."

Chapter Seven

1. Oskar Hintrager, *Südwestafrika in der deutschen Zeit* (Munich, 1955), pp. 163–65. These regions had also played an important part in German emigration to America in the first part of the nineteenth century. Much earlier, in the sixteenth century, they had been a major focus of rebellion in the German Peasants' War.

2. For a selective list of colonial governors and their political affiliations, see Appendix A.

3. See John Iliffe, *Tanganyika under German Rule, 1905–1912* (London, 1969), p. 52 and *passim*.

4. *Ibid.*, p. 54.

5. *Ibid.*, p. 70.

6. *Ibid.*, p. 76.

7. For Theodor Seitz's career, see his *Vom Aufstieg und Niederbruch deutscher Kolonialmacht* (3 vols.; Karlsruhe, 1927–29), and Paul Leutwein, *Afrikanerschicksal: Gouverneur Leutwein and seine Zeit* (Stuttgart, 1929), pp. 175–76.

8. Cited by René Lemarchand, *Rwanda and Burundi* (New York, 1970), pp. 19, 65. The standard history of the area is Wm. Roger Louis, *Ruanda-Urundi, 1884–1919* (Oxford, 1963).

9. Ernst Hamburger, *Juden im öffentlichen Leben Deutschlands . . . 1848–1918* (Tübingen, 1968), p. 85.

10. Reichstag, . . . *Verhandlungen des Reichstags . . .* 9 Legislaturperiode, 4 Session, 13 March 1896, p. 1425.

11. Scharlach was born in Bodenwerder (Braunschweig), studied law at Jena, and was a co-founder of the South-West Africa Company, the Otavi Minen und Eisenbahngesellschaft, the Gesellschaft Süd-Kamerun, the Schantung Eisenbahn, and the Schantung-Bergbaugesellschaft. In addition, he cofounded the Kolonialschule in Witzenhausen and the Hamburg section of

the Deutsche Kolonialgesellschaft, and became an influential member of the German Kolonialrat. During the last years of his life he worked for a railway to serve the German settlement of Blumenau in Brazil. (Data from Heinrich Schnee, ed., *Deutsches Kolonial-Lexikon* [3 vols.; Leipzig, 1920].)

12. Fr. Vieter, "Erinnerungen aus Kamerun" (typescript), Box 8, Quinn Papers, Hoover Institution Archives.

13. Schroeder to Palézieux, 27 December 1890, Palézieux Papers, No. 7, Bundesarchiv Koblenz.

14. See Ida Pippin van Hulten, *An Episode of Colonial History: The German Press in Tanzania, 1901–1914* (Uppsala, 1974).

15. Dr. Karl Weule, *Native Life in East Africa: The Results of an Ethnological Research Expedition* (trans. Alice Werner; London, 1909), p. 41.

16. Iliffe, *Tanganyika under German Rule*, p. 106.

17. H. Zimmermann, "Auszug aus dem Reisebericht . . . über die Reise des Staatssekretär nach Ostafrika," Solf Papers, no. 28, vol. 9, Bundesarchiv Koblenz.

18. Confidential report by Captain Hoepner, senior officer of the East African Station, c. 21 September 1899, RM 5, 5668, Bundesarchiv Freiburg.

19. Heinrich Fonck, *Deutsch Ost-Afrika: Eine Schilderung deutscher Tropen nach zehn Wanderjahren* (Berlin, 1907), p. 69.

20. Kurt von Schwabe, *Dienst in den Kolonien und auf überseeischen Expeditionen* (Berlin, 1903), pp. 3, 4, 6.

21. Ludwig von Estorff, *Wanderungen und Kämpfe in Südwestafrika, Ostafrika und Südafrika, 1894–1910* (ed. Christoph-Friedrich Kutscher; Wiesbaden, 1968), p. 134.

22. Cited by Helmut Bley, *South-West Africa under German Rule, 1894–1914* (Evanston, Ill., 1968), p. 92.

23. See Ralph A. Austen, "Duala vs. Germans in Cameroon: Economic Dimensions of a Political Conflict" (Paper read at the African Studies Association meeting, Chicago, October 31, 1974). See also Robert Cornevin, "The Germans in Africa before 1918" in *The History and Politics of Colonialism, 1870–1914*, eds. L. H. Gann and Peter Duignan (Cambridge, Eng., 1969; vol. 1 of *Colonialism in Africa*, eds. Duignan and Gann), pp. 383–84.

Chapter Eight

1. Herbert Feis, *Europe, the World's Banker, 1870–1914. An Account of European Foreign Investment and the Connection of World Finance with Diplomacy before the War* (New Haven, 1930), pp. 60–78.

2. Jesco von Puttkamer, *Gouverneursjahre in Kamerun* (Berlin, 1912), pp. 103–4. For a scholarly critique of German proceedings in Cameroun seen from the Marxist standpoint, see Helmuth Stoecker, ed., *Kamerun unter deutscher Kolonialherrschaft* (2 vols.; Berlin, 1960–68).

3. For more details, see chapter 1 above; see also Herbert Jäckel, *Die Landesgesellschaften in den deutschen Schutzgebieten* (Jena, 1909); Hans von

Schöllenbach Oelhafen, *Die Besiedlung Deutsch-Südwestafrikas bis zum Weltkrieg* (Berlin, 1913); and for a Marxist critique, Horst Drechsler, *Südwestafrika unter deutscher Kolonialherrschaft: der Kampf der Herero und Nama gegen den deutschen Imperialismus (1884–1915)* (Berlin, 1966).

Chapter Nine

1. These sentiments were expressed during World War I when the Duala had taken the British side. Puttkamer contrasted their behavior with that of the "loyal Bamum" people. He promised the Duala that the Germans, on returning to Cameroun, should "at last make an end of this useless and treacherous scum" who should be deported from their ancestral lands so that "decent tribes of the interior" might take their place. See Jesco von Puttkamer, *Zwölf Kriegsaufsätze* (Berlin, 1915), pp. 56–57.

2. Kayser, also of Jewish origin, owed his start in the German administration to the patronage of Bismarck, whose sons he had tutored. He first entered the Reichsjustizministerium as a legal specialist, then transferred into the Auswärtige Amt.

3. Beit donated 2 million marks to the Kolonialinstitut, and in his will left £1.2 million to the Cape-Cairo railway trust, more than £ 600,000 of which went to various educational institutions—most of them in Africa.

4. Bernhard Dernburg, *Südwestafrikanische Eindrücke: industrielle Fortschritte in den Kolonien* (Berlin, 1909), p. 85. For a full-scale biography, see Werner Schiefel, *Bernhard Dernburg 1865–1937. Kolonialpolitiker und Bankier im wilhelminischen Deutschland* (Zürich, 1974).

5. Ralph A. Austen, *Northwest Tanzania under German and British rule: Colonial Policy and Tribal Politics, 1889–1939* (New Haven, 1968), p. 87.

6. Major C. C. Dundas, "Report on German Administration in East Africa," 1919 [copy], Kleine Erwerbungen, no. 555, Bundesarchiv Koblenz.

7. Commander Fuchs of S.M.S. "Panther," "Militärpolitischer Bericht," 25 February 1908, RM 3, 3025, Bundesarchiv Freiburg.

8. See C. Gillman, "A Short History of the Tanganyika Railways," *Tanganyika Notes and Records*, no. 13 (June 1942), pp. 14–56.

9. The Germans built a line in their neighboring colony of Ruanda in 1914–15, but it was moved by the Belgians in 1917; hence little of the original German-built railroads in East Africa remained after the war.

10. Ludwig von Estorff, "Die Lehren des grossen Aufstandes" in E. G. Jacob, ed., *Deutsche Kolonialpolitik in Dokumenten* (Leipzig, 1938), pp. 297–300.

Chapter Ten

1. Johnston to Foreign Office, July 18, 1891, no. 149, Foreign Office Confidential Print, 6178/91.

2. See Fritz Weidner, *Die Haussklaverei in Ostafrika: geschichtlich und politisch dargestellt* (Jena, 1915), *passim*.

3. For an excellent survey of East African responses to German rule, see O. F. Raum, "German East Africa: Changes in African Tribal Life under German Administration, 1892–1914" in *History of East Africa*, eds. Vincent Harlow et al. (2 vols.; Oxford, 1965), 2:163–207. This section draws heavily on Raum.

4. Patrick M. Redmond, "Maji-Maji in Ungoni: A Reappraisal of Existing Historiography," *International Journal of African Historical Studies*, 8, no. 3 (1975): 407–24, esp. p. 412.

5. Raum, "German East Africa," p. 185.

6. *Ibid.*, pp. 192ff.

7. See Adalbert Bauer, "Der Arbeitszwang in Deutsch-Ostafrika" (doctoral dissertation, Würzburg, 1919), esp. p. 16.

8. Reichskolonialamt, *Medizinalbericht über die deutschen Schutzgebiete 1911–12* (Berlin, 1915), p. 163.

9. Recent studies concerning the general social and economic impact of German colonization on particular territories include Karin Hausen, *Deutsche Kolonialherrschaft in Afrika: Wirtschaftsinteressen und Kolonialverwaltung in Kamerun vor 1914* (Zürich, 1970); Detlef Bald, *Deutsch-Ostafrika 1900–1914: eine Studie über die Verwaltung, Interessengruppen und wirtschaftliche Erschliessung* (Munich, 1970); Rainer Tetzlaff, *Koloniale Entwicklung und Ausbeutung: Wirtschafts- und Sozialgeschichte Deutsch-Ostafrikas 1885–1914* (Berlin, 1970); and Albert Wirtz, *Vom Sklavenhandel zum kolonialen Handel. Wirtschaftsräume und Wirtschaftsformen in Kamerun vor 1914* (Zürich, 1972).

10. For details on the history of Dar es Salaam, see C. Gillman, "Dar es Salaam, 1860–1940: A Story of Growth and Change," *Tanganyika Notes and Records*, no. 20 (December 1945), pp. 1–23.

11. See Marcia Wright, *German Missions in Tanganyika, 1891–1941: Lutherans and Moravians in the Southern Highlands* (New York, 1971), *passim*.

12. Mission schools in East Africa received no subsidy as they did in British Africa; on education, see George Hornsby, "German Educational Achievement in East Africa," *Tanganyika Notes and Records*, no. 2 (March 1964), pp. 83–90.

13. *Ibid.*, p. 85.

14. *Ibid.*, p. 90.

15. The Universities Mission to Central Africa established St. Andrews College and used it for training teachers and African clergy; perhaps 600 men were educated there between 1869 and 1912. See John Iliffe, *Tanganyika under German Rule, 1905–1912* (London, 1969), *passim*.

16. *Ibid.*, quoted on p. 88.

17. Cited in Raymond Leslie Buell, *The Native Problem in Africa* (2 vols.; London, 1965), 1:478.

18. Germany, Reichstag, *Verhandlungen*, 13 Legislaturperiode, 1 Session, *Anlagen zu den stenographischen Berichten*, 304, no. 1421 (1914):2918–19.

The accompanying debate, *Verhandlungen, Reichstags, Legislaturperiode*, 1 Session, vol. 294:7967–97, gives further insight into the state of parliamentary opinion just before the outbreak of World War I.

Chapter Eleven

1. The actual invading force comprised about 50,000 men. Of these some 23,000 were Afrikaners, mainly mounted troops, while the British, primarily infantry units, numbered 27,000.

2. In British East Africa alone, the British conscripted some 150,000 carriers for varying lengths of time.

3. The tip of the African pyramid consisted of *effendis*—Sudanese officers trained in military schools in Egypt or men who had risen from the ranks. Originally these men acted as interpreters as well as subcommanders. They were inferior in rank to all German sergeants. The salary structure of the original Wissmann Schutztruppe was as shown in Table N.2.

TABLE N.2

Rank	Monthly salary (*marks*)	Rank	Monthly salary (*marks*)
German sergeant major	300	African sergeant	65
German sergeant	200	Corporal	58
Effendi	150–300	Sudanese private	40
African sergeant major	75	Zulu private	22–30

SOURCE: George Maercker, *Unsere Schutztruppe in Ostafrika* (Berlin, c. 1893), pp. 60–61).

4. Commander of S.M.S. "Panther," "Militärpolitischer Bericht," 25 February 1909 and 18 October 1909, RM 3, 3025, Bundesarchiv Freiburg.

5. Hannah Arendt, *The Origins of Totalitarianism* (New York, 1966).

6. Theodor Leutwein, *Elf Jahre Gouverneur in Deutsch-Südwestafrika* (Berlin, 1908), pp. 233–34, and Oskar Hintrager, *Südwestafrika in der deutschen Zeit* (Munich, 1955), pp. 73–80.

7. For a detailed discussion, see Helmut Bley, *South-West Africa under German Rule, 1894–1914* (Evanston, Ill., 1968), pp. 212–19. See also Acting Governor von Teckenburg to Auswärtiges Amt [draft framed by Oskar Hintrager], 5 Oct. 1905, Hintrager Papers, no. 8, Bundesarchiv Koblenz; and Paul Leutwein, *Afrikanerschicksal: Gouverneur Leutwein und seine Zeit* (Stuttgart, 1929), pp. 74–75. A Nazi-inspired doctoral dissertation is by Kurt Hedrich, "Der Rassegedanke im deutschen Kolonialrecht. Die rechtliche Regelung der ehelichen und ausserehelichen Beziehungen zwischen Weissen und Farbigen" (Tübingen, 1941).

8. See especially Dirk Stegmann, *Die Erben Bismarcks: Parteien und Verbände in der Spätphase des wilhelminischen Deutschlands. Sammlungspolitik, 1897–1918* (Cologne, 1970), pp. 458–514.

9. See especially the reports submitted by the Kolonialrat, 24 and 26 April 1918 [copies], Solf Papers, No. 46, Bundesarchiv Koblenz.

10. For the views of men like Solf. Delbrück, Oncken, and others, see Emil Zimmermann, *The German Empire of Central Africa as the Basis of a New German World-Policy*, trans. Edwyn Bevan (New York, 1918).

11. See especially the entry by Hans-Joachim Fieber in the article by Helmut Müller and Hans-Joachim Fieber, "Deutsche Kolonialgesellschaft DKG 1882[1887]–1933" in *Die bürgerlichen Parteien in Deutschland* (Leipzig, 1968), 2:390–407.

12. Wolfe W. Schmokel, *Dream of Empire: German Colonialism, 1919–1945* (New Haven, 1964), p. 15. For a different interpretation, see the monumental work by Klaus Hildebrand, *Vom Reich zum Weltreich: Hitler, NSDAP und koloniale Frage, 1919–1945* (Munich, 1969). Hildebrand places more stress on the link between colonialism and totalitarianism than does Schmokel; for a detailed discussion, see Woodruff D. Smith, "The Ideology of German Colonialism, 1840–1914" (doctoral dissertation, University of Chicago, 1972).

13. *Der grosse Brockhaus* (Leipzig, 1928), 4:374; Leutwein, *Afrikanerschicksal*, pp. 770–72; and Berthold von Deimling, *Aus der alten in die neue Zeit: Lebenserinnerungen* (Berlin, 1930).

14. Adolf Hitler, *Mein Kampf* (Munich, 1944), pp. 689, 706.

15. Schmokel, *Dream of Empire*, pp. 22–25, and Hans Buchheim, "The Totalitarian State: Police, Propaganda, National Expansionism, Culture," in *Republic to Reich: the Making of the Nazi Revolution* ed. Hajo Holborn (New York, 1972), p. 260.

16. For details and data concerning the economic dimensions of colonial revisionism, see Müller and Fieber, "Deutsche Kolonialgesellschaft," pp. 390–407.

17. See Hugh Ridley, "Colonial Society and European Totalitarianism," *Journal of European Studies*, no. 3 (1973), pp. 147–59, and Roland N. Stromberg, "The Intellectuals and the Coming of War in 1914," *ibid.*, pp. 109–22.

18. For details see Fritz Fischer, *Griff nach der Weltmacht: die Kriegszielpolitik des kaiserlichen Deutschlands, 1914/18* (Düsseldorf, 1961), and the excellent discussion by Klaus Epstein, *Geschichte und Geschichtswissenschaft im 20. Jahrhundert: Ein Leitfaden* (Frankfurt am Main, 1972), pp. 82–109, esp. p. 91.

Chapter Twelve

1. For Marx's and Engels's views, see Karl Marx, "The Future Results of the British Rule in India" (22 July 1853) and "The British Rule in India" (10 June 1853) in Karl Marx and Friedrich Engels, *On Colonialism: Articles from the New York Tribune and Other Writings* (New York, 1972), pp. 35–41, 81–87. Engels's views regarding the French conquest of Algeria are reprinted in Shlomo Avineri, ed., *Karl Marx on Colonialism* (New York, 1968), p. 43.

2. The pastoral economy of South-West Africa also increased manyfold, as indicated in Table N.3.

TABLE N.3

Farm animals	Number, 1907	Number, 1913
Cattle	52,531	205,643
Horses	3,119	15,916
Sheep bred for meat, and goats	204,954	957,986
Sheep bred for wool	3,526	53,691
Angora goats	3,696	31,400
Pigs	1,202	7,772
Ostriches	0	1,507

SOURCE: Oscar Hintrager, *Südwestafrica in der deutschen Zeit* (Munich, 1955), p. 175.

3. The mining development in South-West Africa is reflected in Table N.4.

TABLE N.4

Product	Value, 1908	Value, 1913
Diamonds	51[a]	58,910
Copper	6,296	7,929
All products	7,795	70,303

SOURCE: Hintrager, *Südwestafrika*, pp. 177–78.
[a] In 1,000 marks.

4. In 1914 South-West Africa had four machine works, two railway depots, a wagon-building shop, two electricity works, three quarries, a cannery, two breweries, two distilleries, two tanning works, and an ice-making factory; in addition, there were numerous small workshops belonging to individual artisans.

Index

Aborigines Protection Society (Great Britain), 34

Adam, Dr. Leonard, 49

Adamawa (Islamic state), 22, 167

Administration, central colonial, 45–55; early period (1890–1906), 45–52; administrative structure, 46, 50–51; 255–56; Reichskolonialamt created, 51f, 57; Dernburg reforms (1906–14), 53–55

Administration, colonial, in Africa, 56–86; military role in, 51, 125; pioneer administrators, 56–67; physicians turned administrators, 57–63; soldiers as explorers, 63–67; successors to early administrators, 67–73; structure of, 67–73, 79, 100 fig., 267; statutory authority, 68, 73; number of administrators by colony, 69–71, 71 table; treatment of Africans by, 73–76, 148–49, 209; techniques of governance, 73–86; coercion in, 74–75; use of African institutions by, 77–79, 80–83; judicial system under, 102–3; civil and military functions shared by same person, 269; ennoblement for service in, 270. *See also* Colonial service

Administration, German civil, 7–8, 263

Agriculture, 98–99, 152–53, 153 table; in Togo, 165–66; in Cameroun, 167–68; research and development in, 189–91; impact of colonialism on, 201–3, 245

Algeciras crisis, 176

Algeria, Engels's view of colonialism in, 243

Alldeutsche Verband (Pan-German League), 36, 40, 113, 169, 249, 264

Allied forces in World War I, 216–22, 275

Ambo people (S.–W. Africa), 18, 75

Amo, Anton Wilhelm, 22

Anglo-German colonial agreement (1890), 15, 61

Antiultramontaner Reichsverband, 105

Arbeitsausschuss Deutscher Verbände, 251

Arendt, Hannah, on colonialism and totalitarianism, xii, 226, 228–29

Aristocracy, German: in government service, 2–3; in military, 4–6, 111, 112 table; in colonial service, 47, 90, 111, 112 table, 138, 139 table, 143 table

Armed forces, 104–30

Army, German, 4–6, 5 table, 263

Army, German colonial: financing of, 54; soldiers as explorers, 63–67; number of units and troops, by colony, 106, 106 table; control of, 107; social background of, 107–15; casualties suffered by, 108, 125–26, 126 table; pay for, 108, 275; geographical origins of, 112; in Togo, 115–16; organization, functions, and campaigns, 115–18; training and tactics, 118–19; and coercion, 118–27; administrative duties of, 119; social function of, 125–30; attitude toward Africans, 158–59; in World War I, 216–22; evaluation of military force usage, 224; and Weimar, 232–34; selected list of general officers, 253–54; civil and military functions exercised by the same person, 269; ennoblement for service in, 270

Askaris (African professional soldiers), 16, 61, 118–19, 220

Atangana, Charles, 85

Auswärtige Amt, colonial affairs and, 46, 255

Baden, Prince Max von, 230

Baden state, 1, 137

Bagamoyo (E. Africa), 77, 196, 205, 211

Ballin, Albert, 31

Banks and bankers, colonial involvement of, 12, 52f, 72

Barth, Heinrich, 27, 37

Basel Missionary Society, 22, 169, 209

Bassermann, Ernst, 250

Basters people (S.–W. Africa), 18, 45, 122, 123–24

Beaulieu, Martin Charles de, 253

Beit, Alfred, 179, 273